# STORYBOOK CULTURE

## THE ART OF POPULAR CHILDREN'S BOOKS

**Joseph Homme and Cheryl Homme**

**PORTLAND, OREGON**

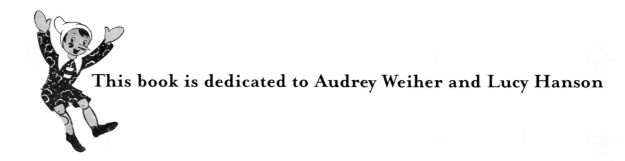

**This book is dedicated to Audrey Weiher and Lucy Hanson**

Copyright ©2002 Collectors Press, Inc.

*For a free catalog write to:*

**Collectors Press, Inc.**

P.O. Box 230986

Portland, Oregon 97281

Toll-free 1-800-423-1848

Design *Evan Holt, Collectors Press*

Based on concept and designs by *Principia Graphica*

Editor *Ann Granning Bennett*

Printed in Hong Kong

First American Edition

1 2 3 4 5 6 7 8 9

Library of Congress Cataloging-in-Publication Data

Homme, Joe, 1959-
    *Storybook culture : the art of popular children's books*  by Joe and Cheryl Homme.
        p. cm.
Includes bibliographical references.
    ISBN 1-888054-71-9 (alk. paper)
    1.  Illustrated children's books--United States. 2.  Illustration of books--20th century--United States.  I. Homme, Cheryl, 1961- II. Title.
    NC975 .H66 2002
    741.6'42'0973--dc21
                                        2002006530

# Contents

# Introduction

Growing up in Palmer, Alaska, I had the pleasure of living within short walking distance of Miss V. Louise Kellogg. She lived alone in a stately, old home, and on rainy afternoons she often allowed us neighborhood kids to play inside. This gave us an opportunity to get to know her. She was well educated and one of the most interesting and independent individuals I have ever met. Miss Kellogg had an enormous library and occasionally would let us look at her precious books. I remember that she didn't refer to them as her books, but rather as her old friends. How wise she was to equate the value of books to that of old friends.

Joseph Homme
July 2001

At the dawn of the last century, Americans were fascinated by America. They had a right to be. The Industrial Revolution powered a strong economy, immigration brought families bursting with hope and optimism in their new country, the western frontier offered cheap land and great opportunity, farming was on the upswing, and cities were flourishing. Technological advances were on the rise, reaching the masses in communications with telephones, in entertainment with moving pictures, and in transportation with automobiles, with flight soon to follow. The lure of the sporting life brought legions of fans to baseball and football. Legitimate theater enjoyed a soaring popularity, small towns had their own vaudeville shows, and circuses crisscrossed the country. The nation's foremost hero and future president, Theodore Roosevelt, was the embodiment of leadership, vigor, and optimism. And it was a time of peace. Perhaps foremost to the fascination was the newness of it all. America was young and full of passion. In all the excitement, this continuously emerging country began to slowly shed the oppressiveness of the preceding Victorian era. There were no greater beneficiaries of this newfound freedom than the nation's youth. Strict conformity to rules and laws were still exacted, but new choices abounded. A proliferation of children's literature and ease of access to books made for variety and independence in thought and in dreams.

The cornerstones of any library are, of course, the classics. At the opening of the twentieth century, much time-honored literature and many authors were deemed acceptable by parents, teachers, and authority figures. These enduring authors and works included James Fenimore Cooper and his "Leatherstocking Tales," action stories that teemed with heroism and adventure. Cooper wrote about life in the American wilderness, of frontiersmen, and Native Americans. He examined the issues of progress in contrast with the loss of forest and virgin waterways. He was a writer of conscience and patriotism and is regarded by many as the first great writer of fiction in America.

**Special Note**
The illustrator listed in the captions is the cover artist; when the cover artist's name is unknown, the illustrator of the book is listed.

The March Hare, the Mad Hatter, and the Cheshire Cat were characters created by an Oxford faculty member and mathematician named Charles Dodgson. He was better known by his pen name, Lewis Carroll. Carroll's *Alice's Adventures in Wonderland* and later *Through the Looking Glass* were nonsensical flights of fancy that were often read and reread, with each reading offering new perspectives and insights into the highly imaginative stories.

Robert Louis Stevenson wrote with entertainment as his goal. His writings were full of romantic images: villainous pirates, gallant knights, and thrilling battles. The adventures included treasure hunts, kidnappings, and daring escapes. His stories, which often dealt with young characters, were well told and fast-paced. But many critics believe his greatest achievement in children's writing was his book of poetry, *A Child's Garden of Verses*.

Through keen observation of human nature, infused with great wit and more than a little satire, Samuel Langhorne Clemens (writing as Mark Twain) provided an enduring picture of the people and their times. His writings fully encompassed the rural and small town lifestyles of Americans in the last half of the nineteenth century. He understood that Americans were fascinated with each other and loved to laugh at themselves. Many of his characters were composites of actual people he had met during the course of his own rather colorful life; these added realism to his stories. He knew boyhood adventure too. His classic tales, *The Adventures of Tom Sawyer* and *The Adventures of Huckleberry Finn*, are unmistakably "all boy." Widely regarded as a master of language, Twain stood at the forefront of American literature at the beginning of the twentieth century.

The classics had competition. Much to the chagrin of their parents and teachers, children and teenagers were choosing another form of reading material. The classics, many children thought, belonged to another generation; they wanted to pursue more topical stories. Much of it wasn't very high-toned or well written, and some of it was not even very respectable. A number of the magazines and "pulps" were adult stories thinly veiled as children's collections. These sometimes violent and lurid tales were a mixed success, but they helped create a niche for characters that shared the idealism and enthusiasm for the country; tales in which virtue was a reward and fair play paramount. The stories were wholesome enough to win at least the grudging acceptance of adults.

So was born the dime novel. The dime novel was little more than a weekly fantasy magazine. Its subject matter is best described by the stories' own banner titles and subtitles: Might and Main Library, Stories of Boys Who Succeed; Fame and Fortune Weekly, Stories of Boys Who Make Money; and Pluck and Luck, Complete Stories of Adventure. There were many more, and each had its own thrilling characters, such as Bowery Billy and Fred Fearnot.

Of all the sensational characters, one stood above the rest in popularity, courage, and goodness. Gilbert Patton, writing under the name of Burt L. Standish, created Frank

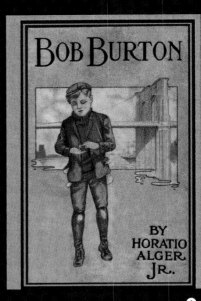

**1**

**BOB BURTON**
Author: Horatio Alger Jr.
Illustrator: Unknown
Publisher: John C Winston Co

**2**

**TIP TOP WEEKLY NO. 251**
Author: Burt L. Standish
Ilustrator: Unknown
Publisher: Street & Smith

**❸** 📖

**TIP TOP WEEKLY NO. 269**
Author: Cover Story by Burt
L. Standish
Illustrator: Unknown
Publisher: Street & Smith

**❹** 📖

**BOWERY BOY LIBRARY NO. 34**
Author: Cover story by John
Conway
Illustrator: Unknown
Publisher: Street & Smith

**❺** 📖

**WORK AND WIN NO. 300**
Author: Hal Standish
Illustrator: Unknown
Publisher: Street & Smith

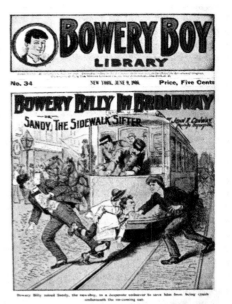

Merriwell, whose very name speaks to honesty, good temperament, and strength of health. Frank Merriwell has it all. He is handsome, fair-minded, athletically gifted, intelligent, and ambitious. He is even described as "kingly." His readers first meet him during his school days, follow his academic career through Yale, then travel the globe with him. His adventures bring him success, always success, in every athletic endeavor. He foils criminals and other assorted scoundrels at each turn, and throughout he remains true to his ideals, never wavering from the straight and narrow. Frank Merriwell's world is clearly defined between good and evil, and stories of his escapades sold prodigiously, reaching an estimated 125 million readers. Just as the character of Frank Merriwell epitomized the dime novel at the century's turn, one nineteenth-century writer had grown to such stature that his very name became a household word. He was Horatio Alger.

Horatio Alger's own unusual success story rivaled those he created. He was born in 1832 in Chelsea (now Revere), Massachusetts. His father, a Unitarian minister, gave Horatio a strongly disciplined, spiritual upbringing. He was home schooled in algebra and Latin — somewhat irregularly — until he enrolled at Gates Academy. Three years later, he was accepted at Harvard College, graduating Phi Beta Kappa in 1852. Alger entered Harvard Divinity School but withdrew to become assistant editor for the Boston Daily Advertiser. In 1857, he returned to the School and graduated in 1860. He volunteered three times for military service in the Union Army during the Civil War, but was deemed unfit each time as a result of near-sightedness, bronchial asthma, and size (he weighed 120 pounds and stood just over five feet).

A short time later, Alger accepted a ministerial post in Massachusetts but left that for a grand tour of England and Europe. He wrote articles for the New York Sun to defray travel and living expenses. On his return, he moved to New York City to write children's books.

In writing about the struggles on the streets, Horatio Alger found his true calling. His characters grew at least partly

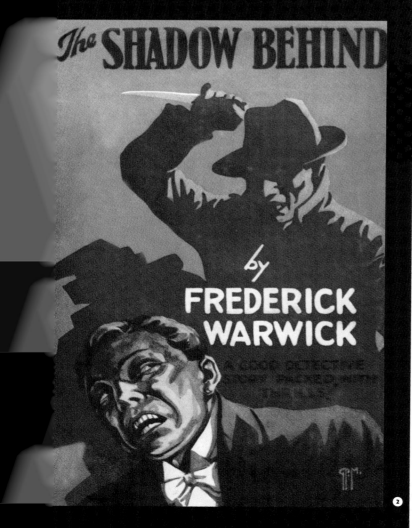

from his observations. He witnessed impoverished and sometimes homeless children hawking newspapers or shining shoes on the streets. Those real life children, he believed, still had hope despite their adversity, and through his writing, he would liberate their dreams. Although Alger's stories were rooted in reality, he soon transfigured them into improbable morality tales. It didn't matter that the yarns of success from rags to riches were implausible. He knew his audience; he wrote stories about boys for boys.

His stories carried a common theme. Alger's hero is of modest upbringing, a sturdy, self-reliant, bright-eyed youngster. Unashamed of his humble beginnings, the lad sets about to make something of himself. Through hard work, ingenuity, and resolve, the boy overcomes tragedy, poverty, and injustice. He is always successful and ultimately gains a measure of respect. The stories were a virtual blueprint for personal growth and ambition that could only happen in America. Readers got the message that their very existence in the United States was their providence. This great land of opportunity championed the underdog. If one possessed the mettle, he or she would prevail. The message of Horatio Alger was a pep talk for the masses.

The nation's youth hungered for each Alger offering, and he did not disappoint them. In the 32 years between his first great success, the "Ragged Dick" series, and his death in 1898, Horatio Alger wrote more than 120 books. His inspirational works continued to have brisk sales into the 1920s. While his writing produced unparalleled sales, it was critically panned. There were claims that while the text espoused hard work as a means to success, the stories routinely provided the hero with a convenient piece of luck to assist him in his quest. This bit of good fortune, critics said, was unrealistic, and even worse, it showed a lack of imagination. Critics further criticized Alger's work for general sloppiness; in some cases, events were left unfinished and characters were lost and unaccounted for. Alger might have deserved this criticism, but he did not seek critical tributes. Through the creation of positive role models, he remained loyal to his upbringing and faith. His lasting achievement bears his name: the label "A Horatio Alger story" is often given today to a real life person who triumphs over adversity.

As a result of exhaustion and illness in the closing years of his life, Horatio Alger was unable to complete his last novel. He had already written two hundred pages, and he longed for a proper finish to the book. His solution was to hire an able ghostwriter who could provide an ending while Alger's name remained under the title. His choice was up-and-coming editor and writer of juvenile books named Edward Stratemeyer. Neither man could have known that this agreement would be a symbolic passing of the torch from Horatio Alger, the dominant writer of juvenile dime novels of the nineteenth century, to Edward Stratemeyer, who would revolutionize and define the business of juvenile books in the century to come.

Stratemeyer's father, Henry Julius Stratemeyer, was a German immigrant participating in the California Gold Rush when word reached him that his brother, who lived in Elizabeth, New Jersey, had died. Henry left the gold fields and journeyed east to assist his brother's widow, Anna, and her four children. Eventually Henry and Anna fell in love and were married; this union produced two children, the younger of whom was Edward.

Edward's upbringing was typical of the strict, obedience oriented, German-American family of the age. The youngster was shy, quiet, and generally serious-minded. And he loved to read, the Alger novels being among his favorites. He loved to write too, using his skills to entertain friends and family. He graduated from high school and continued his education in literature and composition through private tutors. His parents, particularly his father, opposed his interest in writing as a vocation, believing the work was not sufficiently stable nor financially rewarding enough to provide for a family.

But Edward's dream would not die, so while he clerked at his brother's tobacco shop, he continued to write. Some report his devotion to writing was so intense that he sometimes wrote by day on the store's brown wrapping paper and recopied the stories at night for submission to a publisher. He sold only a few, but he was gaining experience in his craft.

Finally, the success he had long dreamed of was his when *Victor Horton's Idea* was published as a dime novel. It was his first notable payday, and the one that gave him the confidence to pursue a career in literature. In the following years, he proved himself a highly competent author of juvenile novels. Although his stories were not long on complexity, they were strong, met publishers' deadlines, and required limited editing.

As his successes increased, so did his ambition. When offered a position as editor for the dime novel publication *Good News*, he readily accepted. His duties were a perfect match for his ambitions. As editor, he learned the business side of writing and became immersed in the whole publication process. If Edward Stratemeyer had previously held any high-handed notions of the work as art, he soon lost them. Among his more pressing concerns now were deadlines and the bottom line. He learned and practiced the team approach to the work: that no individual player is greater than the team. To ensure this, the writer remained anonymous, which allowed substitute writers to be inserted as needed. The author's pseudonym for any given dime novel remained constant; thus the public was unaware that several writers might have worked on a single series. Under this system, writers received a lump sum buyout for their work and agreed to claim no future royalties. Publishers recognized that writers could be an independent lot if given credit for their work; business dictated that it was best to keep them unknown and a little hungry.

In his new position, Stratemeyer flourished. He worked tirelessly editing *Good News*, while supplementing his income by inserting his own stories into the publication. He also found time to write books on the side. But Stratemeyer, for all his success as a writer and editor, was frustrated by his own ambition. The true success of the team (his success) was enjoyed by the publication's owners. It must have seemed to Edward Stratemeyer a waste of his education and talent.

**❶**   📖

**MIGHT AND MAIN LIBRARY NO. 43**
Author: Unknown
Illustrator: Unknown
Publisher: Street & Smith

**❷**  

**THE SHADOW BEHIND**
Author: Frederick Warwick
Illustrator: Unknown
Publisher: Modern Publishing Co

**❸**  

**ARABIAN NIGHTS**
Authors: Kate Wiggin, Nora Smith
Illustrator: Maxfield Parrish
Publisher: Charles Scribner's Sons

**❹**  

**ARABIAN KNIGHTS**
Authors: Kate Wiggin, Nora Smith
Illustrator: Maxfield Parrish
Publisher: Charles Scribner's Sons

❸

❹

**① □□□□**

**ARABIAN NIGHTS "PRINCE CODADAD"**
Author: Kate Wiggin, Nora Smith
Illustrator: Maxfield Parrish
Publisher: Charles Scribner's Sons

**② □□□□**

**TREASURE ISLAND - ENDPAPERS**
Author; Robert Louis Stevenson
Illustrator: N.C. Wyeth
Publisher: Charles Scribner's Sons

**③ □□□□**

**TREASURE ISLAND "OVER THE BARRICADE"**
Author: Robert Louis Stevenson
Illustrator: N.C. Wyeth
Publisher: Charles Scribner's Sons

**④ □□□□**

**TREASURE ISLAND "THE HOSTAGE"**
Author: Robert Louis Stevenson
Illustrator: N.C. Wyeth
Publisher: Charles Scribner's Sons

**⑤ □□□□**

**TREASURE ISLAND "OLD PEW"**
Author: Robert Louis Stevenson
Illustrator: N.C. Wyeth
Publisher: Charles Scribner's Sons

Success may be determined by as many different standards as there are people. Wealth, fame, and power are coveted by some, while peace of mind might spell success for others. Stratemeyer most certainly would have added control to his list. He started his own company, the Stratemeyer Syndicate, in 1905 to gain such control. The Syndicate would allow him greater freedom. There would be risk for sure — even setbacks and failures but the success would be his alone. He had a plan, an aggressive approach to juvenile writing, publishing, and marketing. The business ideas were not necessarily original; he mixed and matched from a variety of existing enterprises. But he had a knack for identifying the strengths of each and enhancing them. He brought to his new company a proven series, "The Rover Boys," and what would prove to be his longest running series, "The Bobbsey Twins." From this foundation, he began his fiction factory.

Stratemeyer thought the present juvenile book catalog was too narrow for America's youth. He believed a series should be created to serve a multitude of interests. If a youth fancied sports, moving pictures, science, or automobiles, they could soon read, under the Syndicate's banner, "Baseball Joe," "Movie Boys," "Tom Swift," or "The Motor Boys." Indeed there would be a series developed for nearly every taste. Publishers balked at first. They complained that the problem with series books was they took time to catch on; often three books were produced before the series found an audience. Stratemeyer's solution was to have the first three books written and on hold, then published together and released nearly simultaneously, thereby creating an instant series without the wait.

Stratemeyer's ambitious plan required a team of writers, a small staff of regulars, and a larger group of ever-changing freelancers whom he would audition by providing a loose story outline from which the writers would supply a two-chapter writing sample. Once chosen, the writers would be offered a contract under which they would sell the Syndicate their story for a one-time flat fee, agree to write under the series' pseudonym, and promise to never reveal that they were the authors behind the pseudonym.

If all terms were accepted, the work would begin, with the authors receiving an outline quite different from the audition outline. This outline contained specific instructions; it described all characters in detail, and provided exact behavior and language directives. The plot was strictly specified, along with major events of each chapter. As a rule, every chapter was to end with a "page turner" or cliffhanger to maintain excitement for the subsequent chapter. The names of previous adventures were to be sprinkled in to promote earlier works; likewise, upcoming story titles were inserted in the book's closing chapters to foster a continued interest in the series. If the Syndicate were to prosper, it would do so on the volume of the work. Therefore, writing quickly within the guidelines was paramount. If the authors accomplished these goals, they could count on future assignments, at the usual flat fee.

Stratemeyer had other ideas as well. In dime novels, the writer usually employed a single lead character to tell the story. Stratemeyer reasoned that if two or even more leads were introduced, the reader would more likely identify with some aspect of a lead character's personality and

KIDNAPPED
THE ADVENTURES OF DAVID BALFOUR
ROBERT LOUIS STEVENSON

*ILLUSTRATED BY*
N.C.WYETH

NEW YORK
CHARLES SCRIBNER'S SONS

❶ ▢▢▢▢▢
**KIDNAPPED-frontispiece**
Author: Robert Louis Stevenson
Illustrator: N.C. Wyeth
Publisher: Charles Scribner's Sons

❷ ▢▢▢▢▢
**KIDNAPPED "SIEGE OF THE ROUND-HOUSE"**
Author: Robert Louis Stevenson
Illustrator: N.C. Wyeth
Publisher: Charles Scribner's Sons

become a devotee of the series. His business plan was simple. It was more characters to love, more titles from which to chose. With all these aspects of the plan under his firm hand and watchful eye, his Syndicate became amazingly prolific and prosperous. He controlled such a prodigious output of salable material that he developed a relationship with his publishers few other writers would ever enjoy. With about thirty titles a year coming to print, an enormous total for a single writer, Stratemeyer had increased leverage for royalty payments. He could also command a larger percentage of the publisher's advertising budget for Syndicate titles. He was a tough negotiator, but if giving in to his business demands was bad, competing with him was worse. His publishers were happy to have him as part of their organization.

Stratemeyer's business experience had taught him not to rest upon his laurels, and he remained driven in his pursuits: outlining, writing, and editing. He was constantly looking to bring new series to publication. He put in full days at the office and was likely to bring work home as well. His home life now included his wife Magdalene and daughters Harriet and Edna. The girls, especially Harriet, took a keen interest in their father's business. In the coming years, this interest caused Stratemeyer some consternation, for Harriet wanted an active role at the Syndicate.

Although she had an undeniable talent for writing and editing, Stratemeyer rebuffed his daughter's ambitions. He believed that if Harriet worked in any capacity at the Syndicate, he might be viewed as a father unable to provide ade-

quately for his daughter's needs, forcing her into the workplace. For a time, she was allowed to perform editing duties in the relative secrecy of the family home. When Harriet married Russell Adams, her father cut her from Syndicate activities altogether, believing that the duties of a wife and mother were a higher calling than any business enterprise. Harriet had little choice but to comply with her father's wishes, but her interest in writing and the Syndicate endured.

Edward Stratemeyer was now outlining more and writing less. He found this to be the best use of his time, for his plot creations came quickly and seemed inexhaustible. New series in development included one centering on two brothers, sons of a famous detective, who would solve mysteries as a team after school and on summer vacations. The series became known as "The Hardy Boys" and featured the crime-solving exploits of Frank and Joe Hardy. The notion of the brothers independently solving mysteries seemed to strike a chord with young readers, and the series grew to become a flagship of the Syndicate. In the Stratemeyer business plan, if a series proved successful, a similar one would follow. "The Nancy Drew" series provided female readers with their own mystery-solving character and rivaled "The Hardy Boys" in sales and popularity.

The Syndicate continued to thrive, but its founder's health was failing. Stratemeyer continued to work, but a succession of heart attacks slowed him and eventually took his life in the early summer of 1930. For Edward

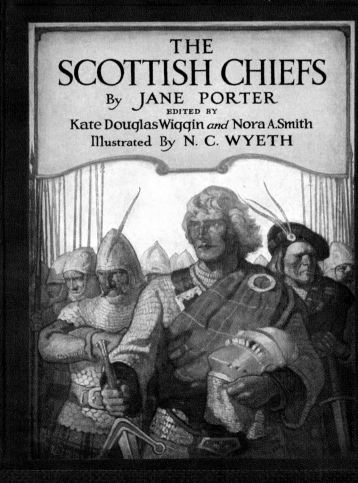

 **3**

**LAST OF THE MOHICANS "THE FIGHT IN THE FOREST"**
Author: James Fenimore Cooper
Illustrator: N.C. Wyeth
Publisher: Charles Scribner's Sons

**4**

**DEERSLAYER**
Author: James Fenimore Cooper
Illustrator: N.C. Wyeth
Publisher: Charles Scribner's Sons
Used by permission of Wyeth Family Archives

**5**

**THE SCOTTISH CHIEFS**
Author: Jane Porter
Illustrator: N.C. Wyeth
Publisher: Charles Scribner's Sons

Stratemeyer there was no great outpouring of national sympathy, for few of his vast readership had ever heard his name. The literary empire, which he alone had controlled, was now leaderless and in some disarray. Manuscripts in various stages of development at the time of his death needed to be completed. Publishers and freelance writers eagerly awaited information on the Syndicate's future.

At the time of her father's death, Harriet Adams had a family of her own with a life far away from her father's business. But ambition and determination must have been a family trait, for shortly after her father's passing, Harriet and her sister Edna assumed control of the Syndicate. These were challenging times for the Stratemeyer Syndicate, with untried leadership at the helm and the economic turmoil of the Great Depression ahead. Harriet carried on her father's outlining and editing duties and began writing stories as well. Of the two sisters, she played the dominant role in the business.

During the Depression and through the war years, the Syndicate limited its output to the more popular series. At the end of the war, Harriet Adams pursued a more aggressive approach in sales and marketing, and added new series, the immensely successful "Happy Hollisters" among them. Since the company's inception, Edward Stratemeyer had retained the rights to all published works. Harriet revived these older stories and reissued them after ghostwriters had performed updates, sometimes infusing the stories with new, more topical plots. The business practices were of her father's creation, but Harriet Adams made the business her own, and it

❷

❶

continued to prosper for another fifty years under her leadership.

As with any innovative, successful enterprise, the Stratemeyer Syndicate had its share of detractors. The emphasis on high output, many thought, limited the literary strength of the work. Likewise, the strict guidelines didn't allow the author as artist to emerge. Another grievance was the exploitive nature of the flat fees accorded the authors. Similarly, that authors didn't receive credit for their work as a result of company-imposed pseudonyms seemed unfair. How Edward Stratemeyer would have answered these allegations is unclear, for he avoided involving himself and his company in controversy, probably because the time spent wasn't productive.

That indeed may be the heart of the matter for Stratemeyer. It was about production and his means to attain maximum production by controlling the creative process. There is no doubt that he loved literature. But he understood that the marrying of literature and business would primarily serve business the most and literature the least. He could accept that. He stands among the great entrepreneurs of his time.

Evidence of this, and perhaps the epitome of his professional life, can be found in his dealings with the estate of his hero, Horatio Alger. Alger had contracted with Stratemeyer to finish or ghostwrite a single piece of fiction that Alger had begun but was too ill to complete. Stratemeyer began writing the novel's conclusion after Alger's death. He soon realized he could

**1** ▢▢▢

**DEERSLAYER-INTERIOR**
Author: James Fenimore Cooper
Illustrator: N.C. Wyeth
Publisher: Charles Scribner's Sons
Used by permission of the Wyeth Family
Archives

**2** ▢▢▢▢

**DEERSLAYER-INTERIOR**
Author: James Fenimore Cooper
Illustrator: N.C. Wyeth
Publisher: Charles Scribner's Sons
Used by permission of the Wyeth Family
Archives

**3** ▢▢

**KING ARTHUR AND HIS KNIGHTS-FRONTISPIECE**
Author: Howard Pyle
Illustrator: Frank Godwin
Publisher: John C Winston Co

**4** ▢▢▢

**THE PRINCE AND THE PAUPER**
Author: Mark Twain
Illustrator: Franklin Booth
Publisher: Harper & Brothers

**5** ▢▢▢

**THE PRINCE AND THE PAUPER**
Author: Mark Twain
Illustrator: Franklin Booth
Publisher: Harper & Brothers

Guinevere Turned from Her Father to the Stranger Knight **3**

**5**

①

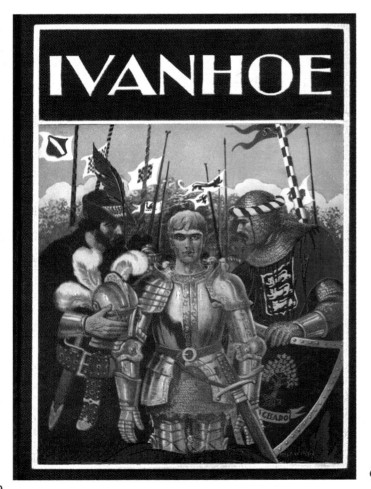

**① ▢▢▢**
**THE SWISS FAMILY ROBINSON**
Author: David Wyss
Illustrator: Frank Godwin
Publisher: John C Winston Co

②

halve Alger's existing work and produce from it two books, which he did, with permission from the Alger estate. He further inquired whether Alger left behind any story fragments or outlines. The estate provided additional unfinished materials, and he fashioned stories around those as well. From the original single book contract came a total of ten volumes, from which Stratemeyer gained the financial reward. All were published under Alger's name, but were the result of Stratemeyer's ambition and hard work. Quite probably Edward Stratemeyer would have been a great success at most any business endeavor he chose, and that his impact in any field would have been significant. It is difficult to fault him for that. For better or for worse, Edward Stratemeyer worked and lived the American Dream. Horatio Alger could not have told Edward Stratemeyer's story any better.

Frank Merriwell and The Rover Boys were creations of the most influential figures in juvenile fiction at the beginning of the twentieth century. Yet despite their many achievements, Burt L. Standish and Edward Stratemeyer are largely unknown names. Each of these men had silent partners of a sort. These silent partners were the books' artists and illustrators whose art was used to advertise and motivate a perspective buyer into picking up a publication. But beyond the sale, the appeal of the artwork might have motivated a reader to retain a treasured volume for his or her own collection.

An illustration may be loosely defined as the connection, for reasons of adornment, of a picture with text. A picture, in general, depicts a pivotal moment, expands a central theme, or helps describe a dramatic event in the written word. Illustrations commonly appeared in American adult novels and other publications through most of the nineteenth century. By 1900, the use of illustrations in adult reading material was gradually limited to scholarly books. Artists and illustrators began to show their portfolios to publishers of children's and juvenile books, and in this arena, they found their niche.

Illustrators rejoiced in the exposure children's books afforded their work, as it was not uncommon for a picture to appear on every page. Books for teenagers required illustrations with greater sophistication, but in more limited quantity. One or two illustrations, generally a black-and-white frontispiece and a pen-and-ink drawing, might make up the whole of the book's interior artwork. A fortunate illustrator was not always confined to an edition's interiors, but was able to showcase his or her best work on a dust jacket.

At first, dust jackets were referred to as "wrappers," and their use was restricted to expensive books awaiting sale. Booksellers championed commercial use of the dust jacket as a means to lessen damage to their inventory. Many dust jackets were removed at the time of sale or soon after, so the ornate bookbinding might be displayed in the buyer's home. Over time, the dust jacket changed from a relatively plain wrapper to one displaying other books in the publisher's catalog. As promotional tools, the jackets proved to be of value, but lacking marketing research, could not be linked to a direct sale. Retailers had long known that once a customer had a product in hand, he or she would strongly consider a purchase. Enticing the prospective purchaser to actually pick up the product naturally interested the seller. Book retailers found they could

3

"I here perceived the whole fleet moving in order"    Page 40

4

5

GULLIVER'S TRAVELS

**1** 📖📖
**ALICE IN WONDERLAND- INTERIOR**
Author: Lewis Carroll
Illustrator: Maraja
Publisher: Grosset & Dunlap

**3** 📖📖
**ALICE IN WONDERLAND- INTERIOR**
Author: Lewis Carroll
Illustrator: Maraja
Publisher: Grosset & Dunlap

**2** 📖📖
**ALICE IN WONDERLAND- INTERIOR**
Author: Lewis Carroll
Illustrator: Maraja
Publisher: Grosset & Dunlap

**4** 📖📖
**ALICE IN WONDERLAND- INTERIOR**
Author: Lewis Carroll
Illustrator: Maraja
Publisher: Grosset & Dunlap

best accomplish this with art on a protective wrapper, no less.

Soon the jackets carried art to enhance the sale of the book it contained, and promotion of other volumes was moved to jacket flaps. Some editions arrived at the point of sale without jackets, but many of these had hand-applied, paste-on illustrations on the front cover. Such was the power of art to sell.

Book illustration, of course, was a boon to the art community; soon illustrators realized an abundance of potential assignments existed. That children's and juvenile books were at the forefront of this explosion of illustrations was further good fortune for them. Though children and teenagers were tough and demanding of their art, they were also receptive, and illustrators found new freedom in producing honest artwork for an adoring public. With the offering of such great opportunities, it is no surprise that the finest illustrators in the country were drawn to the field of illustrating children's and juvenile books.

Without doubt, Howard Pyle is rightly called the Father of American Illustration. During an age when the whole nation engaged in reading as a pastime, Pyle and his faithful followers shaped the use of illustration with creations that were at once modern, relevant, and faithful to the stories to which they were tied. Howard Pyle was a man of many and varied talents. He was a prodigious reader and researcher, from which he profited as a writer. His tales of pirates and knights were products of his research and were widely praised for their truth and accuracy. Of course, these books were strongly illustrated with characters costumed so richly and with such authority that Pyle's depiction of knights and pirates became the accepted historical version, surviving to the present. The illustrations' historical accuracy was important to Pyle, but so was their drama. He was a student of the human experience, and from this he brought real life emotions to his illustrations. Surely the truth in Pyle's illustrations accounts for its continued appreciation. With his reputation for greatness in the field assured, his respect and devotion to his art compelled him to start a career in teaching. And as a teacher, Pyle may have equaled his influence as an artist. Without question, he was a master in both realms.

His first foray into the teaching profession was well received but, by his own high standards, mixed. Pyle believed that standard art class sizes were unmanageably large and that they contained students at such varying levels of ability that he could measure little real progress. His solution was to form his own school of art. It was located in the Brandywine River Valley of Pennsylvania and became known as the Brandywine School. His class sizes ranged from six to twelve students. Pyle personally selected his students from hundreds of applicants. Tuition was nominal, if collected at all.

Pyle's teaching techniques were highly innovative. He observed that most art curricula taught imitative art based on the works of the masters. Pyle implored his students to adopt a style of their own based primarily on their own life experience. He believed that illustrators must encounter a wide variety of people and places, and thus he encouraged his students to travel and study the drama in life. He said that the world would reveal the look of hatred or greed in a man's eye and that a hard man's face could soften at the birth of his child. He suggested that such drama was common, but its capture and reproduction was not. The studio therefore was a place for work; the world was the place for learning.

Pyle conducted many classes outdoors — not in the studio — so that his charges could observe natural light and learn to utilize its subtle and dramatic characteristics. He preached accuracy and truth in illustration. He demanded his students pay attention to every detail and realize that growth in their art must be unending. They listened to him, for emerging from the Brandywine School were the masters of the next century, among them, Maxfield Parrish and Newell Convers (N.C.) Wyeth.

If anyone took Pyle's lessons of developing one's own style to heart, it was Maxfield Parrish. His schooling began early. His father Stephen, himself a painter and etcher, recognized his son's extraordinary gifts and set about to foster them. His parents had sufficient means to allow him to travel to Europe to study. He graduated from Haverford College and attended Pennsylvania Academy of Fine Arts and Drexel Institute. The education he received in technique, coupled with his fertile imagination, produced early success.

# Little Women

by¹
Louisa May Alcott

Centennial Edition

## EIGHT COUSINS

BY LOUISA MAY ALCOTT

COMPLETE AUTHORIZED EDITION

*Then all drew to the fire*

sa May Alcott
ssie Willcox Smith
ttle, Brown, & Co.
mission by Little,

**② ▢▢▢**
**EIGHT COUSINS**
Author: Louisa May Alcott
Illustrator: Pelagie Doane
Publisher: Grosset & Dunlap

**③ ▢**
**LITTLE WOMEN- FRONTISPIECE**
Author: Louisa May Alcott
Illustrator: Jessie Willcox Smith
Publisher: Little, Brown, & Co.
Used with permission by Little,
Brown, & Co.

Maxfield Parrish's search for an audience was brief, for something in his pieces appealed to nearly everyone. From connoisseur and critic to the blue-collared Everyman, Parrish fascinated all with his unique use of color and his highly decorative images. His illustrations showed such intricacy that each viewing led to yet another. His work embodied a pleasant, even soothing tone, without resorting to sentimentality. His illustrations for *The Arabian Nights, Their Best Known Stories* characterizes his early work. The twelve illustrations complement the narration of Scheherazade, as she entices and entertains the Sultan (who has her life in his hands) with tales of magic, humor, high adventure, and suspense. From this edition is the illustration entitled "Prince Codadad," which is notable for the sensation of speed and determination it communicates. The illustration depicts a sturdy craft at full sail, the boat's speed emitting a spray of mist from her bow as she crests a swell; the crew stands forward together, locked in a single purpose. Illustrations of this kind fulfill their intended purpose by enhancing, even strengthening, the text.

Parrish's work in other youth volumes was no less impressive. These works include *Mother Goose in Prose* and *Poems of Childhood*. Parrish was, to say the least, prolific; he produced prints, posters, and illustrations into the 1960s. But in the first two decades of the century, Maxfield Parrish and his peers presided over what may be viewed as the classic age of children and juvenile book illustration. Books at this time combined the country's finest illustrators with the best of the world's authors. A contemporary of Parrish, another student of Pyle, perhaps best exemplified this era. He was Newell Convers Wyeth.

Wyeth was interested in art and displayed natural ability at an early age. In his teens, he was inclined to follow those interests at the expense of his schoolwork. In fact, young Wyeth wanted to be an artist, and he was determined. His father found his son's behavior troubling. The boy's staunchest ally, his mother, sought to intercede on her son's behalf before his father disciplined him. She traveled to Boston, where she presented several of her son's drawings for artistic assessment, and was informed that the work showed promise. With this validation, she championed Wyeth's future education in art. His father, though still not completely convinced, relented.

First, Wyeth studied drafting at Mechanic's Art School in Boston, followed by classes at Massachusetts Normal Art School, then the Eric Pape School of Art. Next came the coveted acceptance to Howard Pyle's Brandywine School. Wyeth was in awe of Pyle, honored to be chosen, overwhelmed, and excited about what lay ahead. His letters home spoke of the lessons and work at the school. He wrote that those who thought an artist's life was easy were greatly mistaken — this was hard work! Despite this, he proved to be a remarkably fast learner. His strength as an illustrator, beyond his extraordinary artistic gift, was soon apparent; his passion for life, which Pyle constantly emphasized, was a vital component to his success as an illustrator. Wyeth harnessed his enthusiasm and infused this into the characters in his illustrations. In short order, he was selling his work to the nation's leading, most prestigious magazines. He was twenty.

Following the advice of his teacher, Wyeth journeyed west to experience the rich romance of cowboys, Indians, and the wilderness of the plains. He did not conduct his observations of the west as a bystander; instead, he became a participant. He served as a cowpuncher and rode in a roundup. He

**❹** 🗔

**GRACE HARLOWE'S FIRST YEAR AT OVERTON COLLEGE**
Author: Jessie Graham Flower, A.M.
Illustrator: Unknown
Publisher: Altemus

**❺** 🗔

**ROSE IN BLOOM**
Author: Louisa May Alcott
Illustrator: Clara M. Burd
Publisher: John C Winston Co

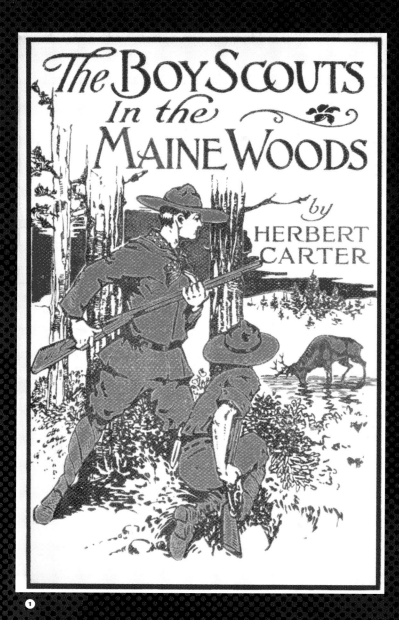

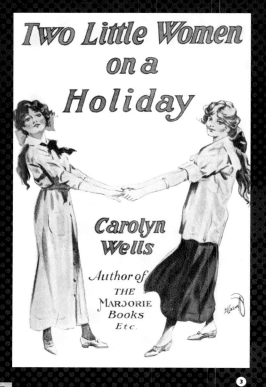

**3** 📖

**TWO LITTLE WOMEN ON A HOLIDAY**
Author: Carolyn Wells
Illustrator: E.C. Caswell
Publisher: Grosset & Dunlap

**4** 📖

**TWO LITTLE WOMEN AND TREASURE HOUSE**
Author: Carolyn Wells
Illustrator: Pelagie Doane
Publisher: Grosset & Dunlap

**5** 📖📖

**THE LITTLE ENGINE THAT COULD**
Author: Watty Piper
Illustrators: George & Doris Hauman
Publisher: Platt & Munk

4

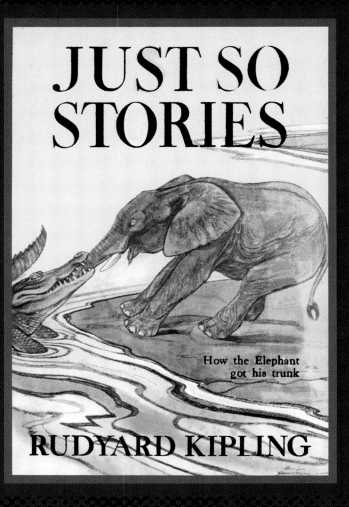

5

6

**6** 📖

**JUST SO STORIES**
Author: Rudyard Kipling
Illustrators: Paul Bransom, J.M. Gleeson
Publisher: Garden City Publishing Co

visited Indian reservations. He rode in a posse in search of bandits. At first, he had planned to sketch what he saw but soon abandoned this, realizing that he could best learn by sharing the work and hardships of his fellow man. He was right. The respect and appreciation he gained for rough men performing hard tasks never left him.

His western journeys complete, Wyeth returned home and married Carolyn Bockius. They built their home in the Brandywine Valley where they were to raise their five children. Wyeth was now much in demand as an illustrator and could freely choose the projects that interested him. He undertook a number of children's books, the first of which was Robert Louis Stevenson's *Treasure Island*. The illustrations are nothing short of masterpieces; this was one of Wyeth's favorite assignments, and it shows.

As we turn to the endpapers, the illustrations introduce the adventure immediately, depicting a menacing throng of pirates hell-bent for plunder. Read on, the illustration beckons, if you are to learn of their victims' plight. Inside the book, there are more treasures to be discovered. The painting of Old Pew is widely considered to be one of the finest of American illustrations. It depicts a blind man, Old Pew, abandoned by his cohorts in a moment of danger. He can clearly hear a group of riders bearing down upon him as he frantically taps with his cane to find his direction of escape. His hand is raised in a futile gesture for help, but who would risk his neck to assist this old blind man? Old Pew knows that he is doomed, and we know too because of Wyeth's illustration.

Another noteworthy illustration, "Over the Barricade," depicts doom, not for Old Pew, but this time for us. We are inside the relative safety of a stockade when we are beset by a band of pirates. The pirates are not conducting an ordinary raid; they are coming after us with murderous intent. Witness for yourself: they are armed with muskets, knives, and cutlasses as they clamor over the walls. Soon they will be upon us. How are we to defend ourselves against this lot? They are enormously powerful, evidenced by their immense forearms and huge hands. Why, these men don't even need weapons to destroy us! A thirst for destruction emanates from their faces — there will be no pity from these

HE LONGED TO BUY ONE AT ONCE FOR HIS LITTLE BROTHER IN ENGLAND

**❶** 📖📖

**HANS BRINKER OR THE SILVER SKATES**
Author: Mary Mapes Dodge
Illustrator: Alice Carsey
Publisher: Whitman

**❷** 📖📖

**HANS BRINKER OR THE SILVER SKATES - INTERIOR**
Author: Mary Mapes Dodge
Illustrator: Alice Carsey
Publisher: Whitman

**❸** 📖📖

**HANS BRINKER OR THE SILVER SKATES- FRONTISPIECE**
Author: Mary Mapes Dodge
Illustrator: Alice Carsey
Publisher: Whitman

THEIR MOTHER'S TALL FORM STOOD IN THE DOORWAY

pirates. Here Wyeth gives us the chaos inherent in battle. The light is cast upon the pirate at center, our focal point, but another ahead of him, almost in the shadows, is rushing forth with musket in hand. One must wonder if still more are ahead of this man and if the battle is beginning, or near its end. It is clear that there are more pirates on the way; we don't know the number. Wyeth's treatment of the siege, for a moment, removes some of the veneer of adventure and allows us to feel our own fear. This supplies the text with a potent dose of reality, exactly what a swashbuckling tale requires. Critical praise for the art of *Treasure Island* was overwhelming, and with it began a succession of assignments for Wyeth illustrating classic books for young people. The titles included *Kidnapped, Rip Van Winkle, Robin Hood*, and a great many more.

The matching of a James Fenimore Cooper book with N.C. Wyeth as illustrator seemed a natural. Both author and artist found nature to be the purest element for their respective talents. Both loved the romance of the wilderness and its indigenous people. The pairing was indeed golden. Wyeth illustrated two volumes of Cooper's work, first *The Last of the Mohicans*, then *Deerslayer*. The results were typical of Wyeth's stunning sense of drama and detail, but again, the addition of realism made it all valid.

In *The Last of the Mohicans*, a plate entitled "The Fight in the Forest" features two Indians wrestling on the ground with knives in a life and death struggle. Above them is another Indian about to wade into the fray, he too with knife drawn. To the right of the standing Indian is a frontiersman. He is holding his musket by the barrel as a club, the weapon cocked slightly over his head. In a moment, he will bring it down upon his enemy in a crushing blow. The faces of the participants are distorted by their quest for survival or for killing. The savagery is evident; their mouths are open and their white teeth are bared like vicious animals. The placement of the characters is purposeful, for while the center of the illustration is at once eye catching, the action radiates from it

**❹** ☐☐

**HEIDI**
Author: Johanna Spyri
Illustrator: Goldy-Young
Publisher: Whitman

**❺** ☐☐

**REBECCA OF SUNNYBROOK FARM**
Author: Kate Douglas Wiggin
Illustrator: F.C. Yohn
Publisher: Grosset & Dunlap

**❻** ☐☐

**HEIDI- FRONTISPIECE**
Author: Johanna Spyri
Illustrator: Goldy-Young
Publisher: Whitman

*"I Want to See What You Have Inside the House."*

# HEIDI'S CHILDREN

by CHARLES TRITTEN
JOHANNA SPYRI'S TRANSLATOR

GROSSET & DUNLAP

by CHARLES TRITTEN
JOHANNA SPYRI'S Translator

**①**

# THE STORY OF
# THE WIZARD OF OZ

708 **③**

*"Just see what Tobi's found!" Marta cried.*

**②**

**①** 📖

**HEIDI'S CHILDREN**
Author: Charles Tritten, Johanna Spyri's translator
Illustrator: Pelagie Doane
Publisher: Grosset & Dunlap

**②** 📖

**HEIDI'S CHILDREN- FRONTISPIECE**
Author: Charles Tritten, Johanna Spyri's translator
Illustrator: Pelagie Doane
Publisher: Grosset & Dunlap

**③** 📖📖📖

**THE STORY OF THE WIZARD OF OZ**
Author: Unknown
Illustrator: Henry E. Vallely
Publisher: Whitman

**④** 📖📖📖

**PINOCCHIO- THE STORY OF A PUPPET**
Author: C. Collodi
Illustrator: Esther Friend
Publisher: Rand McNally & Co

# PINOCCHIO
### The Story of a Puppet

**④**

like degrees from a compass.

And as always, there is more. Framing this great struggle is the wilderness. The scene, apart from the men, is a virgin forest in all its tranquility. The artist's implication is that after the battle has ended, with no regard to the victor, the forest would remain the same. The participants were indeed men of courage and purpose, but finally they were merely transient. The forest would endure.

As well received as these books were by both critic and readership, the trend in illustration began to turn elsewhere. Wyeth unquestionably had a great understanding of young people and their needs for realistic imagery. But he began to divide his time between book illustrations and his other art interests, which included the painting of murals and commercial projects. N.C. Wyeth never abandoned his roots in illustration, however, even when moving on to other ventures such as impressionistic painting. His purest gifts were for illustration, and he gave of them freely. His favored audience remained young readers of the classics.

Just as the trend in illustration began to change, so did young America's interest in reading material. Book themes were more topical, and the art mirrored this change. With the highly sensationalistic dime novels came covers depicting dramatic situations that could only be described as pure fantasy. The illustrations have a number of common elements. A good many picture the rescue of a woman or child from some onrushing mode of transportation: a runaway carriage bearing down upon a helpless damsel, or a newspaper boy being tripped in front of a trolley. In all cases, they are, of course, rescued by quick-thinking passersby with nerves of steel and courage to match. The world of dime novels was fraught with peril of all sorts. There are men catching children who had fallen from high windows and townspeople to be rescued from marauding circus animals. The saving of life on railroad tracks never seemed to go out of style. Most of the scenes take place in urban areas. The characters are generally well dressed, especially the women, who maintain an air of fashion, wholesomeness, and vulnerability. Bright colors are used throughout the illustrations, especially deep dramatic reds.

As sensational and successful as they were, the dime novel and its form of illustration began to give way to more mainstream reading. High adventure and intrigue still carried the day, but with a little less melodrama. The emerging Stratemeyer Syndicate publications came with illustrations of young people sporting automobiles and learning to fly. These depictions show less struggle and toil and more smiling characters. It seems that bravery, adventure, and mystery-solving need not be undertaken with gritted teeth and heavy heart. The pictures soften somewhat to coincide with the fun and amusement the stories bring.

The illustrations proved what children and juveniles already knew, that it was great to be young and an American. The classic illustrations of Pyle, Parrish, and Wyeth were to endure and be held in highest esteem, but there was increasing call for art depicting popular culture. As a form, it too would endure.

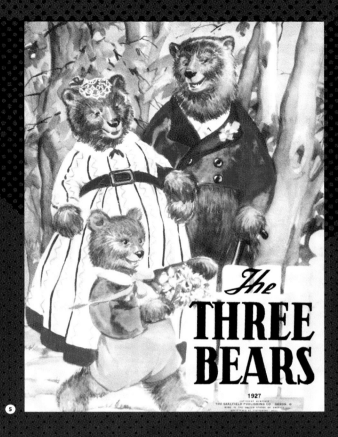

**5**

**5**

**THE THREE BEARS**
Author: Unknown
Illustrator: Unknown
Publisher: Saalfield

**6**

Regarded as one of America's finest illustrators, Newell Convers Wyeth. Courtesy of the Wyeth Family Archives.

**6**

**M**ystery/detective stories have been produced in one form or another since the eighteenth century, but none was written, even remotely so, in the style of the modern genre. The early mystery was thick with atmosphere and added a mix of horror. The stories did not readily invite the reader to help solve the puzzle. In fact, the solution often resulted from some important piece of information that a character had declined to expose until the end of the story. Readers who were inclined to read mysteries, understandably, did not care to be frustrated by improbable, last minute, "trick" endings. As a result, the mystery story did not sell well and few publishers sought the material. But through the influence of Edgar Allan Poe and his story *The Murders in the Rue Morgue*, the style of the mystery/detective story was forever changed.

The tale is of a seemingly unsolvable double homicide. The clues left behind are random and out of place in a murder scene. Poe's detective, Dupin, through analytic thought and acute observation, solves the murders. The tale's innovation lies in its telling. Poe leads us through his detective's crime-solving methods from which we gain entertainment and learn something of detective work as well. Poe allows us to participate in the story, as we become fellow travelers with the sleuth, something that would become a time-honored tradition in the writing of crime detection.

Sir Arthur Conan Doyle, in his creation of Sherlock Holmes, expanded further upon Poe's innovations by adding development to his principal character's personality. Now the mystery lover could solve crimes with a personal acquaintance. The series of stories involving Sherlock Holmes became enormously popular. Aside from fiction, crime writing was becoming big business. Newspapers of the day reported sensational true crimes in typical yellow journalism fashion. Actual police crime detection methods improved and netted results, all of which fueled the public's imagination. Increasingly, fictional stories involving crime or mystery were often thinly veiled true crime stories. The murders perpetrated by Jack the Ripper sprouted its own cottage industry of books and periodicals. These stories were steeped in gruesome images with elements of madness and horror. They were strictly for the adult readership.

Young people too had an interest in mystery and crime solving but not within the framework of the adult works. Understandably, juveniles growing up in a world of authority figures did not wish to entertain themselves with adult fare during their pleasure reading hours. So was born the juvenile mystery/amateur detective story whose sleuth was a teenager. So much the better that our young detectives were foiling adult criminals and were often requested to intervene in matters that police and other authority figures could not resolve.

Teenagers solving mysteries, as a concept for a series, was employed sporadically until the mid 1920s when Edward Stratemeyer introduced the Hardy Boys to the country's juvenile readers. The boys, Frank and younger brother Joe, reside in Bayport, a small town on Barmet Bay. The boys are the offspring of the renowned sleuth Fenton Hardy. It seems, therefore, a natural that the boys would fall into or be called upon to solve mysteries in the family tradition. The characters are assigned contrasting personalities. Frank is the more reserved and disciplined while Joe is the impulsive and somewhat reckless brother. Fenton Hardy is on hand for occasional advice and to express fatherly concern. The boys have friends, or in the vernacular of the day, chums, to assist them in their pursuits. Chet Morton, the beefy country boy, adds a dose of comic relief. Biff Hooper is another cohort who can be counted on in times of trouble. The principal characters in the series remain, of course, Frank and Joe, and together they search for buried treasure, stolen paintings, lost stamp collections, and hijacked

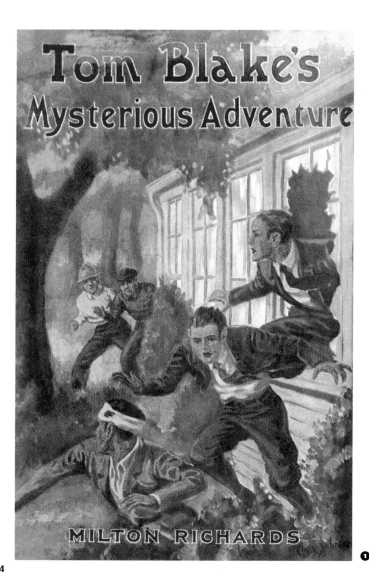

**❶** ▢▢

**TOM BLAKE'S MYSTERIOUS ADVENTURE**
Author: Milton Richards
Illustrator: Chris Schaare
Publisher: Saalfield

**❷** ▢▢▢▢▢

**THE TOWER TREASURE**
Author: Franklin W. Dixon
Illustrator: Walter S. Rogers
Publisher: Grosset & Dunlap
Reprinted with the permission of Pocket Books, a division of Simon & Schuster, Inc.
Copyright © 1927, 1959 by Simon & Schuster. Hardy Boys™ is a registered trademark of Simon & Schuster, Inc.

# THE HARDY BOYS
# THE MISSING CHUMS
## FRANKLIN W. DIXON

**⑤** 🔖

**TEDDY AND THE MYSTERY PARROT**
Author: Howard R. Garis
Illustrator: Unknown
Publisher: Cupples & Leon

**④** 🔖

**THE SEVEN SLEUTHS' CLUB**
Author; Carol Norton
Illustrator: Roy Mendenhall
Publisher: Saalfield

THE SEVEN
SLEUTHS' CLUB

**④**

**③** 🔖🔖🔖🔖

**THE MISSING CHUMS**
Author: Franklin W. Dixon
Illustrator: Walter S. Rogers
Publisher: Grosset & Dunlap
Reprinted with the permission of Pocket Books, a division of Simon & Schuster, Inc.
Copyright © 1928, 1962 by Simon & Schuster. Hardy Boys™ is a registered trademark of Simon & Schuster, Inc.

**③**

TEDDY
AND THE MYSTERY PARROT

HOWARD
R . GARIS

**⑤**

**①** █████

**BEVERLY GRAY FRESHMAN**
Author: Clair Blank
Illustrator: Unknown
Publisher: Grosset & Dunlap

**②** ████████

**THE SECRET OF THE OLD CLOCK**
Author: Carolyn Keene
Illustrator: Russell H. Tandy
Publisher: Grosset & Dunlap
Reprinted with the permission of Pocket Books, a division of Simon & Schuster, Inc.
Copyright © 1930, 1959 by Simon & Schuster. Nancy Drew™ is a registered trademark
of Simon & Schuster, Inc.

**③** ██████████

**THE HIDDEN STAIRCASE**
Author: Carolyn Keene
Illustrator: Russell H. Tandy
Publisher: Grosset & Dunlap
Reprinted with the permission of Pocket Books, a division of Simon & Schuster, Inc.
Copyright © 1930, 1959 by Simon & Schuster. Nancy Drew™ is a registered trademark
of Simon & Schuster, Inc.

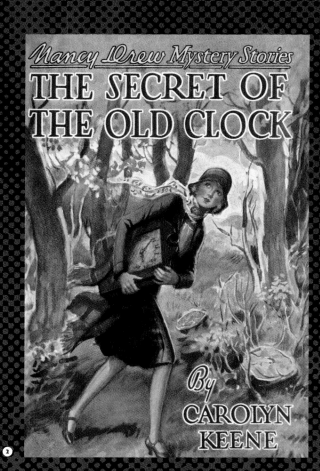

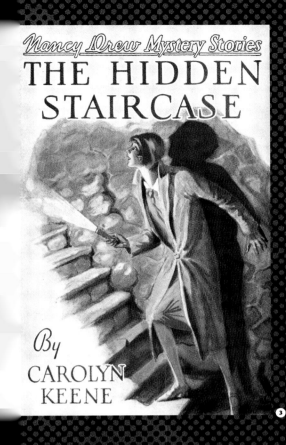

**THE SECRET OF RED GATE FARM**
Author: Carolyn Keene
Illustrator: Russell H. Tandy
Publisher: Grosset & Dunlap
Reprinted with the permission of Pocket Books,
a division of Simon & Schuster, Inc.
Copyright © 1931, 1961 by Simon & Schuster.
Nancy Drew™ is a registered trademark of
Simon & Schuster, Inc.

**THE BUNGALOW MYSTERY**
Author: Carolyn Keene
Illustrator: Russell H. Tandy
Publisher: Grosset & Dunlap
Reprinted with the permission of Pocket Books,
a division of Simon & Schuster, Inc.
Copyright © 1930, 1960 by Simon & Schuster.
Nancy Drew™ is a registered trademark of
Simon & Schuster, Inc.

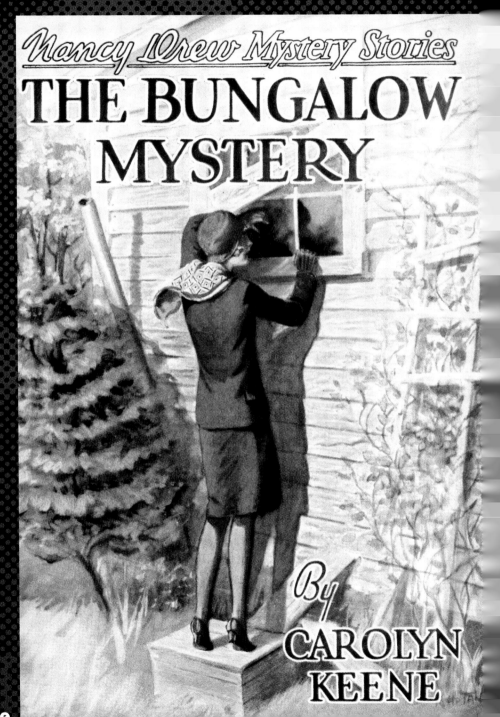

loads of cargo. They break up smuggling, counterfeiting, and spy rings. And throughout it all they remain wholesome in nature, their characters never tinged by the ruffians and criminals they encounter.

The means at their disposal for mystery solving are formidable. There is an at-home laboratory with up-to-date equipment for use in crime scene analysis. Apparently, they are unrestrained by need for capital for their adventures. Transportation is not an issue either as they freely travel by automobile, motorcycle, powerboat, airplane, and even iceboat. Unfettered by adult involvement and with unlimited means, these are a couple of teenagers who can get things, big things, accomplished. Unrealistic as the plots might have been, they were of tremendous appeal to the teenage reader, most of whom, as teenagers do, believed that they were not properly listened to or were under appreciated in their personal lives.

Sales of "Hardy Boys" material remained brisk, but changes were afoot. In 1959, a massive undertaking to reedit and, in some cases, rewrite the stories got underway. The stories' staples of fast-paced adventure with cliffhanging chapter finishes were maintained, but the move to modernize had begun. Terms such as "roadster" were deemed old-fashioned and were replaced. Such was the case with passages of

dialogue that, in the changing usage of the teen population, seemed laughable after nearly thirty years. Some of the Boys' old fans cried "foul" for they wanted the old stories to stay intact, but the stories were not intended for an older readership. Instead, they were for an ever-changing audience, new mysteries for new generations.

The one "Hardy Boys" constant was truly not a constant at all. The series authorship was credited to Franklin W. Dixon, which was actually a Stratemeyer Syndicate house name. More than a dozen writers were to assume the Dixon pen name over the years. The Hardy's first author was the young newspaper reporter, Leslie McFarlane, who many regard as the finest of the series' writers. McFarlane wrote the books from carefully prepared story outlines and chapter summaries, standard procedure with all the ghostwriters the Syndicate employed. For his efforts, he would earn $125 per completed manuscript, forfeiting future royalties. McFarlane wrote the first sixteen books, but he eventually left the Syndicate over financial considerations. His talents were missed, and the Syndicate lured him back for an additional five stories. Other writers who contributed to the series include Andrew Svenson, John Almquist, and James Lawrence. From 1927 to 1970, with the exception of 1958, at least one and as many as three new

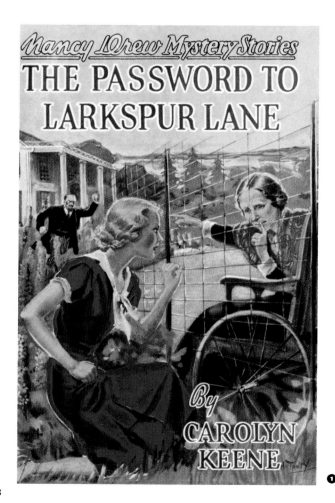

**❶** ▫▫▫▫

**THE PASSWORD TO LARKSPUR LANE**
Author: Carolyn Keene
Illustrator: Russell H. Tandy
Publisher: Grosset & Dunlap
Reprinted with the permission of Pocket Books, a division of Simon & Schuster, Inc. Copyright © 1966 by Simon & Schuster. Nancy Drew™ is a registered trademark of Simon & Schuster, Inc.

**❷** ▫▫▫▫▫

**THE CLUE IN THE DIARY**
Author: Carolyn Keene
Illustrator: Russell H. Tandy
Publisher: Grosset & Dunlap
Reprinted with the permission of Pocket Books, a division of Simon & Schuster, Inc. Copyright © 1932, 1962 by Simon & Schuster. Nancy Drew™ is a registered trademark of Simon & Schuster, Inc.

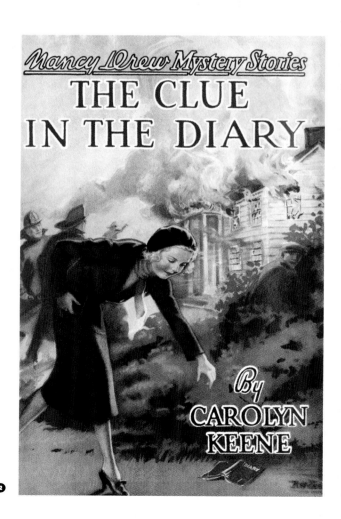

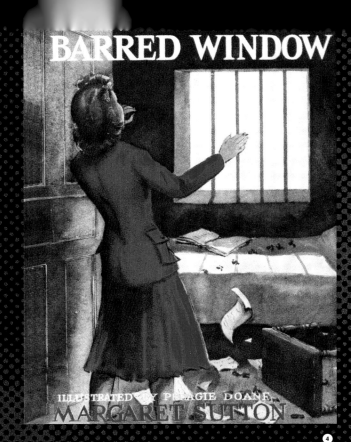

# THE YELLOW PHANTOM

## BY MARGARET SUTTON
### ILLUSTRATED BY PELAGIE DOANE

❸

# BARRED WINDOW

ILLUSTRATED BY PELAGIE DOANE
MARGARET SUTTON

❹

A JUDY BOLTON MYSTERY
# THE CLUE IN THE PATCHWORK QUILT

Illustrated by PELAGIE DOANE
MARGARET SUTTON

❺

---

❸ ▢▢▢

**THE YELLOW PHANTOM**
Author: Margaret Sutton
Illustrator: Pelagie Doane
Publisher: Grosset & Dunlap

❹ ▢▢▢

**THE SECRET OF THE BARRED WINDOW**
Author: Margaret Sutton
Illustrator: Pelagie Doane
Publisher: Grosset & Dunlap

❺ ▢▢▢

**THE CLUE IN THE PATCHWORK QUILT**
Author: Margaret Sutton
Illustrator: Pelagie Doane
Publisher: Grosset & Dunlap

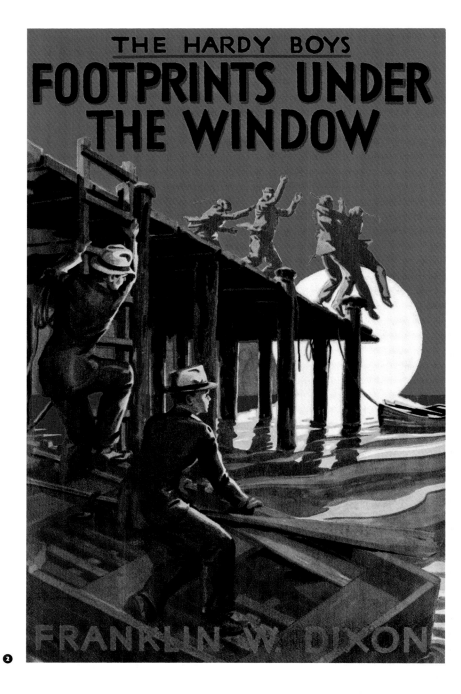

**❶** ▫▫▫▫

**THE SINISTER SIGN POST**
Author: Franklin W. Dixon
Illustrator: J. Clemens Gretter
Publisher: Grosset & Dunlap
Reprinted with the permission of Pocket Books, a division of Simon & Schuster, Inc. Copyright © 1936, 1968 by Simon & Schuster. Hardy Boys™ is a registered trademark of Simon & Schuster, Inc.

**❷** ▫▫▫▫

**FOOTPRINTS UNDER THE WINDOW**
Author: Franklin W. Dixon
Illustrator: J. Clemens Gretter
Publisher: Grosset & Dunlap
Reprinted with the permission of Pocket Books, a division of Simon & Schuster, Inc. Copyright © 1933, 1965 by Simon & Schuster. Hardy Boys™ is a registered trademark of Simon & Schuster, Inc.

**❸** ▫▫▫▫▫

**WHILE THE CLOCK TICKED**
Author: Franklin W. Dixon
Illustrator: J. Clemens Gretter
Publisher: Grosset & Dunlap
Reprinted with the permission of Pocket Books, a division of Simon & Schuster, Inc. Copyright © 1932, 1962 by Simon & Schuster. Hardy Boys™ is a registered trademark of Simon & Schuster, Inc.

**THE SECRET WARNING**

Author: Franklin W. Dixon
Illustrator: Paul S. Laune
Publisher: Grosset & Dunlap
Reprinted with the permission of Pocket
Books, a division of Simon & Schuster, Inc.
Copyright © 1938, 1966 by Simon &
Schuster. Hardy Boys™ is a registered
trademark of Simon & Schuster, Inc.

**THE HAUNTED ATTIC**

Autho: Margaret Sutton
Illustrator: Pelagie Doane
Publisher: Grosset & Dunlap

**SEVEN STRANGE CLUES**

Author: Margaret Sutton
Illustrator: Pelagie Doane
Publisher: Grosset & Dunlap

❹

❺

❻

"Hardy Boys" mystery stories were produced each year. "Author" Dixon's output was remarkable and was only rivaled in the Syndicate's mystery department by one other, "author" Carolyn Keene.

The pseudonym is most prominently linked to the "Nancy Drew" series of mysteries, written primarily for girls. Carolyn Keene was also the designated author for the "Dana Girls" series, which was, in the style of "Hardy Boys," two mystery-solving siblings, Louise and her sister Jean, and their tales of intrigue. Keene, like Hardy's Dixon, was a Syndicate house name employed by several writers, though two primarily. They were Mildred Wirt and Harriet Stratemeyer Adams.

Adams's degree of authorship is of some dispute, although she was, without question, an editor on the series. She outlined the stories and was certainly capable of writing an entire "Nancy" manuscript. As her father's chief heir to the Syndicate, Adams's influence on the series is obvious, and she is due much of the credit for the lasting success of the series. But did her role merely border on or was it indeed as author of a large portion of the "Nancy Drew" catalog? A marketing strategy of the Syndicate had long been the guarding of the actual names of the series' authors. This practice and the extensive use of pseudonyms have clouded many of the individual roles within the company. Some claims of authorship may never be entirely proved or, for that matter, disproved. However, it may be said that Harriet Adams's contributions to the tremendous success of "Nancy Drew" are at the very least substantial.

Mildred Wirt grew up in the nation's heartland where her pluck and athleticism as a child brought her the reputation of a tomboy. Her love of writing was evident at an early age and continued into her chosen field of study. She graduated from the University of Iowa with a degree in journalism. She applied for employment as a writer to the Stratemeyer Syndicate, which accepted her based on the writing sample she provided. Positions within the Syndicate were by no means secure for the writers as they were to prove themselves with each new assignment, which in turn might lead to the next assignment. Apparently, Wirt was up to the task. She began her Syndicate career with the ongoing "Ruth Fielding" series, for which she wrote several volumes.

Stratemeyer's "Fielding" series was nearing the end of its run, but he had a new series in development. It was a series for girls to be called the "Nancy Drew Mystery Stories." Mildred Wirt was chosen by Edward Stratemeyer himself to write the initial "Nancy Drew" offerings. Stratemeyer, in his review of Wirt's finished manuscript, was somewhat tepid about how his newest creation's personality was portrayed. He believed that several of Nancy's traits were unbecoming of a young lady's preferred behavior. Stratemeyer had a keen sense of public reaction and he knew his readership, but this time he was wrong. The series was an immediate success. A part of the Syndicate's business strategy had always been to keep a winning formula unaltered. So it was that Wirt would continue to write the mysteries, twenty-three in all, before her departure from the Syndicate. Her

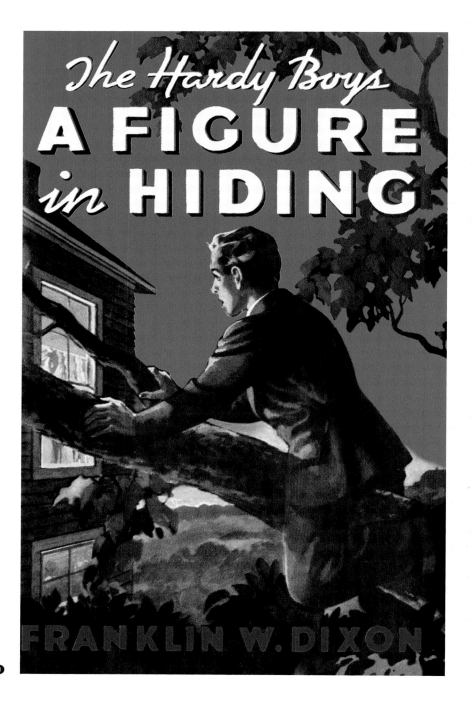

**A FIGURE IN HIDING**
Author: Franklin W. Dixon
Illustrator: Paul S. Laune
Publisher: Grosset & Dunlap
Reprinted with the permission of Pocket Books, a division of Simon & Schuster, Inc.
Copyright © 1937, 1965 by Simon & Schuster. Hardy Boys™ is a registered trademark of Simon & Schuster, Inc.

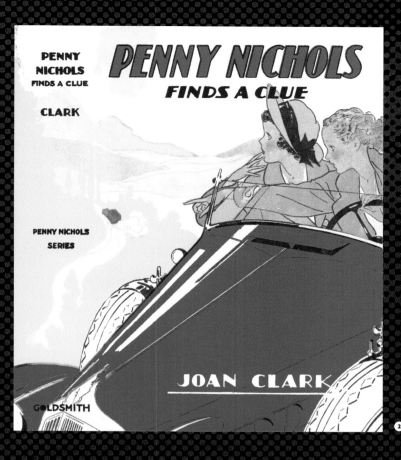

**2**

**PENNY NICHOLS FINDS A CLUE**
Author: Joan Clark
Illustrator: Unknown
Publisher: Goldsmith Publishing Co

**3**

**BEVERLY GRAY'S PROBLEM**
Author: Clair Blank
Illustrator: Unknown
Publisher: Grosset & Dunlap

**4**

**BEVERLY GRAY REPORTER**
Author: Clair Blank
Illustrator: Unknown
Publisher: Grosset & Dunlap

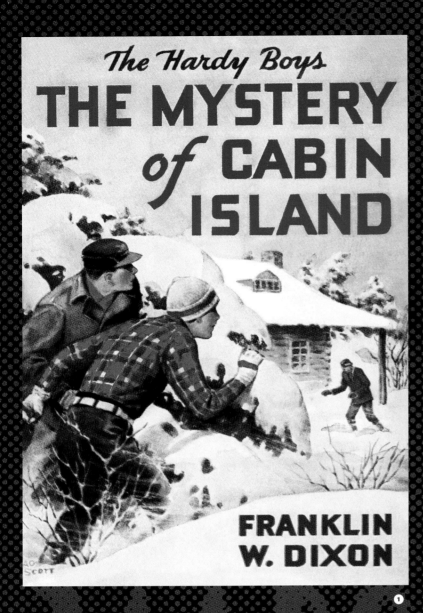

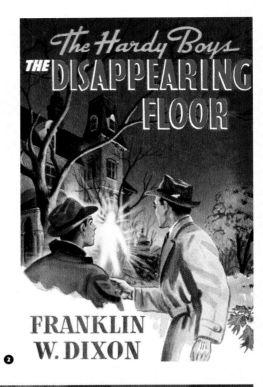

**②** ⊡⊡⊡

**THE DISAPPEARING FLOOR**

Author: Franklin W. Dixon

Illustrator: Paul S. Laune

Publisher: Grosset & Dunlap

Reprinted with the permission of Pocket Books, a division of Simon & Schuster, Inc. Copyright © 1940, 1964 by Simon & Schuster. Hardy Boys™ is a registered trademark of Simon & Schuster, Inc.

**③** ⊡⊡⊡

**THE MIDNIGHT VISITOR**

Author: Margaret Sutton

Illustrator: Pelagie Doane

Publisher: Grosset & Dunlap

**①** ⊡⊡⊡

**THE MYSTERY OF CABIN ISLAND**

Author: Franklin W. Dixon

Illustrator: A. O. Scott

Publisher: Grosset & Dunlap

Reprinted with the permission of Pocket Books, a division of Simon & Schuster, Inc.

Copyright © 1929, 1966 by Simon & Schuster. Hardy Boys™ is a registered trademark of Simon & Schuster, Inc.

**④** ⊡⊡⊡⊡

**THE MYSTERIOUS HALF CAT**

Author: Margaret Sutton

Illustrator: Pelagie Doane

Publisher: Grosset & Dunlap

**⑤** ⊡⊡⊡⊡

**THE MYSTIC BALL**

Author: Margaret Sutton

Illustrator: Pelagie Doane

Publisher: Grosset & Dunlap

writing days were far from over after "Nancy Drew." Her work continued in the writing of a great many additional juvenile stories on a variety of subjects. She also continued her writing endeavors in the newspaper business. Her name may not have appeared on the "Nancy Drew" covers, but Mildred Wirt was indeed Carolyn Keene, and although she did not create the character, she did share in the upbringing of the country's favorite girl detective.

Nancy Drew was raised by a single parent, her mother having passed away when Nancy was a little girl. As a result, her father, Carson Drew, plays a larger role in the stories than most parents in the juvenile titles. He is, of course, a wonderful dad, brimming with encouragement for his daughter's every endeavor. There is fatherly concern to be sure, but clearly Carson respects his teenage daughter's judgment, realizing at times that she knows best. Proof of this can be found in a number of the books in which respected attorney Carson calls upon daughter Nancy for advice and help in investigative matters. He is not the only one, for Nancy is something of a celebrity outside of her hometown of River Heights. Through her notoriety gained from newspaper articles reporting her latest triumph, she receives calls for help from those in dire need of detective services only Nancy can provide. It is Nancy they turn to when the police and private agencies need help. She never disappoints. Nancy's cases, in general, are of a more feminine interest than those of the Hardys. She always solves the mystery by story's end just as Frank and Joe did, but there are mentions of fashion, jewelry, and style along the way. And, unlike the Hardys, Nancy has a continuing love interest. Ned Nickerson and Nancy's subtle romance provides subplots in several editions. A pair of girlfriends, George Fayne and Bess Marvin, aid in her adventures. These two cousins are Nancy's best friends and are of great assistance, but there is never any question as to who among the three is the most beautiful, clever, and resourceful. How could any teenager compete with one who is so respected that law enforcement seeks her advice in important matters such as the release of a jailed suspect? As for resourcefulness, how many teenage girls have been expert fliers and marksmen while possessing the skills of a dramatist and art connoisseur? Nancy is indeed golden in an age that seeks near perfection in young female role models.

Much later, critics would pan Nancy's character as boring and repetitive in her perfection. They would also decry aspects of the stories that might easily be viewed as racist or class oriented. These elements would be overhauled with the updates and rewrites of the 1960s, but still they existed.

Perhaps the early "Nancy Drew" stories should be viewed as a portal to the past where the old axiom of art imitating life can be viewed in full measure. That was the America of that age, expressed in the juvenile mystery fiction warts and all or, more aptly, pimples and all. One thing is most certainly true, the country changed and Nancy Drew did too, with the exception that she is and was America's most loved teenage female gumshoe.

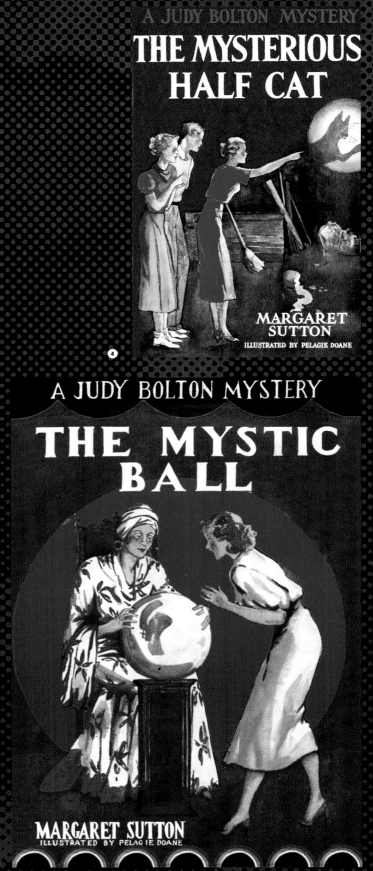

**① ▢▢▢**

**THE VANISHING SHADOW**
Author: Margaret Sutton
Illustrator: Pelagie Doane
Publisher: Grosset & Dunlap

**② ▢▢▢▢**

**THE INVISIBLE CHIMES**
Author: Margaret Sutton
Illustrator: Pelagie Doane
Publisher: Grosset & Dunlap

**③ ▢▢▢▢**

**THE VOICE IN THE SUITCASE**
Author: Margaret Sutton
Illustrator: Pelagie Doane
Publisher: Grosset & Dunlap

② 

①

③

**1** ☐☐☐☐

**THE CLUE IN THE JEWEL BOX**
Author: Carolyn Keene
Illustrator: Russell H. Tandy
Publisher: Grosset & Dunlap
Reprinted with the permission of
Pocket Books, a division of
Simon & Schuster, Inc.
Copyright © 1943, 1972 by
Simon & Schuster. Nancy
Drew™ is a registered trademark
of Simon & Schuster, Inc.

**2** ☐☐☐☐

**THE QUEST OF THE MISSING MAP**
Author: Carolyn Keene
Illustrator: Russell H. Tandy
Publisher: Grosset & Dunlap
Reprinted with the permission of
Pocket Books, a division of
Simon & Schuster, Inc.
Copyright © 1942, 1969 by
Simon & Schuster. Nancy
Drew™ is a registered trademark
of Simon & Schuster, Inc.

**❶**

**❷**

If the sons of a great detective and daughter of a respected attorney could solve mysteries, entertain young readers, and sell enormous quantities of books, imagine what an entire family devoted to the solving of mysteries could accomplish. From this marketing perspective came "The Happy Hollisters" series. The Hollisters were never intended as competition for Nancy or the Hardys; that would be counterproductive to the Stratemeyer business strategy. Instead, the series was meant to appeal to a far younger audience. As a result, the themes of the mysteries are far less threatening to the series characters and contain fewer, if any, frightening images of villains and peril. The stories are so wholesome and family oriented that danger can never quite gain a foothold.

The Hollisters, who live on Pine Lake in Shoreham, are a family of seven. In addition to Mr. and Mrs. Hollister, there is the eldest son Pete, followed by Pam, Ricky, Holly, and Sue. Family pets include dog Zip and the cat White Nose and her five kittens. The family-owned business is the "Trading Post," which sells amongst its wares toys and sports equipment. The mysteries are straightforward and uncluttered by subplots or, for that matter, by plots that even approach a medium level of complexity. These mysteries focus as much on families and role models as they do on mystery storylines. They speak of traditional family themes such as nurturing, security, and loyalty within a light framework of a simple mystery. In general, story topics involve some kind of treasure hunt the family undertake, as only the fictional fam-

**THE MYSTERY OF THE FLYING EXPRESS**
Author: Franklin W. Dixon
Illustrator: Paul S. Laune
Publisher: Grosset & Dunlap
Reprinted with the permission of
Pocket Books, a division of Simon &
Schuster, Inc.
Copyright © 1941, 1970 by Simon &
Schuster. Hardy Boys™ is a
registered trademark of Simon &
Schuster, Inc.

**THE TWISTED CLAW**
Author: Franklin W. Dixon
Illustrator: Paul S. Laune
Publisher: Grosset & Dunlap
Reprinted with the permission of
Pocket Books, a division of Simon &
Schuster, Inc.
Copyright © 1939, 1969 by Simon &
Schuster. Hardy Boys™ is a
registered trademark of Simon &
Schuster, Inc.

**THE SHORE ROAD MYSTERY**
Author: Franklin W. Dixon
Illustrator: A.O. Scott
Publisher: Grosset & Dunlap
Reprinted with the permission of
Pocket Books, a division of Simon &
Schuster, Inc.
Copyright © 1928, 1964 by Simon &
Schuster. Hardy Boys™ is a
registered trademark of Simon &
Schuster, Inc.

THE HARDY BOYS
*The House on the Cliff*
THE HOUSE on the CLIFF
FRANKLIN W. DIXON

THE
HOUSE
ON THE
CLIFF

F.W.
DIXON

THE
HARDY
BOYS
STORIES

GROSSET
& DUNLAP

By the author of the NANCY DREW BOOKS

BY THE LIGHT
OF THE
STUDY LAMP

THE DANA GIRLS MYSTERY STORIES
By CAROLYN KEENE

By the author of the NANCY DREW BOOKS

IN THE SHADOW
OF THE TOWER

THE DANA GIRLS MYSTERY STORIES
By CAROLYN KEENE

**1**

**THE HOUSE ON THE CLIFF**
Author: Franklin W. Dixon
Illustrator: A.O. Scott
Publisher: Grosset & Dunlap
Reprinted with the permission of
Pocket Books, a division of Simon &
Schuster, Inc.
Copyright © 1927, 1959 by Simon &
Schuster. Hardy Boys™ is a
registered trademark of Simon &
Schuster, Inc.

**2**

**BY THE LIGHT OF THE STUDY LAMP**
Author: Carolyn Keene
Illustrator: Unknown
Publisher: Grosset & Dunlap
Reprinted with the permission of
Pocket Books, a division of Simon &
Schuster, Inc.
Dana Girls, Copyright © 1934

**3**

**IN THE SHADOW OF THE TOWER**
Author: Carolyn Keene
Illustrator: Unknown
Publisher: Grosset & Dunlap
Reprinted with the permission of
Pocket Books, a division of Simon
& Schuster, Inc.
Dana Girls, Copyright © 1934

ily might, with sunny dispositions, helpfulness, and respect for the order of the day. Simply put, it is the ideal family in an ideal family business with the ideal family hobby: treasure hunting and mystery solving. The books had a target audience with an upper age projection of about eleven years, and for this age group of entry-level mystery lovers they fit the bill entirely. "The Happy Hollisters" series was among the best-loved of children's mystery books.

"The Hollisters" series was the creation of Andrew Svenson who wrote the books under the pseudonym of Jerry West. Svenson was a man of writing, editing, and administrative talents. He was hired initially as a writer for the Syndicate, and from that position he rose through the ranks of the company and was eventually accepted as a partner, the first so named from outside the family business.

It would seem the Stratemeyer Syndicate had a monopoly on the publication of juvenile mysteries with "The Hardy Boys," "Nancy Drew," and "The Happy Hollisters" taking so much of the share of the market. But the demand was huge for stories of the mystery genre, and a host of independent writers and characters stood ready to fill the niche. These autonomous writers included Charles Spain Verral and George Wyatt who each contributed to the "Brains Benton Mystery" series. Brains Benton, with right-hand man Jimmy Carson in tow, solves mysteries in a more scientific manner than his peers. Whereas many teen detective types are known and respected by law enforcement agencies, Benton and crew are viewed as youthful intruders — especially when showing up the authorities.

Also among the successful series were the "Ken Holt" mysteries. Ken Holt, teenage newspaper reporter, and his sidekick Sandy Allen, ace photographer, undertake their mysteries from a reporter's angle. These two boys, both from famous newspaper families, work for the Brentwood Advance. Their escapades offer the same thrilling fare as others in the mystery line, but are perhaps somewhat more realistic. The boys at times seem overwhelmed by their situations and actually call for adult intervention. Overall, their adult relationships appear more in line with those traditionally found in American society. The books were written under the name of Bruce Campbell, the pseudonym employed by Samuel Epstein for the series. Epstein was an amazingly prolific fiction and nonfiction writer. Many of his writing projects were undertaken with his wife Beryl; together they produced a wide assortment of titles involving diverse subject matter from mysteries to educational works.

Many more teenage detectives each distinguished themselves with their own merits: Trixie Belden, The Power Boys, and The Three Investigators to name a few, but there was yet another who stands out among her peers. The strength of author Margaret Sutton's writing and her evolving Judy Bolton character make this series noteworthy.

Judy Bolton was something of an anomaly in the highly formulistic world of juvenile mystery fiction. To begin with, many elements in each story did not read as fiction at all. Of course, the very premise of the series was that

NANCY DREW MYSTERY STORIES
The Clue of the Leaning Chimney
CAROLYN KEENE

NANCY DREW MYSTERY STORIES
The Mystery of the Tolling Bell
CAROLYN KEENE

**❶** ▢▢▢

**THE GHOST OF BLACKWOOD HALL**
Author: Carolyn Keene
Illustrator: Russell H. Tandy
Publisher: Grosset & Dunlap
Reprinted with the permission of
Pocket Books, a division of Simon &
Schuster, Inc.
Copyright © 1948, 1967 by Simon &
Schuster. Nancy Drew™ is a
registered trademark of Simon &
Schuster, Inc.

**❷** ▢▢▢

**THE PHANTOM FREIGHTER**
Author: Franklin W. Dixon
Illustrator: Russell H. Tandy
Publisher: Grosset & Dunlap
Reprinted with the permission of
Pocket Books, a division of Simon &
Schuster, Inc.
Copyright © 1947, 1970 by Simon &
Schuster. Hardy Boys™ is a registered
trademark of Simon & Schuster, Inc.

**❸** ▢▢

**WHAT HAPPENED AT MIDNIGHT**
Author: Franklin W. Dixon
Illustrator: Paul S. Laune
Publisher: Grosset & Dunlap
Reprinted with the permission of Pocket
Books, a division of Simon & Schuster,
Inc.
Copyright © 1931, 1967 by Simon &
Schuster. Hardy Boys™ is a registered
trademark of Simon & Schuster, Inc.

**❹** ▫▫▫

**THE RIDDLE OF THE FROZEN FOUNTAIN**

Author: Carolyn Keene
Illustrator: Unknown
Publisher: Grosset & Dunlap
Reprinted with the permission of Pocket Books, a division
of Simon & Schuster, Inc.
Dana Girls, Copyright © 1964, 1972

**❺** ▫▫

**THE SECRET AT THE HERMITAGE**

Author: Carolyne Keene
Illustrator: Unknown
Publisher: Grosset & Dunlap
Reprinted with the permission of Pocket Books, a division of
Simon & Schuster, Inc.
Dana Girls, Copyright © 1936, 1949

of the Mansion

**1**

# BITSY FINDS THE CLUE

Bitsy and her college friends in a mystery of historic Williamsburg

## AUGUSTA HUIELL SEAMAN

NANCY DREW MYSTERY STORIES

# The Sign of the Twisted Candles

CAROLYN KEENE

**2**

**3**

**2**

**3**

the stories were based upon actual incidents. But beyond that, Judy was written with a well-developed personality. She has her own dreams, which do not always come true, and her own burdens to bear, some of which she overcomes. This touch of realism gave the reader something to care about in the leading character beyond the action and derring-do; her sole existence was not based upon serving as a character to solve a given mystery story. Her background is firmly rooted in the middle class. Her father, Henry Bolton, is a physician, a respected position in the community but not necessarily a prosperous one, for in his practice he accepts patients based upon health needs, not on ability to pay. Dr. Bolton sees in his medical profession a higher calling that holds rewards in service surpassing monetary considerations. Judy's mother, Stella, fills the role of a supporting housewife. Judy's older brother Horace is a reporter for the local newspaper. Their first home in the fictional town of Roulsville, Pennsylvania was destroyed in a flood, a man-made disaster that Judy exposes. The family then moves north to the city of Farringdon. The series follows Judy through her high school years, her entry into the workplace, through romance, including a broken engagement (by Judy), to eventual marriage, and a family.

Along her life's journey, she shares with her readers a great many events — both joyful and sorrowful — that they also have experienced. Joy is the simple emotion of youth and therefore is easier to write; sorrow is trickier. Sorrow, as in the passing of Judy's beloved grandparents, was an emotion largely alien to youth fiction. To achieve realism in the fantasy-based youth stories it was sometimes necessary to explore real life's harsh realities through the characters. The development of Judy's character was extraordinary given the prevailing juvenile series wisdom that characters must be frozen in time in terms of age, personality, and most definitely, sexual maturity. The portrayal and circumstances of Judy and her family were inspired, to be sure,

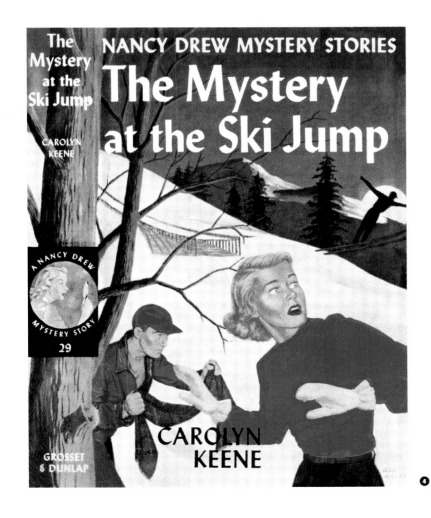

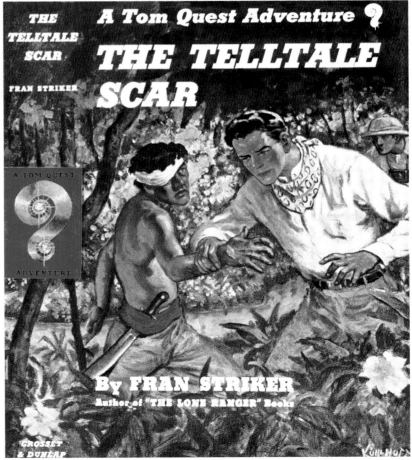

but it was the storylines as well that set Judy apart from the other series. Of course, they were standard juvenile mystery fare, but each contained, whether as the main story or in the subplot, a larger social issue. For example, while Judy solves mysteries involving haunted houses, missing persons, and theft rings, she also takes on issues such as fraudulent construction practices, harassment of minorities, and even concerns regarding subliminal messages. What other series would so consistently explore issues as complex as religious persecution, child custody cases, and land development schemes?

The series examination of class struggles is especially interesting given that most Americans wanted to believe they lived in a classless society. But there is Judy in the middle of the issue, trying to bring her wealthy friends and her friends of lesser means together to break down prejudices. The story indicates that prejudice is built upon perception rather than fact. Judy is not entirely successful in joining the differing parties, but again this seeming failure aids the realism. Perhaps it's enough that she maintains her friendships in both camps and accepts people based upon merit instead of privilege. These are the sorts of life lessons contained under the umbrella of each "Judy Bolton Mystery" story. It isn't preachy; it is merely the goings on in a fictional character's life, common enough so that the reader readily identifies with the situation or would soon be able to. They are expressions of lofty ideals considering the venue. The Stratemeyer Syndicate was amazingly successful with an entirely different approach, one which avoided controversy altogether.

Was the author's intent in the Bolton series to offer a role model to the young female readership? Probably. Writers of youth fiction generally want to contribute to young lives beyond the telling of a story. Providing role models for young girls was a delicate issue in the 1930s through the 1960s. If she were not the era's best-loved girl detective, could Judy's claim be that of the era's best female role model? Stratemeyer's vision of female role models appears to rely on perfection as the standard for girls. Judy Bolton, while still the heroine, is far from perfect; she does, however, strive for that elusive perfection. This simple difference in approach actually defines and identifies the better role model, for perfection in a role model is a useless blanket approach to life. The standard here must be based upon honesty, blemishes and all. Higher goals expressed by a character possessing a great deal of humanity makes Judy Bolton's character the foremost role model of her era in the mystery genre or, for that matter, in any other category.

Margaret Sutton was not a pseudonym; she was indeed a real person. Born in the early part of the new century, Sutton grew up in Pennsylvania, where she attended public school and, for a short time, was schooled at home. She loved to read. In one instance, a portent of the future, she asked a librarian for additional books involving a character from a book she was returning; she was told that none existed. Sutton vowed that she would someday write stories with continuing characters for young people

**①** 🔲🔲
**THE SECRET OF THUNDER MOUNTAIN**
Author: Fran Striker
Illustrator: Kuhlhoff
Publisher: Grosset & Dunlap

**②** 🔲🔲
**THE MYSTERY OF THE TIMBER GIANT**
Author: Fran Striker
Illustrator: Israel Doskow
Publisher: Clover Books

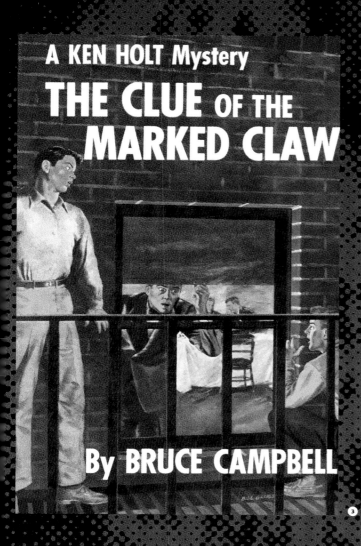

**A KEN HOLT Mystery**

## THE CLUE OF THE MARKED CLAW

**By BRUCE CAMPBELL**

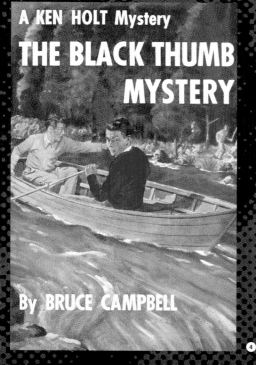

**A KEN HOLT Mystery**

## THE BLACK THUMB MYSTERY

**By BRUCE CAMPBELL**

**A KEN HOLT Mystery**

# THE CLUE OF THE COILED COBRA

**By BRUCE CAMPBELL**

**THE CLUE OF THE MARKED CLAW**
Author: Bruce Campbell
Illustrator: Bill Gillies
Publisher: Grosset & Dunlap
Used by permission of Bill Gillies, Jr.

**THE BLACK THUMB MYSTERY**
Author: Bruce Campbell
Illustrator: Bill Gillies
Publisher: Grosset & Dunlap
Used by permission of Bill Gillies, Jr.

**THE CLUE OF THE COILED COBRA**
Author: Bruce Campbell
Illustrator: Bill Gillies
Publisher: Grosset & Dunlap
Used by permission of Bill Gillies, Jr.

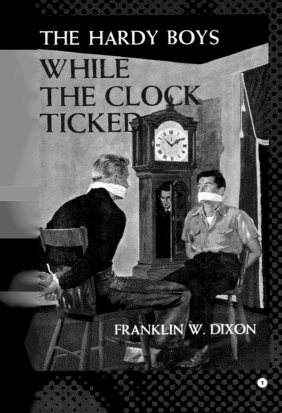

**①** ▢▢▢

**WHILE THE CLOCK TICKED**
Author: Franklin W. Dixon
Illustrator: Bill Gillies
Publisher: Grosset & Dunlap
Reprinted with the permission of
Pocket Books, a division of Simon &
Schuster, Inc.
Copyright © 1932, 1962 by Simon &
Schuster. Hardy Boys™ is a
registered trademark of Simon &
Schuster, Inc.

**②** ▢▢▢

**FOOTPRINTS UNDER THE WINDOW**
Author: Franklin W. Dixon
Illustrator: Bill Gillies
Publisher: Grosset & Dunlap
Reprinted with the permission of
Pocket Books, a division of Simon &
Schuster, Inc.
Copyright © 1933, 1965 by Simon &
Schuster. Hardy Boys™ is a
registered trademark of Simon &
Schuster, Inc.

**③** ▢▢▢

**THE CLUE IN THE RUINED CASTLE**
Author: Margaret Sutton
Illustrator: Unknown
Publisher: Grosset & Dunlap

**④** ▢▢▢

**THE HIDDEN WINDOW MYSTERY**
Author: Carolyn Keene
Illustrator: Rudy Nappi
Publisher: Grosset & Dunlap
Reprinted with the permission of Pocket Books,
a division of Simon & Schuster, Inc.
Copyright © 1956, 1975 by Simon & Schuster.
Nancy Drew™ is a registered trademark of
Simon & Schuster, Inc.

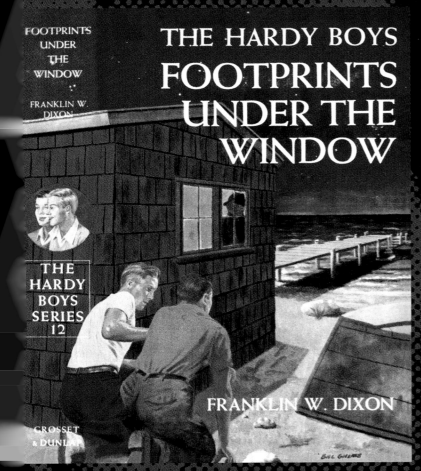

to follow and enjoy. In her early high-school years, a series of personality conflicts contributed to Sutton's quitting school and pursuing an education elsewhere. She attended Rochester Business Institute, from which she graduated. She obtained work shortly thereafter as a stenographer. Her other occupations included that of a waitress and variety store clerk. When she married, she and her husband moved to Brooklyn and started a family. She continued her interest in reading and began to write book reviews for the Brooklyn Daily Times.

Sutton also began to tinker with the idea that she could write as well as some of the authors in the field of juvenile fiction. She acquired an agent through whom she submitted a book-length manuscript for publication. A publisher accepted it with the provision that two more manuscripts accompany the first story, part of the "breeder" plan of creating an instant series. So was born the "Judy Bolton Mystery" series. The books found their audience almost immediately and sold very well.

In addition to her Bolton output, Sutton's publisher requested that she assist in writing other works for which she did not receive an author's credit. One such project was the "Heidi" series. Several "Heidi" books by Swiss author Johanna Spyri suffered in their translation from German to English. Sutton was employed in the sometimes extensive rewrite process.

**5**

**THE VANISHING SHADOW**
Author: Margaret Sutton
Illustrator: Unknown
Publisher: Grosset & Dunlap

Sutton wrote and was credited for many other books. She was the author of "The Magic Makers," a series of three volumes, and penned several non-serial books, among them a historical biography of Daniel Boone's daughter, Jemima. The "Judy Bolton" series, however, was the mainstay of her writing career.

Sutton enjoyed unsurpassed artistic freedom in her work in comparison with that of her peers writing for the Syndicate. Chiefly, she remained an active participant in editing her manuscripts. A common complaint of Syndicate writers was that the formula was so rigidly adhered to and the house so top heavy with editors that in many instances the authors found their printed work rendered unrecognizable from their original submissions. Because she was part of the editing process, Sutton was able to fight for the continued development of her Bolton character, and she was able to speak to editing concerns over her stories' depiction of sensitive subject matter. Her artistic freedom was complete in the initial manuscript submission in that she was not required to write from a prepared outline; her stories were her own. This freedom made her work credible, for she was allowed to insert her own experiences into her books.

Sutton's vacations with her family became the backdrops in many of her stories, her own interpersonal relationships appeared in the books, and a good bit of her own outspoken nature made it into the character of Judy Bolton. The "Bolton" series had a number of other benefits for her and her readership. Among those were that Sutton retained the use of her name as author and was compensated with royalties. She was the sole author of the "Bolton" series, which contributed greatly to its continuity. The series enjoyed a successful run for more than thirty-five years. Her place among the greatest writers of juvenile mysteries remains open to debate, but it is clear that the work was her own, unencumbered by the over-editing and the formula that diminished so many books. Clearly her heart was in her work, and she cared about her readers. That remains the sum total of

**❶** 🕮

**DAN CARTER AND THE GREAT CARVED FACE**
Author: Mildred A. Wirt
Illustrator: Marquerita Gayer
Publisher: Cupples & Leon

**❷** 🕮

**DAN CARTER AND THE MONEY BOX**
Author: Mildred A. Wirt
Illustrator: Marquerita Gayer
Publisher: Cupples & Leon

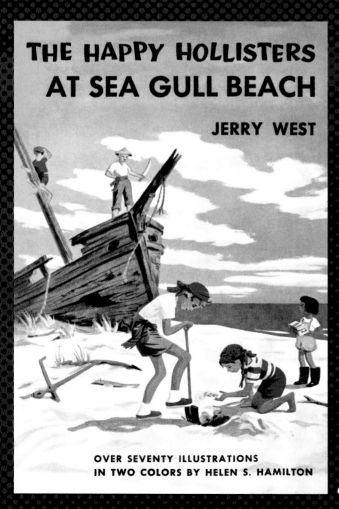

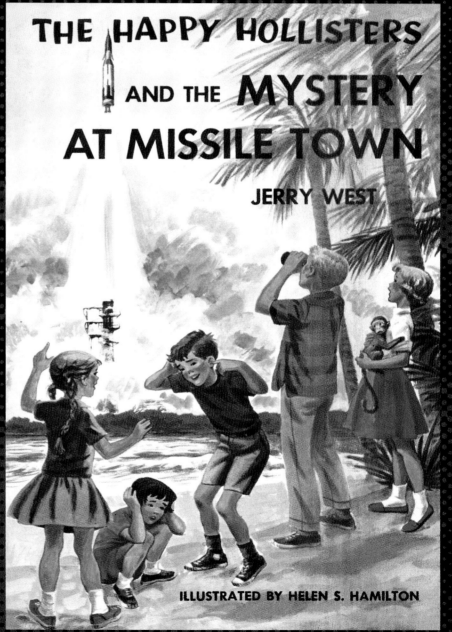

**③**

**THE HAPPY HOLLISTERS AND THE COWBOY MYSTERY**
Author: Jerry West
Illustrator: Helen S. Hamilton
Used by permission of Random House Children's Books, a division of Random House, Inc.

**④**

**THE HAPPY HOLLISTERS AT SEA GULL BEACH**
Author: Jerry West
Illustrator: Helen S. Hamilton
Used by permission of Random House Children's Books, a division of Random House, Inc.

**⑤**

**THE HAPPY HOLLISTERS AND THE MYSTERY AT MISSILE TOWN**
Author: Jerry West
Illustrator: Helen S. Hamilton
Used by permission of Random House Children's Books, a division of Random House, Inc.

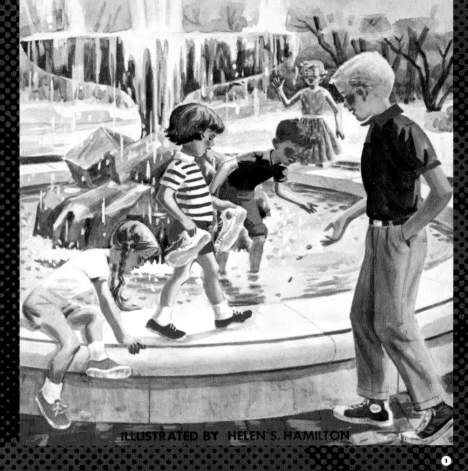

**1**

**THE HAPPY HOLLISTERS AND THE SECRET OF THE LUCKY COINS**
Author: Jerry West
Illustrator: Helen S. Hamilton
Used by permission of Random House Children's
Books, a division of Random House, Inc.

**2**

**THE HAPPY HOLLISTERS AND THE PUNCH AND JUDY MYSTERY**
Author: Jerry West
Illustrator: Helen S. Hamilton
Used by permission of Random House Children's Books,
a division of Random House, Inc.

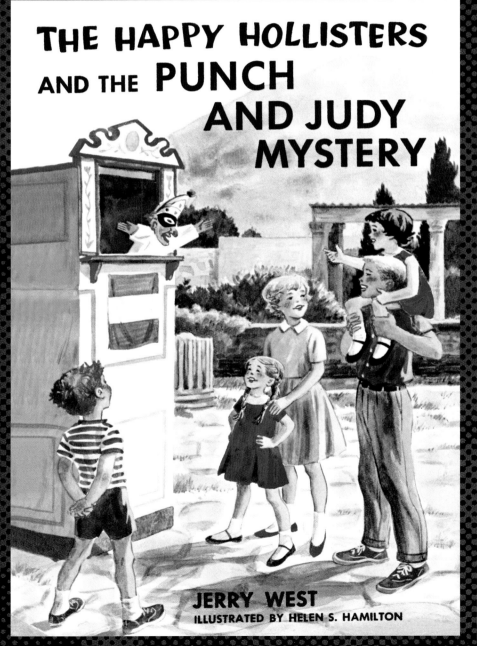

**③** 🔲🔲

**GINNY GORDON AND THE BROADCAST MYSTERY**
Author: Julie Campbell
Illustrator: Margaret Wesley
Publisher: Whitman

**④** 🔲🔲🔲🔲

**THE MESSAGE IN THE HOLLOW OAK**
Author: Carolyn Keene
Illustrator: Rudy Nappi
Publisher: Grosset & Dunlap

**⑤** 🔲🔲

**TRIXIE BELDEN AND THE MYSTERY OFF GLEN ROAD**
Author: Julie Campbell
Illustrator: Mary Stevens

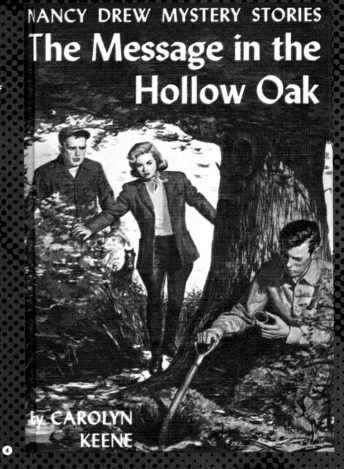

④

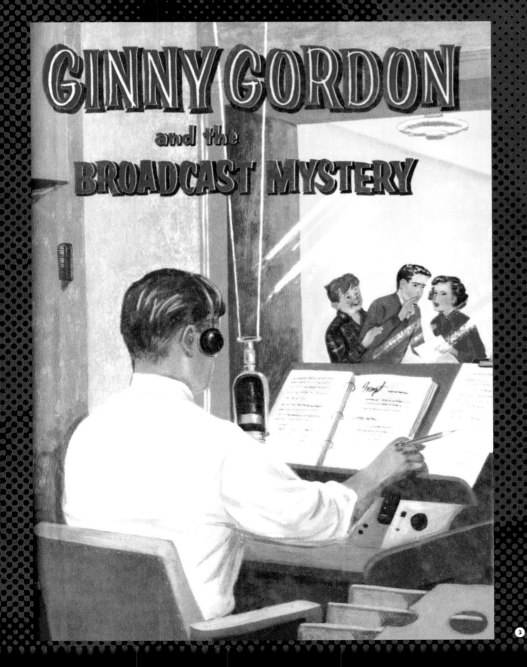

③

⑤

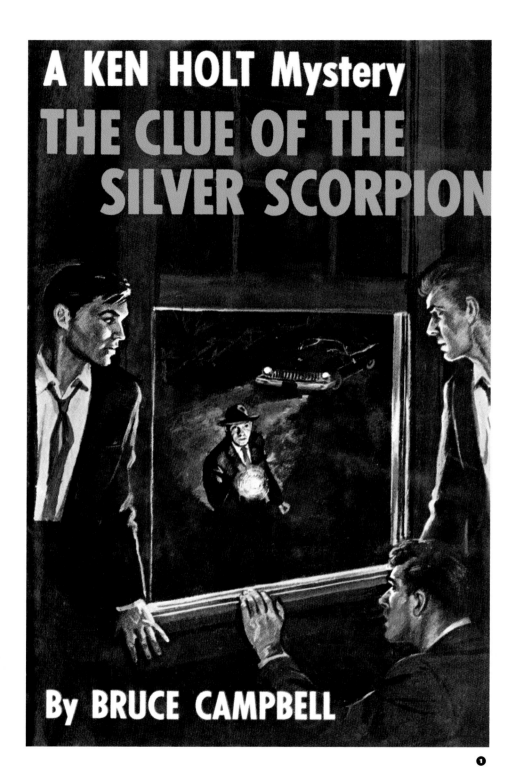

**❶**

**THE CLUE OF THE SILVER SCORPION**
Author: Bruce Campbell
Illustrator: Unknown
Publisher: Grosset & Dunlap

**❷**

**THE CLUE OF THE PHANTOM CAR**
Author: Bruce Campbell
Illustrator: Baby
Publisher: Grosset & Dunlap

**❸**

**THE MYSTERY OF THE SHATTERED GLASS**
Author: Bruce Campbell
Illustrator: Unknown
Publisher: Grosset & Dunlap

**❹**

**THE GHOST AT SKELETON ROCK**
Author: Franklin W. Dixon
Illustrator: Rudy Nappi
Publisher: Grosset & Dunlap
Reprinted with the permission of Pocket Books, a division of Simon & Schuster, Inc. Copyright © 1957, 1966 by Simon & Schuster. Hardy Boys™ is a registered trademark of Simon & Schuster, Inc.

**❷**

all that can be expected from an honest writer plying his or her craft.

In the application of their art, no group, outside of or within the Syndicate, possessed more artistic freedom than did the illustrators. While writers came and went under a house pseudonym, the house retained its illustrators for extended periods. They were able to work under their own names and sign their art. The publishers knew that readers would readily identify characters with their depiction on dust jackets and in interior illustrations. The publishers therefore made every effort to keep their series characters consistent in appearance. A gifted illustrator was assigned a dual role, that of artist and salesman. In mystery illustration, they had to harness the author's suspense and intrigue and, with this combination, sell the book. Further, the illustrator had to possess an understanding of what juveniles conceived of as suspense. A slight misstep in style might cause an illustration to be seen as silly, which, of course, would have been poison in the world of whodunits.

The process of creating jacket art was developed in several ways. The illustrator might receive a full manuscript to read before undertaking a project. Sometimes the publisher supplied a physical description of the characters along with a particular scene's narrative. Next, depending on the illustrator, came a series of submissions of sketches followed by pen-and-ink drawings. A few artists insisted upon submitting full color illustrations in the first step of the process. The illustrations chosen for publication must have met all criteria, which included potentially attracting the customer's eye and portraying the excitement and mystery between the covers.

Early mystery illustrations resemble those intended for the pulp market. The dust jackets are printed in dark blue or black. The characters are often portrayed as assailant and victim, their faces contorted in hate and fear. The subjects brandish weapons implying sudden doom. They have more qualities of horror than mystery, and they are not appropriate for a young audience.

In marketing the teenage sleuth, the publishers replaced much of the overt violence with mild suspense wrapped into the adventure tales inherent to solving crimes. Juvenile mystery illustration began a tradition of cover themes that told as much about the readership as it did the fiction it depicted. Illustrators retained a little of the horror and played on basic childhood fears: fear of the dark, with a host of night scenes replete with full moon and characters with dim flashlights; fear of being watched made more intense when the watcher was also being watched. And illustrators created scenes in which the main character was searching intently for clues, or again watching, while the sidekick was seen partially turned, looking over a shoulder in apprehension and fear. For that matter, perhaps they were looking back over the reader's shoulder, too. Throw in a secret passageway, abandoned building, or dark cellar, and the stage was set for mystery.

Dust jacket and later picture cover illustrations for the "Hardy Boys"

THE HARDY BOYS
THE MYSTERY OF THE CHINESE JUNK

FRANKLIN W. DIXON

**1**

**1** 🕮🕮🕮

**THE MYSTERY OF THE CHINESE JUNK**
Author: Franklin W. Dixon
Illustrator: Rudy Nappi
Publisher: Grosset & Dunlap
Reprinted with the permission of Pocket Books, a division of Simon & Schuster, Inc. Copyright © 1960 by Simon & Schuster. Hardy Boys™ is a registered trademark of Simon & Schuster, Inc.

**2** 🕮

**THE MISSING CHUMS**
Author: Franklin W. Dixon
Illustrator: Rudy Nappi
Publisher: Grosset & Dunlap
Reprinted with the permission of Pocket Books, a division of Simon & Schuster, Inc. Copyright © 1928, 1962 by Simon & Schuster. Hardy Boys™ is a registered trademark of Simon & Schuster, Inc.

**3** 🕮

**A FIGURE IN HIDING**
Author: Franklin W. Dixon
Illustrator: John Leone
Publisher: Grosset & Dunlap
Reprinted with the permission of Pocket Books, a division of Simon & Schuster, Inc. Copyright © 1937, 1965 by Simon & Schuster. Hardy Boys™ is a registered trademark of Simon & Schuster, Inc.

**4**

Hardy Boys dust jacket advertising piece. Used by permission. Courtesty of Pocket Books, a division of Simon & Schuster.

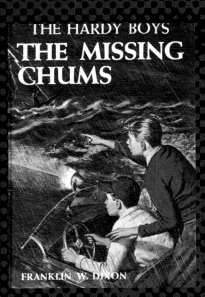

THE HARDY BOYS
THE MISSING CHUMS

FRANKLIN W. DIXON

**2**

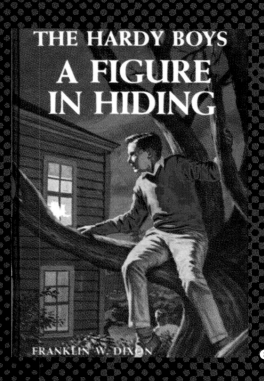

On the Trail of Clues and Criminals

Frank and Joe Hardy are sons of a celebrated
detective. Often the boys help him in his investiga-
tions. In their spare hours and during vacations they
follow up clues "on their own hook." These activities
lead them into many strange adventures and dangerous situations. Yet their efforts are usually successful
in tracking down criminals. These stories are
packed with action, adventure and mystery.

## The Hardy Boys Stories

By FRANKLIN W. DIXON

THE TOWER TREASURE
THE HOUSE ON THE CLIFF
THE SECRET OF THE OLD MILL
THE MISSING CHUMS
HUNTING FOR HIDDEN GOLD
THE SHORE ROAD MYSTERY
THE SECRET OF THE CAVES
THE MYSTERY OF CABIN ISLAND
THE GREAT AIRPORT MYSTERY
WHAT HAPPENED AT MIDNIGHT
WHILE THE CLOCK TICKED
FOOTPRINTS UNDER THE WINDOW
THE MARK ON THE DOOR
THE HIDDEN HARBOR MYSTERY
THE SINISTER SIGN POST
A FIGURE IN HIDING
THE SECRET WARNING

GROSSET & DUNLAP : Publishers : NEW YORK

series are exceptional. Walter S. Rogers illustrated the earliest volumes. Rogers's dust jacket art is highly stylized and displays a unique approach to the subject. The style, while not without charm, is oddly out of place in the mystery format. Mystery writing, to be effective, requires realism and to a great extent so does its art. Rogers's Hardy Boys appear stiff and a little out of proportion on the jackets. The interior line illustrations by Rogers are superior to his cover work, largely due to their realistic nature and to the absence of the garish color that slightly mar the covers. Rogers's jacket illustrations, while interesting, remain the most dated in the series.

J. Clemens Gretter was next to assume the role of illustrator for the series. Gretter's work displays a sharp departure from that of Rogers and sets the tone for much of the dust jacket art that followed his tenure with the Boys. Gretter makes full use of the night and its implied mystery. His oversized full moons serve as lighting for unfolding drama. The use of color, though not entirely accurate, is by its very boldness a catalyst to the action. The characters are pictured in hazardous locations, struggling with dangerous men. One only has to buy the book to find out why the characters are in such dire straits.

Paul S. Laune's covers continued in the style of Gretter by using strong, vivid colors to dramatic effect. His backlighting of the characters and use of shadows to heighten the mystery further benefit Laune's illustrations.

An additional enhancement to the jacket was a change in the books' design. A cursive-style font replaced the block lettering above the title adding to the jackets' overall appeal. Russell H. Tandy, known for his excellent work in the "Nancy Drew" series, contributed several covers with increased emphasis on modernizing the look of the characters. By now much of the "Hardy Boys" back catalog was being reissued with new jackets, revised action, and more contemporary interpretation of the characters and their clothing. Artists A.O. Scott, Bill Gillies, and John Leone were involved in this effort and contributed much to its success. Rudy Nappi's dust jacket art was the culmination of the move to update the scenes and characters. His straightforward illustrations brought realism to the characters and provided them with a consistent look that would long endure. Nappi reworked older titles for reissue, created original artwork for new offerings, and was prolific enough to be employed in the restyling of his own original work for reissue. Nappi and the other "Hardy Boys" illustrators added to the point-of-sale appeal of the books. The illustrations remain instantly recognizable to the readership long after the books' plots have been forgotten.

Nancy Drew's depiction on the dust jacket, in comparison to that of the Hardy Boys, is a different matter. Nancy is rarely in imminent danger. She isn't engaged in physical confrontations. Her actions and those of her assistants are more in keeping with the mystery tradition, as they are usually looking for clues. Nancy is shown as a determined sleuth. She listens in on conversations, peers in windows, and even climbs a tree for a better view if the situation warrants. On a number of covers, Nancy is in the

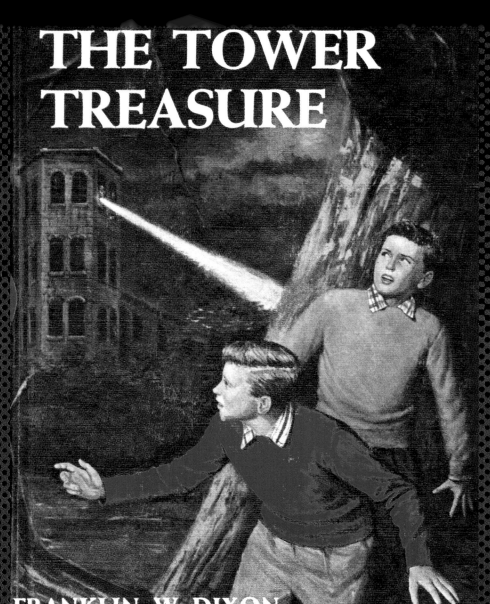

# THE TOWER TREASURE

**FRANKLIN W. DIXON**

THE CASE OF THE PAINTED DRAGON
Author: George Wyatt
Illustrator: Hamilton Greene
Publisher: Whitman
Used by permission. Golden Books
Publishing Company, Inc.
Copyright © 1961, 1989. All rights
reserved.

ALASKA GHOST GLACIER MYSTERY
Author: Andy Adams
Illustrator: Unknown
Publisher: Grosset & Dunlap

➊

**THE TOWER TREASURE**

Author: Franklin W. Dixon
Illustrator: Rudy Nappi
Publisher: Grosset & Dunlap
Reprinted with the permission of Pocket Books, a
division of Simon & Schuster, Inc. Copyright ©
1927, 1959 by Simon & Schuster. Hardy Boys™ is a
registered trademark of Simon & Schuster, Inc.

➋

Thomas Vreeland, nephew of the illustrator,
models as both Joe and Frank Hardy for
Rudy Nappi's cover illustration for *The Tower
Treasure*. Note the illustrator's paint splatters
on the photographs. Used by permission of
Rudy Nappi. Photos courtesy of Tony &
Mary Carpentieri.

company of senior citizens, implying a respect for the elderly. All young mystery lovers understood that the best time to seek clues and sneak around was at night. Nancy does not disappoint. The jackets have a number of night scenes, many of which are partially framed by a large tree. A young reader viewing such a cover might easily conjure up the sounds of the old tree rustling in the breeze, its branches swaying, perhaps every now and then dipping down to brush against someone who lies in wait.

As a result of the limited action and danger portrayed in the cover illustrations, Nancy herself is the focal point of the jackets. Illustrator Russell Tandy created the original Nancy "look" and in doing so drew heavily upon his background as a commercial artist specializing in fashion illustration. Nancy's appearance is inspired. She wears the latest, most elegant fashions, and she wears them well, possessing the grace and figure that complemented the latest designs. Even when engaged in vigorous outdoor activities such as horseback riding, she remains properly attired, outfitted in jodhpurs and boots. Her hair is beautifully coifed, and all accessories seem understated and refined. Nancy's hands are often noticeable on the dust jackets. Her long fingers and manicured nails enhance her femininity. This is the Nancy of Tandy's creation, and she continued to grace the dust jackets with style and sophistication during Tandy's twenty-year reign as illustrator.

Two of the illustrators following Tandy's tenure included Bill Gillies and Rudy Nappi. These illustrators began the subtle movement from the highly polished, cosmopolitan Nancy to the teenage girl-next-door Nancy. She remains beautifully dressed and displays impeccable hygiene, but she is now more approachable with a friendlier appearance. Gillies and Nappi allowed Nancy to change with the times while maintaining the appearance of the all-American girl detective.

With her grandfather a sculptor, her mother having highly artis-

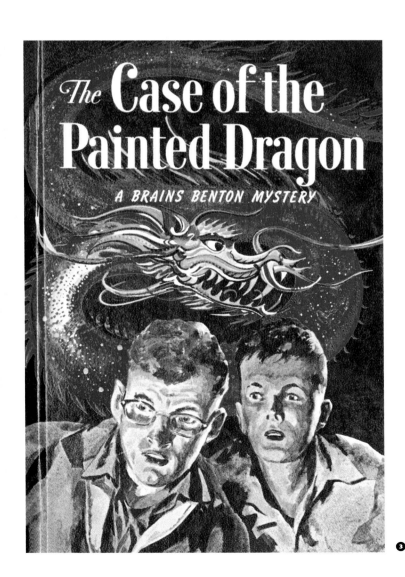

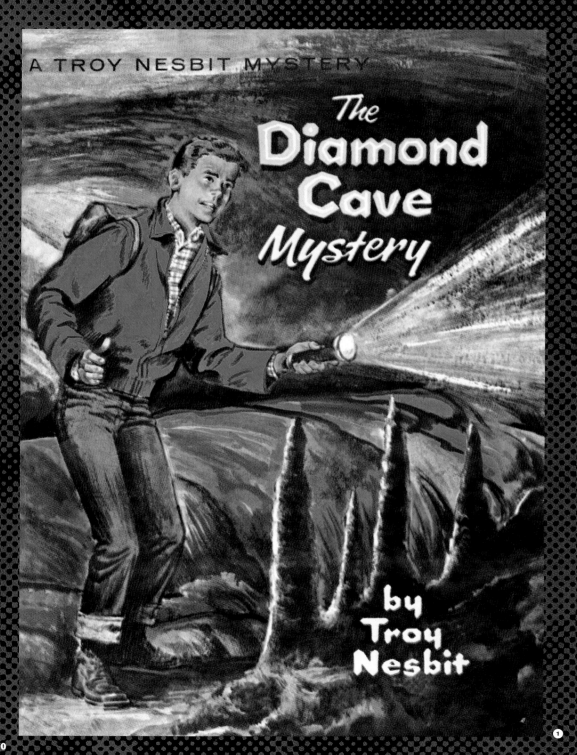

A TROY NESBIT MYSTERY

The Diamond Cave Mystery

by Troy Nesbit

A BIFF BREWSTER MYSTERY ADVENTURE

Mystery of the Caribbean Pearls

BY ANDY ADAMS

**①**

**THE DIAMOND CAVE MYSTERY**
Author: Troy Nesbit
Illustrator: Paul Frame
Publisher: Whitman
Used by permission.  Golden Books Publishing Company,
Inc.  Copyright © 1964, 1984.  All rights reserved

**②**

**MYSTERY OF THE CARIBBEAN PEARLS**
Author: Andy Adams
Illustrator: Unknown
Publisher: Grosset & Dunlap

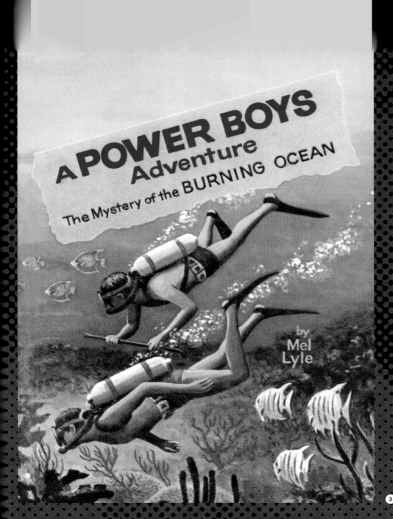

**3**

**THE MYSTERY OF THE BURNING OCEAN**
Author: Mel Lyle
Illustrator: Raymond Burns
Publisher: Whitman
Used by permission. Golden
Books Publishing Company, Inc.
Copyright © 1965, 1993.

**4**

The prolific illustrator, Bill Gillies, who
made significant advances in the cause of
realism in his work for the Hardy Boys,
Nancy Drew, and Ken Holt series. Used by
permission. Photo courtesy of the Gillies
family.

**5**

**THE MYSTERY OF THE DOUBLE KIDNAPPING**
Author: Mel Lyle
Illustrator: Raymond Burns
Publisher: Whitman
Used by permission. Golden Books
Publishing Company, Inc. Copyright ©

tic interests, and her father an editor, it would seem that Pelagie Doane would have been a natural to play an important role in the field of illustration. She did. A graduate of Moore Institute in Philadelphia, she majored in interior decorating. Her real interest, however, was in illustration. Following graduation, she traveled to New York with a portfolio of her work. Upon presentation of the portfolio, she was also encouraged to submit samples for use in the greeting card industry. She complied and found her first success as a professional illustrator. This early accomplishment emboldened her to shop her samples to book publishers where she was met with further success.

The first volume for which Doane provided an illustration was a book for children. This began a long rich career as an illustrator in the field of children's and juvenile literature. For Doane it was a varied profession. She was not to be limited in the subject matter for which she illustrated. Her book illustrations ranged from the classics, Stevenson's *Child's Garden of Verses*, to works for small children, such as *Mother Goose*. They included works of religious content, *Tell Me About the Bible* by Mary Alice Jones and illustrations for secular textbooks for grade-schoolers, *Something Different* by Eva Knox Evans. She wrote more than a dozen works herself and provided the illustrations, among them *The Big Trip* and *Book of Nature*.

Doane was clearly a woman of numerous and diverse talents, but she gained lasting notoriety in the field of illustration for her highly stylized contributions to the "Judy Bolton Mystery" series. Her depiction of Judy Bolton, indeed the entire cover design, was a departure from the norm of the mystery dust jacket illustration. Doane's efforts seemed to border on the experimental, with variations on style and realism throughout her tenure on the "Bolton" series. Her early cover illustrations tend less toward realism and more in favor of the surrealistic. There is something afoot and uncontrolled in the illustrations. Doane composed the figures and scenes in a slightly incongruous manner offering a sense of the inherent mystery in chaos. The subjects express little overt emotion. The picture's focal point is often defused, sacrificed for effect. Judy's character is portrayed as a girl of fashion, her hair styled impeccably. That much could have been expected. But Doane gives her figure a slightly angular sharpness that is somewhat harsh and imperfect. These are not ordinary illustrations. Doane's use of shadows tells a tale of its own indicating imminent peril to the unsuspecting story characters. Here the atmosphere is nearly palpable, for the characters are clearly in harm's way, while we as bystanders, drawn into the fray, are unable to warn them. The bystander's only solace is to read the mystery and discover its outcome.

Over time, Doane modified her illustrations in the direction of realism. Harsh expressions soften and natural backdrops replace the surreal. Images are less haunting and the colors more subtle. They are, however, no less interesting. In the jacket illustration for *The Secret of the*

**❶**
Mary Agnes Gillies, who modeled as Nancy Drew for her husband, illustrator Bill Gillies. Used by permission. Photo courtesy of the Gillies family.

**❷** 📖📖

**THE CASE OF THE COUNTERFEIT COIN**
Author: George Wyatt
Illustrator: Hamilton Greene
Publisher: Whitman

Barred Window, a later work, Judy's face is almost entirely hidden, highly unusual in the depiction of a heroine. We do not need to see Judy's surprised, shocked expression, for the mystery is apparent. She has entered a room with barred windows. The room is in disarray, documents spread about, furniture overturned. A page is wafting through the air, evidence that Judy has upset someone or something in mid-search of the premises. The window's light reveals a set of footprints belonging to an animal. But neither man nor beast occupies the room, for it is empty of life. And what of those bars? Were they intended to keep evil in? Or out? We could only be sure of this: Judy already knew, or she would find out. Such is the illustration's desired effect to generate interest and give rise to sales. Illustrators such as Pelagie Doane were able to accomplish these goals while maintaining an artistic voice.

The mystery category remained a nearly perfect match for author and illustrator, for the mystery lover would freely admit that the success of a good whodunit is not based upon on the revelation of a solution or perpetrator; instead it is in the puzzle itself and its depiction.

**③** The illustrator's nephew, Thomas Vreeland, models as both Hardys for Rudy Nappi's cover illustration of *The Secret of the Old Mill.* Used by permission of Rudy Nappi. Photos courtesy of Tony & Mary Carpentieri.

**④**
**THE SECRET OF THE OLD MILL**
Author: Franklin W. Dixon
Illustrator: Rudy Nappi
Publisher: Grosset & Dunlap
Reprinted with the permission of Pocket Books, a division of Simon & Schuster, Inc. Copyright © 1927, 1962 by Simon & Schuster. Hardy Boys™ is a registered trademark of Simon & Schuster, Inc.

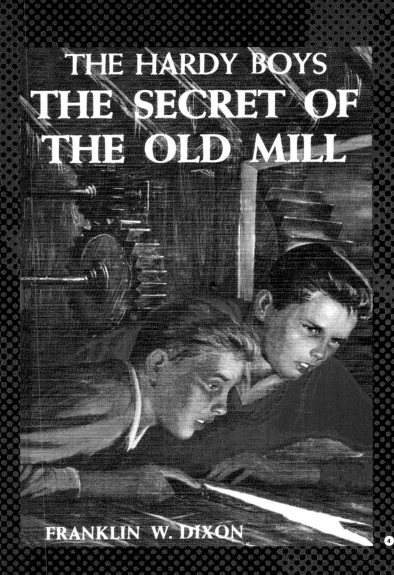

THE HARDY BOYS
THE SECRET OF
THE OLD MILL

FRANKLIN W. DIXON

The western portion of the United States may well be the most highly romanticized piece of real estate on the planet. This has held true almost since the birth of the new nation and is the result of numerous factors. The magnificence of the geography, from the vast plains to the towering mountain ranges to the arid desert expanses, the West held within its loosely defined boundaries a wide variety of wilderness. The vistas of the West simply surpassed young America's capacity to dream. The West spelled opportunity, with large tracts of low-cost, rich land. Opportunity gave rise to hope that a man and his family might set their own course to freedom, independence, and perhaps a little adventure. And the West produced a people unlike any seen in recorded history.

The Native American was viewed from a broad range of perspectives. These perceptions were often motivated by fear and ignorance and resulted in monikers such as "bloodthirsty redman" or at best, "noble savage." Ultimately the American Indian was named a deterrent to westward expansion and was conquered. The people of the West would soon include the settlers traversing the land with hope as their compass, blissfully unaware of hardships ahead. There would follow a cast of characters, which only this new frontier could have assembled. There were the cavalry, railroaders, and buffalo men. There too were the cattle barons, gold seekers, and lawmen. But there was none the equal of the West's finest creation: the cowboy.

The cowboy was the very definition of what the country was seeking to express raw individualism. The image of the solitary cowboy working cattle and sleeping under the stars would seem idealistic enough, but add an element of danger and sacrifice and the cowboy rises to the top of the occupational and cultural hierarchy. In popular mythology, the cowboy avoided violence when possible and prevailed when it was not, much in the way that the country expected itself to perform. Even in the great cattle drives, from grassland to railhead, when the individual cowboy was lost in the group effort, there was still that sense of the heroic: fending off rustlers, service to the greater good — food for the families in the cities in the East. In a future time, motion pictures would be credited with inventing the American cowboy, but his rise to prominence began much

**THE SADDLE BOYS OF THE ROCKIES**
Author: Captain James Carson
Illustrator: Walter S. Rogers
Publisher: Cupples & Leon

**GUNSMOKE GOLD**
Author: Tom West
Illustrator: Unknown
Publisher: E P Dutton & Co

**THE LONESOME TRAIL**
Author: B.M. Bower
Illustrator: Unknown
Publisher: Grosset & Dunlap

**THE PONY RIDER BOYS IN THE ROCKIES**
Author: Frank Gee Patchin
Illustrator: Russell H. Tardy
Publisher: Saalfield

earlier. Prior to motion pictures, the cowboy was already a cultural icon, the subject of poems and songs. The literature of the day recorded his every exploit.

The very notion that the West was won implies that it was fought for, and indeed it was. The men and women of the West fought the elements of nature and the constant threat of illness and injury beyond the reaches of civilization. There was another kind of fight as well. These fights erupted into war. There were the Indian wars involving a number of tribes from Canada to Mexico. And earlier, there was war with Mexico. Eventually, great battles represented these wars, including the Battle of Little Big Horn and the siege at the Alamo. These famous battles, and in particular their participants, entered into the country's folklore; names such as Custer, Crazy Horse, Bowie, and Crockett gained legendary status. Critics of the United States have long held that these cultural icons represent a national conscience steeped in war. In response to this criticism, most Americans

would cite that war heroes are praised for their sacrifice and that their actions rose out of the pursuit of freedom. Of course, opinions held by Americans on this subject are as diverse as its population. But in general, Americans are proud of their nation's history, and wars have been, without question, pivotal points in that history.

Indeed, America's most important war was one contained almost wholly within its borders and waged against itself, the Civil War or the War Between the States. A unique aspect of the American Civil War was its media coverage. Correspondents were not required to travel extensively to cover newsworthy events. Advances in the publishing industry allowed for the timely printing and distribution of the news from the front. Americans were hungry for news about friends and relatives engaged in the conflict. Following the war's end, books and periodicals were published recounting the battles and other events. Sales were brisk as the country examined its great shared experience and attempted to put it into perspective.

**1** 📖

**YOUNG EAGLE OF THE TRAIL**
Author: J. Allan Dunn
Illustrator: Machtey
Publisher: Grosset & Dunlap

**2** 📖

**THE X BAR X BOYS ON THE RANCH**
Author: James Cody Ferris
Illustrator: Walter S. Rogers
Publisher: Grosset & Dunlap
Reprinted with the permission of
Pocket Books, a division of Simon &
Schuster, Inc. Copyright © 1926

**3** 📖

**THE X BAR X BOYS IN THUNDER CANYON**
Author: James Cody Ferris
Illustrator: Walter S. Rogers
Publisher: Grosset & Dunlap
Reprinted with the permission of Pocket
Books, a division of Simon & Schuster,
Inc. Copyright © 1926

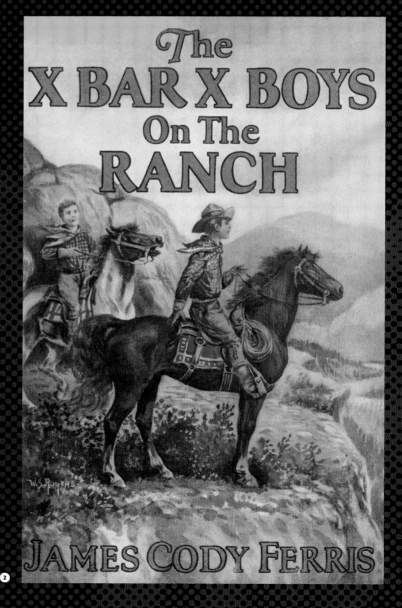

**1**　　**2**

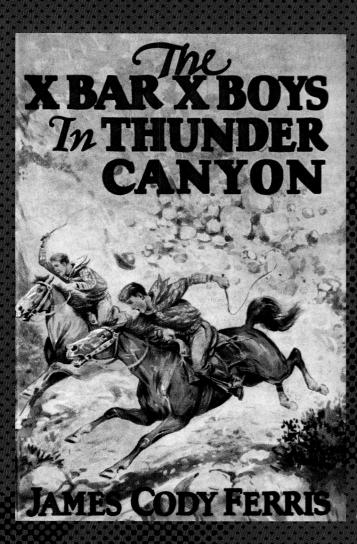

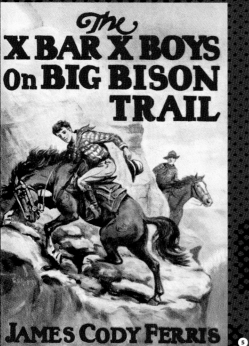

Youngsters for years to come would read of the Civil War and see in it nothing less than high romance and adventure.

By the beginning of the twentieth century, dime novelists had seized upon the lure of the West and the patriotism inherent in times of war and made them salable commodities for juveniles. The dime novel already had a proven track record with western titles containing tales of hired pistolaros and gruesome Indian massacres. On occasion, a minor western celebrity was chosen for his or her marketability and, through the dime novel, was delivered to an adoring public in wait of the latest adventure. William Cody, better known as Buffalo Bill, was a scout and railroad buffalo hunter of some renown, but in the hands of the writer Ned Buntline, he became a national treasure. In the case of Cody, he was up to the part. He parlayed his fame into a traveling Wild West Show, a kind of western circus, in which he would headline for two decades. His success stemmed from the dime novel that created the legend, which in turn made the man. Eventually the more gruesome western dime novels gave way to a more sanitized version of history. The western lost a bit of its grit in the passing of the dime novel and gained some gloss in the process.

Juvenile literature with a war theme received a significant boost from America's triumph in the Spanish-American War. Books on the subject were rushed to press on the heels of the conflict. One writer who would make a career and forge an industry by being prepared to quickly identify a trend or niche was Edward Stratemeyer. His portrayal of the war, several years prior to the launch of his Syndicate, solidified his reputation as a bankable writer. Stratemeyer began his "Spanish-American War" series with *Under Dewey at Manila*, a fictionalized account of Admiral George Dewey's naval conquest of the Spanish fleet in the Philippines. This book introduces the reader to brothers Larry and Ben Russell and their friend Gilbert Pennington, characters whose wartime adventures could be followed through several campaigns in the "Old Glory" series of six titles. The character of Gilbert Pennington is spun off to fight a few battles of his own during the Boxer Rebellion and in the Russo-Japanese War. The books' popularity hinged on their topical nature as well as on the general rise in patriotism.

The subject of war in juvenile literature sold best during the actual time of conflict. When a war wasn't handy, the books turned to stories of military life such as the "West Point" series by author H. Irving Hancock featuring the character of Dick Prescott. Cadet Herb Kent was another West Pointer, the creation of Graham Dean. Young readers desiring tales of battle during times of peace could seek out historical volumes such as the "Revolutionary War" series and "War for the Union" series. Unfortunately, and in short order, the future would provide plenty of topical war-themed books.

Westerns and war books were enjoying brisk sales in the second decade of the new century. They had lost a good deal of their pulp tone and had built a foundation for the respective genres to continue. The legitimizing of the western book owed a debt to the author Zane Grey. His books were meticulously researched, realistic, and well written. The popularity of his work also spawned a host of juvenile books, among them the "X Bar X Boys" series. The "X Bar X Boys" stories followed the western adventures of teenagers Roy and Teddy Manley who live on a ranch with

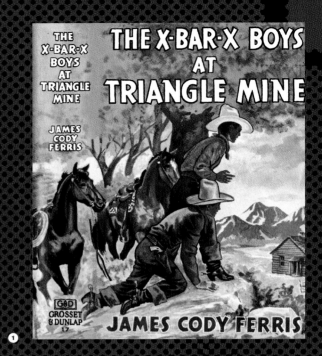

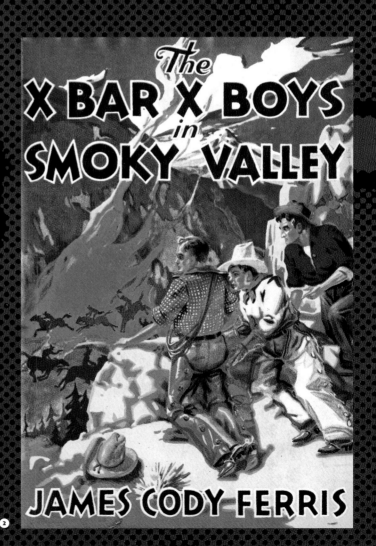

# HOMEGOODS
PORT JEFFERSON STATION, NY
SAVE WITH STYLE.
(631) 331-4674

CUSTOMER SALE                0233/0005/6282-8
0042 JACQUE                   OCT-23-06 11:01

54 FOOD
043384  1@1.49                        1.49N
54 FOOD
043384  1@1.49                        1.49N
54 FOOD
265410  1@2.49                        2.49N
36 TOWELS
047863  1@2.00                        2.00T
36 TOWELS
070839  1@2.00                        2.00T
36 TOWELS
047863  1@2.00                        2.00T
58 JUVENILE
181527  1@15.00                      15.00T

    7 ITEMS SUBTOTAL                  26.47
      21.00 TAX T NY 8.625            1.81

          TOTAL                       28.28
              CASH                    30.00
          DUE CUSTOMER
              CHANGE                   1.72

*REFUNDS WITHIN 30 DAYS WITH RECEIPT*
THANK YOU FOR SHOPPING AT HOMEGOODS
Sign up for email at HomeGoods.com

HomeGoods

HomeGoods®

HomeGoods®

HomeGoods®

HomeGoods®

**1** ▪▪▪

**THE X-BAR-X BOYS AT TRIANGLE MINE**
Author: James Cody Ferris
Illustrator: Paul S. Laune
Publisher: Grosset & Dunlap
Reprinted with the permission of Pocket
Books, a division of Simon & Schuster, Inc.
Copyright © 1938.

**2** ▪▪▪

**THE X-BAR-X BOYS IN SMOKY VALLEY**
Author: James Cody Ferris
Illustrator: J. Clemens Gretter
Publisher: Grosset & Dunlap
Reprinted with the permission of Pocket
Books, a division of Simon & Schuster, Inc.
Copyright © 1932.

**3** ▪▪▪▪▪

**THE X-BAR-X BOYS SEEKING THE LOST TROOPERS**
Author: James Cody Ferris
Illustrator: Paul S. Laune
Publisher: Grosset & Dunlap
Reprinted with the permission of Pocket
Books, a division of Simon & Schuster, Inc.
Copyright © 1941.

**4** ▪▪▪

**THE X-BAR-X BOYS AT COPPERHEAD GULCH**
Author: James Cody Ferris
Illustrator: J. Clemens Gretter
Publisher: Grosset & Dunlap
Reprinted with the permission of Pocket
Books, a division of Simon & Schuster, Inc.
Copyright © 1933.

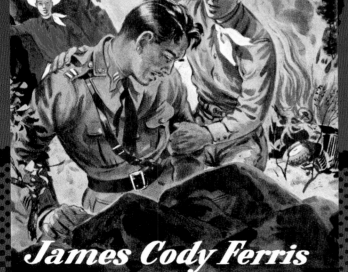

**3**

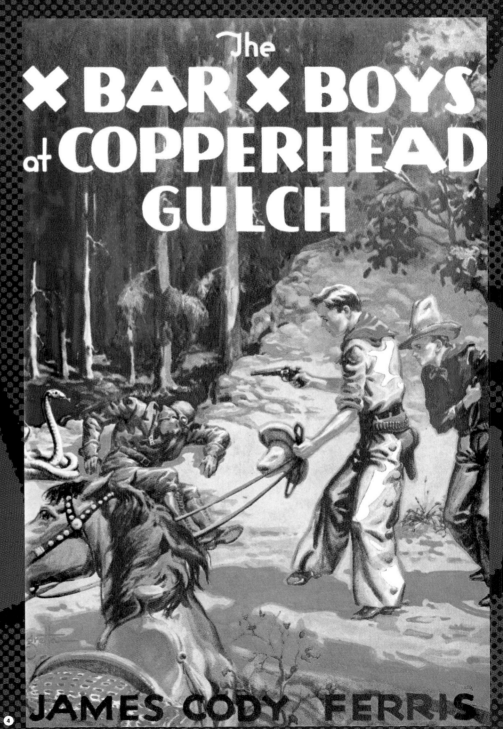

**4**

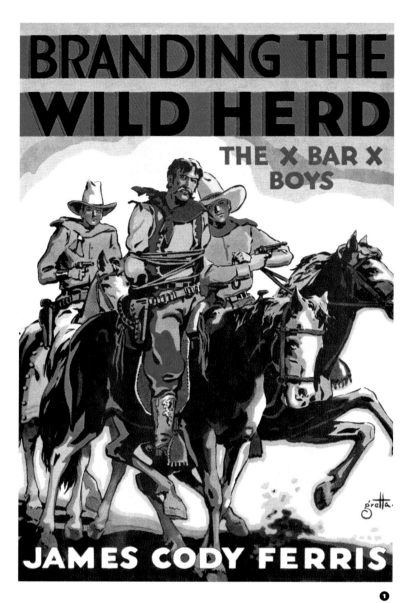

**②** ☐☐☐

**THE X BAR X BOYS WITH THE SECRET RANGERS**

Author: James Cody Ferris

Illustrator: J. Clemens Gretter

Publisher: Grosset & Dunlap

Reprinted with the permission of Pocket Books, a division of Simon & Schuster, Inc. Copyright © 1936.

**❶** ☐☐☐

**THE X BAR X BOYS BRANDING THE WILD HERD**

Author: James Cody Ferris

Illustrator: J. Clemens Gretter

Publisher: Grosset & Dunlap

Reprinted with the permission of Pocket Books, a division of Simon & Schuster, Inc. Copyright © 1934

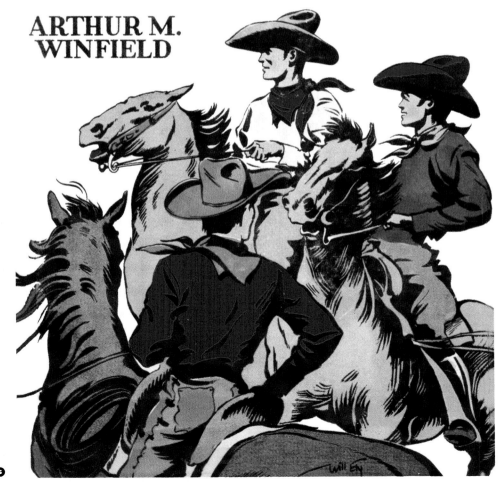

**③** □□□

**THE X-BAR-X BOYS HUNTING THE PRIZE MUSTANGS**
Author: James Cody Ferris
Illustrator: Paul S. Laune
Publisher: Grosset & Dunlap
Reprinted with the permission of Pocket
Books, a division of Simon & Schuster,
Inc. Copyright © 1937.

**④** □□□□□

**THE X-BAR-X BOYS IN THE HAUNTED GULLY**
Author: James Cody Ferris
Illustrator: Paul S. Laune
Publisher: Grosset & Dunlap
Reprinted with the permission of
Pocket Books, a division of Simon &
Schuster, Inc. Copyright © 1940.

**⑤** □□

**THE ROVER BOYS ON THE PLAINS**
Author: Arthur M. Winfield
Illustrator: Will Ely
Publisher: Whitman

their father Bardwell, mother Barbara, and sister Belle Ada. The brothers have a close relationship in spite of their opposing personalities. In keeping with the tried and true formula of the series book, one boy, Roy, is serious in nature, while Teddy is portrayed as the high-spirited younger brother. Other continuing characters include friends from a neighboring ranch and various ranch hands. But it is Roy and Teddy who, with their trusty mounts Star and Flash, carry the day. They team up to foil jailbreaks and kidnappings, and to prevail over more than a few cattle rustlers. Together they sort out claims concerning water rights, perform rescues, and fight range fires. They search for stolen loot and take part in a gold rush. Through their adventures they maintain the western code of justice and fair play above all else. They display a freedom of movement unknown to their youthful readers, but that too serves the western theme of autonomy and self-reliance. The stories are of high adventure and contain violent aspects. But the violence is measured and defensive; for instance, a

passage might involve the wounding of a desperado during his capture. Given that the series is of a two-fisted subject matter, it is — while exciting — remarkably restrained.

The bloodless violence carries the stamp of the series creator Edward Stratemeyer. As was his custom, Stratemeyer outlined the stories, which were then given to a ghostwriter of his choosing. Upon completion of the manuscript, it was returned for editing by Stratemeyer and his staff. Writers contributing to the "X Bar X Boys" series, under the pen name of James Cody Ferris, included Frank Hopley, Walter Karig, Howard Garis, and later his son Roger Garis. After Stratemeyer's death, his daughter Harriet assumed control of the Syndicate. She and her sister, Edna, provided outlines to the series. The adventures of Roy and Teddy Manley had a run of sixteen years, ranking it with the most successful of the juvenile western series.

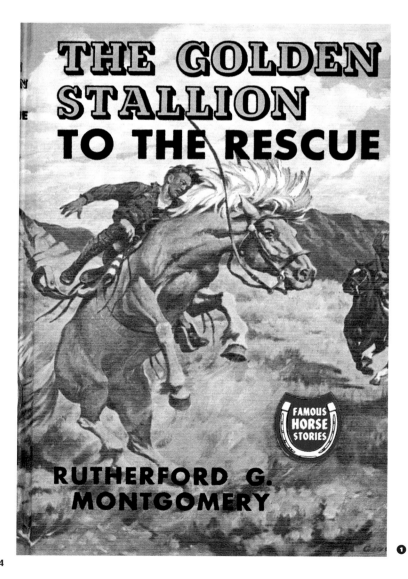

**❶**

**THE GOLDEN STALLION TO THE RESCUE**
Author: Rutherford G. Montgomery
Illustrator: George Giguere
Publisher: Grosset & Dunlap

**❷**

**THE GOLDEN STALLION'S REVENGE**
Author: Rutherford G. Montgomery
Illustrator: George Giguere
Publisher: Grosset & Dunlap

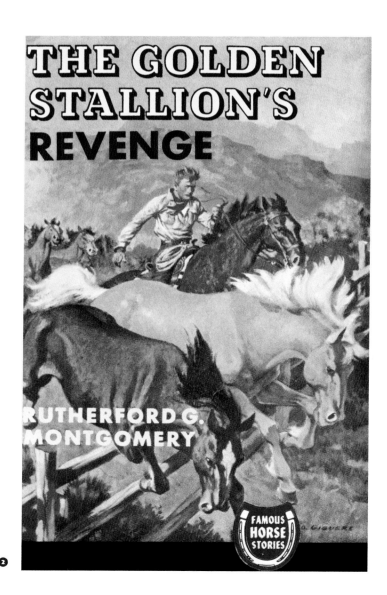

THE STORY OF
Daniel Boone

By WILLIAM O. STEELE
ILLUSTRATED BY WARREN BAUMGARTNER **1**

THE STORY OF
Buffalo Bill

By EDMUND COLLIER
ILLUSTRATED BY NICHOLAS EGGENHOFER **2**

During World War I and directly after, several volumes of juvenile literature were written to herald the heroic actions of our young fighting men and their friends from across the sea. One such series, "The Boy Allies," is actually two, a naval set and an army version. The author Clair W. Hayes, who used his own name for the army series and the pen name of Ensign Robert L. Drake for the navy books, was a veteran of the newspaper business. His army characters, Hal Paine and Chester Crawford, are lads of only seventeen when they set out to the rescue of Europe. They possess skills beyond their years including marksmanship, linguistics, and boxing to name but a few. And, of course, those fencing lessons prove convenient when our heroes are reduced to the hand-to-hand combat of trench warfare. By war's end they, of course, are decorated with nearly every known medal for bravery and both earn the rank of colonel, such was their glorious service.

The navy's Frank Chadwick and Jack Templeton are nearly carbon copies of the army characters. The naval duo's acts of courage are just as impressive. They attain such stature that they are received at the White House for a personal debriefing by Woodrow Wilson, their commander in chief. The accolades are pleasant, after all, but the real fighting, of course, does not take place in Washington. It is on the briny where our boys earn the rank of captain for Templeton and first officer for Chadwick. The "Boy Allies" series was relatively short-lived with titles produced over a five-year period, but that was more than enough time for four teenage boys to conquer the German Empire.

The 1930s and 1940s saw the continued success of juvenile western and war books. For the war volumes, it was a clear result of history's greatest conflict, World War II. The "Dave Dawson" series of war books provided the nation's youth with an American fighting hero before the United States entered the war. The series' author, R. Sidney Bowen, was no paper tiger. As a teenager serving in World War I, Bowen achieved ace status by shooting down eight enemy aircraft. His combat experiences would enrich his later youth stories with realism. Following his war service, Bowen wrote for several newspapers. But his true love was aviation, and he eventually assumed the position of editor-in-chief for Aviation Magazine. He was also an editor of Flying News. He would soon broaden his career to include fiction writing.

With the war underway in Europe and U.S. involvement all but certain, Bowen began his "Dave Dawson" series which became an instant hit in America as well as in England. The title character is an all-American boy of seventeen, a champion of the skies, who flies for Great Britain's Royal Air Force. His adventures are undertaken with the assistance of Freddy Farmer, his English chum. Dave and Freddy bring the war to teenagers on both sides of the ocean with their thrilling global exploits in Dunkirk, Casablanca, and Libya. Dave Dawson sees action in the Pacific Theater of War with adventures at Truk, Guadalcanal, and Singapore. Dawson's wartime service is not limited to flying. He becomes a commando, takes to the high seas, and is also involved in espionage. Clearly, a young man must wear many hats when confronting the Axis powers in the cause of liberty.

The 1930s and 1940s was also the time for an American hero of a different

**1** 📖

**THE STORY OF DANIEL BOONE**
Author: William O Steele
Illustrator: Warren Baumgartner
Publisher: Grosset & Dunlap

**2** 📖

**THE STORY OF BUFFALO BILL**
Author: Edmund Collier
Illustrator: Nicholas Eggenhofer
Publisher: Grosset & Dunlap

**3** 📖

**THE STORY OF GERONIMO**
Author: Jim Kjelgaard
Illustrator: Charles Banks Wilson
Publisher: Grosset & Dunlap

**4** 📖

**INDIAN CHIEFS**
Author: Dorothea J. Snow
Illustrator: E. Joseph Dreany
Publisher: Whitman
Used by permission. Golden Books Publishing
Company, Inc. Copyright © 1959, 1987. All rights
reserved.

**5** 📖

**INDIAN CHIEFS- BACK COVER**
Author: Dorothea J. Snow
Illustrator: E. Joseph Dreany
Publisher: Whitman
Used by permission. Golden Books
Publishing Company, Inc. Copyright ©
1959, 1987. All rights reserved.

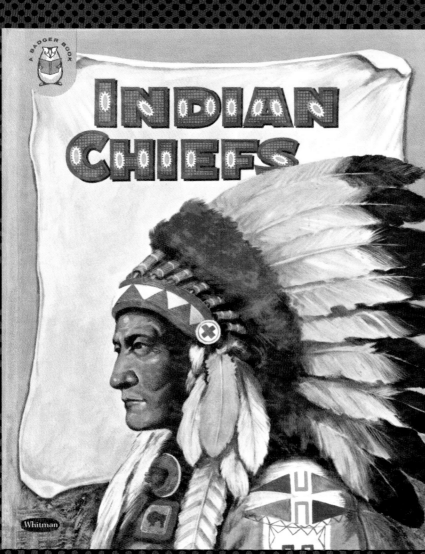

# THE STORY OF
# Crazy Horse

By ENID LAMONTE MEADOWCROFT

ILLUSTRATED BY WILLIAM REUSSWIG

**THE STORY OF CRAZY HORSE**

Author: Enid Lamonte Meadowcroft
Illustrator: William Reusswig
Publisher: Grosset & Dunlap

**INDIANS AND THE OLD WEST**

Author: Anne Terry White
Illustrator: Alfred Jacob Miller
Publisher: Simon & Schuster

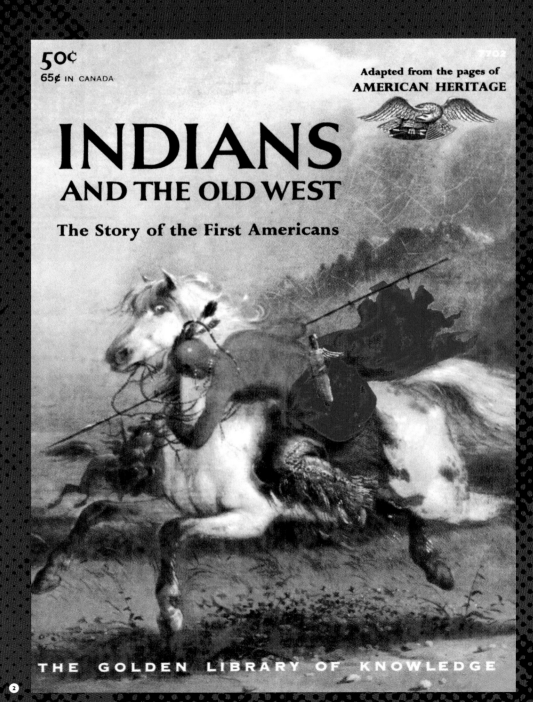

50¢
65¢ IN CANADA

Adapted from the pages of
AMERICAN HERITAGE

# INDIANS
## AND THE OLD WEST

### The Story of the First Americans

THE GOLDEN LIBRARY OF KNOWLEDGE

sort. It was a new creation and perhaps the greatest personification of the western hero. Series creators George W. Trendle and Fran Striker originally conceived of this new character as a composite of Robin Hood and Zorro. Their western hero would be called the Lone Ranger.

The Lone Ranger storyline had its origins in radio. Trendle, the owner of a Detroit radio station, developed a radio program for use at his station. If the show were a success he hoped to syndicate it to reach a larger audience. Striker, a radio scriptwriter, took Trendle's idea and developed it further. The program first aired in 1933. "The Lone Ranger's" audience grew steadily and within four years, the series had gained nationwide popularity. Striker, when not writing radio scripts, penned nineteen "Lone Ranger" books for the series' young fans.

The now classic storyline begins with the ambush of a unit of Texas Rangers. Ranger John Reid, suffering from his wounds and barely alive, is saved from certain death by a passing Indian. Reid, during his convalescence, vows to continue the fight for justice, law, and order. His vow is partly motivated by the death of his older brother and fellow ranger who was killed in the attack. In a dramatic act of respect for the ideals his brother fought and gave his life for, Reid takes a swatch of material from his brother's vest and fashions a mask from it. From that point forward he is known as the Lone Ranger. The Indian who had saved his life is Tonto. They forge a friendship as well as a partnership and together they ride the West on their faithful steeds, Silver and Scout, in search of those in distress. Their quest brings them no monetary compensation. Instead, they find their reward in bringing justice to the American frontier.

Tales of western adventure were not entirely of the fast-draw, cattlepunching, and outlaw-fighting breed. There too were tales of ordinary frontier life that held more than enough real-life drama to captivate the reader's interest. At the age of sixty-five, Laura Ingalls Wilder embarked on a career as an author, bringing to young America tales of the struggles and hardships of the western frontier. Her work was historical fiction, autobiographical in nature. While the books described the tremendous toil and struggle of frontier life, they did not sink into complaint and self-pity. Her characters' acceptance of their circumstances and events allowed them a measure of dignity.

Wilder wrote largely of her childhood experiences in books tailored to a youthful audience that made the historical aspects invisible and the books fun. Her stories involved a number of themes that transcend time, childhood trouble with peers and the awkward shyness one would feel in moving to a new community. These were issues that children understood, and

**❸** ▢

**MAVERICK**
Author: Charles I. Coombs
Illustrator: Alexander Toth
Publisher: Whitman

**❹** ▢▢▢

**LITTLE HOUSE ON THE PRAIRIE**
Author: Laura Ingalls Wilder
Illustrator: Garth Williams
Publisher: HarperCollins Publishers
Used by permission of HarperCollins
Publishers. Text Copyright © 1935 by
Laura Ingalls Wilder, renewed 1963 by
Roer L Macbride. Little House™ is a
registered trademark of HarperCollins
Publishers.

*Laura Ingalls Wilder*

# BY THE SHORES OF SILVER LAKE

PICTURES BY GARTH WILLIAMS

*Laura Ingalls Wilder*

# FARMER BOY

PICTURES BY GARTH WILLIAMS

**❶**

**❶**

**BY THE SHORES OF SILVER LAKE**
Author: Laura Ingalls Wilder
Illustrator: Garth Williams
Publisher: HarperCollins Publishers
Used by permission of HarperCollins
Publishers.

**❷**

**❷**

**FARMER BOY**
Author: Laura Ingalls Wilder
Illustrator: Garth Williams
Publisher: HarperCollins Publish
Used by permission of HarperCol
Publishers.

**THE LONG WINTER**

**LITTLE TOWN ON THE PRAIRIE**

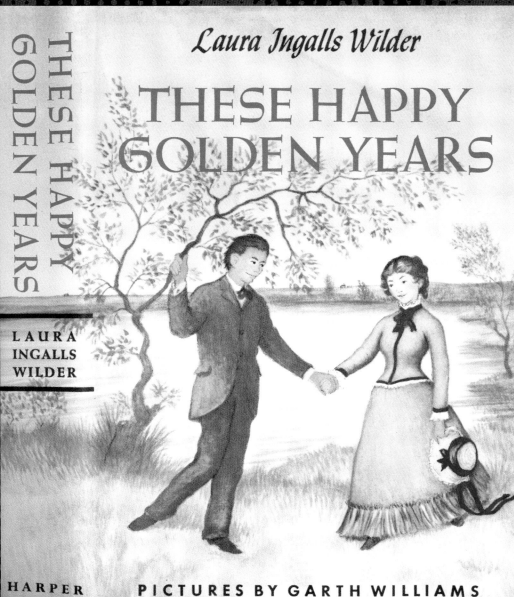

**THESE HAPPY GOLDEN YEARS**

**3**

**THE LONG WINTER**
Author: Laura Ingalls Wilder
Illustrator: Garth Williams
Publisher: HarperCollins Publishers
Used by permission of HarperCollins
Publishers.

**4**

**LITTLE TOWN ON THE PRAIRIE**
Author: Laura Ingalls Wilder
Illustrator: Garth Williams
Publisher: HarperCollins Publishers
Used by permission of HarperCollins
Publishers.

**5**

**THESE HAPPY GOLDEN YEARS**
Author: Laura Ingalls Wilder
Illustrator: Garth Williams
Publisher: HarperCollins Publishers
Used by permission of HarperCollins
Publishers.

**PICTURES BY GARTH WILLIAMS**

**4** 📖

**LITTLE HOUSE IN THE BIG WOODS- INTERIOR**
Author: Laura Ingalls Wilder
Illustrator: Garth Williams
Publisher: HarperCollins Publishers
Used by permission of HarperCollins
Publishers. Little House™ is a registered
trademark of HarperCollins Publishers,
Inc.

**4** 📖

**LITTLE HOUSE IN THE BIG WOODS- INTERIOR**
Author: Laura Ingalls Wilder
Illustrator: Garth Williams
Publisher: HarperCollins Publishers
Used by permission of HarperCollins
Publishers. Little House™ is a registered
trademark of HarperCollins Publishers,
Inc.

**1** 📖

**THE FIRST FOUR YEARS**
Author: Laura Ingalls Wilder
Illustrator: Garth Williams
Publisher: HarperCollins Publishers
Used by permission of HarperCollins
Publishers.

**2** 📖

**LITTLE HOUSE IN THE BIG WOODS**
Author: Laura Ingalls Wilder
Illustrator: Garth Williams
Publisher: HarperCollins Publishers
Used by permission of HarperCollins Publishers.
Little House™ is a registered trademark of
HarperCollins Publishers, Inc.

they added realism to the stories. Further, children began to realize that there did exist a link between the past and present, that the lessons learned in one age could be readily applied to another. The books written by Laura Ingalls Wilder were, after all, about the value of the human experience.

In her first book, entitled *Little House in the Big Woods*, Wilder describes her early childhood growing up on a farm in rural Wisconsin. It is the story of a loving family, Ma and Pa Ingalls and their daughters Mary, Laura, and Carrie who make their living from the land. There is plenty of work, to be sure, but there is time for fun too. The girls play games, and sometimes Pa joins in. It is a period of contentment. In the next volume, *Little House on the Prairie*, the family moves west from Wisconsin to a new home in Kansas. Traveling in the 1870s over a great distance with family and possessions is adventure enough, but after weathering the journey much work lies ahead, including building a family domicile. It is all for naught. In short order, the family loses its new home, a heartbreaking event both for the Ingalls and for the reader as well. This is a family who is easy to care about.

In the books that followed *Little House on the Prairie*, the Ingalls family seem alternately cursed and blessed in life. They journey north to Minnesota where their circumstances improve, only to endure terrible storms and a great grasshopper plague that robs the area of its crops. Mary contracts scarlet fever and loses her sight. The Ingalls are gripped in near poverty. The family, in search of new opportunity, moves westward again, this time to the Dakota Territory. A child, Grace, is born and Pa finds work. The family is tried, and will be again, but determination continues to sustain them. Even amid hard times the family, the girls in particular, have fun. The books maintain in the characters a certain level of mental well-being with passages of humor. It seems that a sense of humor is required for life on the frontier.

In the later books, family life changes as the children grow up. Laura, while still in her mid-teens, qualifies for a teaching position after passing an examination and receives a certificate. She accepts a job offer and is courted by Almanzo Wilder, whom she eventually marries. Laura and her husband move into a home of their own and begin their life together. Here the main series ends. Wilder wrote other books involving her family in a similar vein, including a work that chronicled her husband's youth, but her best loved works were those concerning her childhood on the prairie.

Wilder's professional life in both her writing and teaching careers was somewhat unusual. She had attended several schools in a number of communities in the course of her family's many moves, yet she never received a diploma from any of them. Indeed, the first and only document she received was a teaching certificate. She began her book-writing career at a rather advanced age and might not have done so then had it not been for the encouragement of her daughter Rose. Though Wilder had written articles for newspapers years earlier, it was Rose, herself an accomplished working writer, who gave her mother writing lessons and assisted her in finding her literary voice. Certainly it was an odd beginning to both careers. But Wilder was an unusual person who had lived an unusual life. There probably wasn't a great deal that could surprise

*Chapter* 1

# Little HOUSE
# In the Big WOODS

CHRISTMAS

SUNDAYS

her, even about herself.

To Laura Ingalls Wilder, the stories she shared with her readers were precious. They were the memories of her life, perhaps the most deeply personal possession any person can share with another. Her audience must have sensed that too, for her legions of fans have endured on a worldwide scale. At first glance, her books, steeped in hardship and even tragedy, might be viewed as mere tales of survival from a time long since past, but they were much more than that; they were stories of the American West and its people, who quietly displayed unparalleled heroism in their everyday lives.

Illustration for juvenile western books is a unique undertaking. In most any other genre the emotion, action, and suspense are depicted in the human form. The concept of most dust jacket illustration is, after all, to commence a relationship between the reader and the story's characters. Often this is not the case with illustrations of the American West. The West carries such a degree of romanticism that humans are not of primary importance, an unthinkable concept in any other genre. Instead, the environment is the principal element of Western illustration. The Western environment with its varying topography, flora, and fauna speaks to a wide range of emotions. The Western landscape is at once a place of hope and a place of danger, plentiful in natural resources as well as a desert wasteland. A man might venture west and make his mark, or be swallowed up and never heard from again. It is all of these scenarios and more. There is no other place of its kind on earth, nowhere that can draw upon its heritage as does the American West.

Early juvenile western illustration, particularly the pulp trade, drew heavily upon the violent aspects of the frontier age. Here the West is portrayed through the raw brutality of man, frequently in the image of the bloodthirsty savage. Trading on violence, the illustrations do not invoke the richness of the landscape, and their effectiveness is diminished due to the narrow scope. Later illustrators understood

**❹** 📖

**THE STORY OF GENERAL CUSTER**
Author: Margaret Leighton
Illustrator: Nicholas Eggenhofer
Publisher: Grosset & Dunlap

**❺** 📖

**GETTYSBURG**
Author: MacKinlay Kantor
Illustrator: Donald McKay
Publisher: Random House
Used by permission of Random House Children's Books, a division of Random House, Inc. Copyright © 1952 by MacKinlay Kantor. Copyright © renewed 1980 by Irene Layne Kantor, Tim Kantor, and Layne Kantor Schroder.

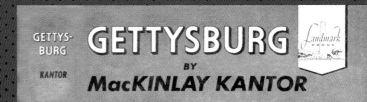

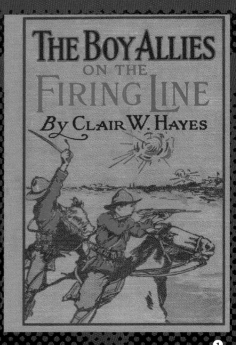

 THE BOY ALLIES ON THE FIRING LINE

**THE BOY ALLIES ON THE FIRING LINE**
Author: Clair W. Hayes
Illustrator: J. Walton Davis
Publisher: A L Burt Co

 **DICK PRESCOTT'S THIRD YEAR AT WEST POINT**
Author: H. Irving Hancock
Illustrator: Unknown
Publisher: Altemus

 **HERB KENT WEST POINT FULLBACK**
Author: Graham M. Dean
Illustrator: Unknown
Publisher: Goldsmith Publishing Co

the storytelling aspects of the Western terrain and employed them successfully in their work. Among these illustrators were Frederic Remington and Charles M. Russell. The depiction of conflict between Indian and expansionist are common themes in their work, but the Indian is increasingly portrayed with dignity and even in heroic form. These two masters of Western illustration were gifted in their understanding of the environment and visionary in their treatment and portrayal of native peoples.

Their insights extended to the representation of animals as well. Animals, particularly horses, are the most dramatic elements in Western illustration. It is the horse that offered the illustrators the opportunity to present their vision of the physical form. With its great muscled frame, huge emotional eyes, and large mouth, the horse is an oversized dramatic piece. The horse, like the land itself, is a study in contrasting images. It is a friend of man and even his affable beast of burden, though its sometimes unpredictable temperament might fail him in times of emergency. The horse was the single most important piece of property to the Westerner in terms of transportation, work, safety, and recreation. To illustrate the West, one had to possess the skills to accurately depict the horse.

When tamer juvenile reading material replaced the violence-ridden pulps, illustrations changed as well. Dust jackets continued to carry themes of adventure and danger, but the trend clearly shifted to more environmental approaches. The jacket art of the popular "X Bar X Boys" series is indicative of this trend. Illustrators contributing to this series were well known for their work in other Stratemeyer Syndicate books, chiefly the "Hardy Boys." Walter S. Rogers was the original illustrator for the "X Bar X Boys" books, and his work adorned the first ten covers of the series. Rogers's work on the "X Bar X Boys" covers was superior to his "Hardy Boys" illustrations. His western art was more realistic, and the colors were better suited.

Rogers's depiction of the horse may be his greatest accomplishment. Through the horses he captures the drama of the scene. For the cover of *The X Bar X Boys in Thunder Canyon*, a scene that depicts the boys racing their steeds down a steep, rocky pass ahead of some unknown danger (or perhaps in pursuit of that danger), Rogers is able to successfully tell the story through the boys' mounts. The boys are shown in dramatic form as well, leaning forward in their saddles, cracking their whips, intent upon their objective. Their hats are torn from their heads and cast backward, a testimony to the speed of their movement. But the horses tell the tale through their alarm and exertion. As they hurtle down the slope, the horses struggle for breath with their large nostrils flaring and their mouths straining against the bits. Their huge eyes show white as they scan the terrain and struggle to keep their near panic in check. Their bodies appear to glisten with sweat, their huge muscles driving them forward over uncertain footing. Rogers shows the horse in the foreground with all four feet simultaneously off the ground. He understood that even under these torturous conditions these magnificent creatures would maintain a grace, strength, and agility unmatched in any other living form.

The work of illustrator J. Clemens Gretter was a sharp departure from that of Rogers. Gretter's emphasis was in the use of color with bold, vivid images. The illustrations are awash in bright reds and blues. While some aspects of realism may have been sacrificed, the overall approach with the use of dazzling color is so dramatic that the usual rules of western illustration seemed not to apply. Gretter's jacket illustration for *The X Bar X Boys in Smoky Valley* is such a work. In the distance we see a group of riders traversing a switchback trail along a deep green mountainside. Red flames silhouette several of these riders. The red flames are far brighter than those existing in nature, and oddly, these massive flames trail into a very few narrow wisps of smoke and instead of showing a gray or whitish hue, are depicted as yellow against a blue sky. Our heroes are gathered in watch in the foreground, hidden behind yellow boulders. They are shown appropriately enough in western attire, but the clothing is spotless and brightly colored, hardly the clothes of working cowboys. The reality of the unfolding drama is not served, but again, the effect is so visually stunning that grand drama is derived from the improbable colors.

Paul S. Laune, who had followed Gretter in the "Hardy Boys" line as well, was the last contributing illustrator to the series. Laune's illustrations are similar to Gretter's in the use of color, but Laune's work tends toward images that are more realistic. His first illustration for the series is representative of his western work.

The dust jacket illustration accompanying *The X Bar X Boys Hunting the Prize Mustangs* displays the boys rounding up wild horses. The colors are an unusual mix, with a purple sky taking up nearly a third of the cover, serving as a striking backdrop for the title lettering. At a distance, the boys and their mounts are seen in orange and brown, with a touch of black added to further define the images. The prairie comprises several colors, including red, green, and yellow mixed into a kind of blur. In the immediate foreground, covering a full one-third of the illustration is the focus of the work, the wild mustang. The horse is white, with black mane and tail, readily distinguishable from the identically colored domestic horses the boys are riding. The colors tell the tale in part, but it is the realism of the characters that completes the illustration.

Laune exhibits a fine grasp of the figures and the unfolding drama in such a western scene. In the capture of their quarry, the riders hold the strategic high ground. One rider parallels the mustang's course and has cast his lariat above the horse. The lariat's loop appears to be on the mark; perhaps in only a moment it will catch the fleeing animal. The remaining rider is bearing down directly upon the mustang. He is twirling his lariat, set to throw it as well. If an escape is to be found, it would be short-lived, for these boys are obviously fit for the task. The wild horse is allowed some measure of personality also. The mustang is depicted with its ears back, its eyes coal black and hard as if angered that other creatures are meaning to deny it freedom.

Laune produced high-quality illustrations throughout the series. His style varies somewhat as he experiments with color and realism, sometimes emphasizing one more than the other; but his vision of the romanticism of the West remains constant.

The stories written by Laura Ingalls Wilder were in contrast to the gunplay and two-fisted action of many juvenile westerns. The illustrations for Wilder's books are also unique compared to the standard western book format. Of these illustrations, those that have longest endured were the creations of Garth Williams. It was neither by luck nor accident that Williams's illustrations so complement Wilder's work. It was the

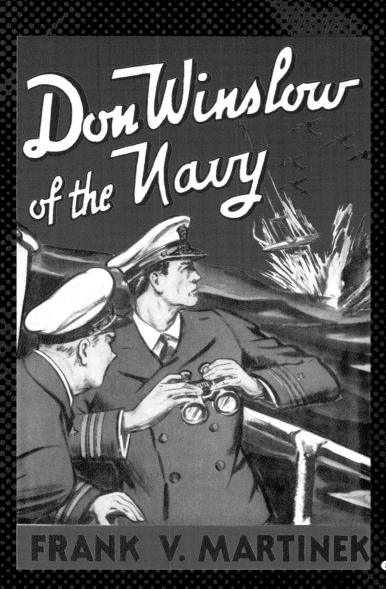

**③**

**④**

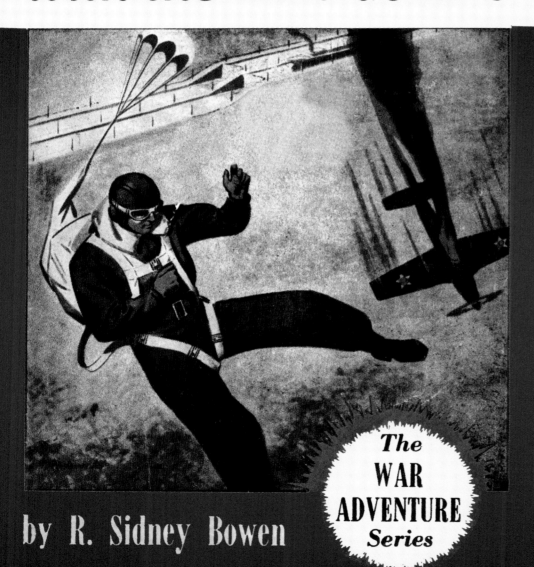

**1**

**DAVE DAWSON WITH THE AIR CORPS**
Author: R. Sidney Bowen
Illustrator: Unknown
Publisher: Saalfield

**2**

**DAVE DAWSON WITH THE FLYING TIGERS**
Author: R. Sidney Bowen
Illustrator: Unknown
Publisher: Saalfield

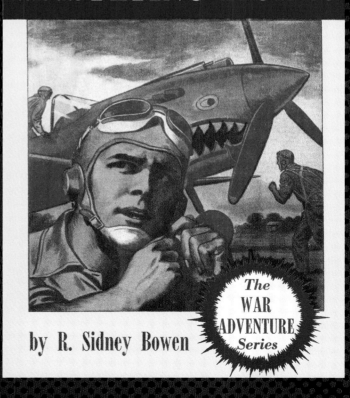

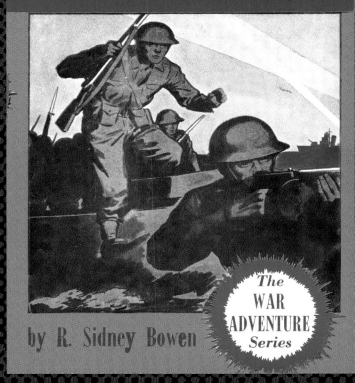

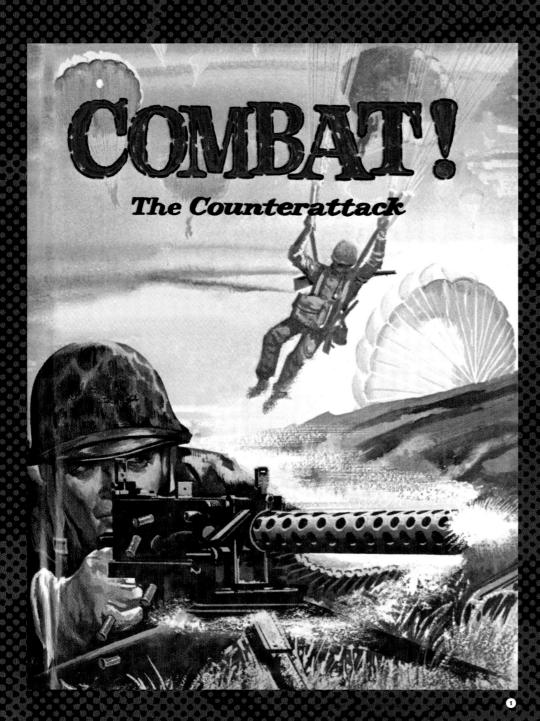

**1**

**COMBAT! THE COUNTERATTACK**

Author: Franklin M. Davis, Jr.
Illustrator: Unknown
Publisher: Whitman

**2**

**CHERRY AMES FLIGHT NURSE**

Author: Helen Wells
Illustrator: Ralph Crosby Smith
Publisher: Grosset & Dunlap

result of research. Upon acceptance of the assignment, Williams began a period of intensive research, first by reading Wilder's books and by studying frontier cabins and their construction. He examined the logs and how they were hewn. He inspected the chinking material and how it was applied. His aim was not to learn how to build a log cabin. It was to understand the labor involved in such an undertaking and to appreciate the pride of ownership a family must have had in creating something from the earth, something of its own in a time of few material possessions.

Williams needed to know more, so he journeyed west to meet the author. His interview with Wilder compelled him to journey farther west, then north, retracing the travels of the Ingalls family. He wanted to see the places with his own eyes and, with the stories fresh in his mind, through Laura's eyes too.

The resulting illustrations reflect Williams's research, his travels, and commitment to his craft. The illustrations are understated and simple, much like the age they depict. Foremost, they are illustrations of family life, and here Williams excels by bestowing love and warmth on the characters.

In the nearly five hundred illustrations for the series, he gives the girls playfulness, innocence, and a sense of adventure. It is apparent in Williams's illustrations, just as in the books, that there is hopefulness in what lies ahead. He knew that hope was the birthright of the American West, a timeless sense that the best was yet to come. Williams understood that hope is most accurately portrayed on the faces of children.

Just as the focal point of western dust jacket illustration is the land, for juvenile war books it is the people. A natural desert scene is capable of evoking some level of emotion, if for nothing else but for its raw beauty. A battle-ravaged landscape devoid of people is of little emotional value. Certainly, it would not entice a potential book buyer to give it more than a cursory glance. It would seem then, given the intended audience, that the illustrations for juvenile war books fit into one of two dramatic and opposing categories: heroic patriotism bordering on propaganda or grim realism. Though both approaches were used, the former was in far greater numbers that the latter.

Patriotism and propaganda are key elements in any war and, of course,

**3**

**CHERRY AMES ARMY NURSE**
Author: Helen Wells
Illustrator: Frank Vaughn
Publisher: Grosset & Dunlap

**4**

**THE STORY OF D-DAY JUNE 6, 1944**
Author: Bruce Bliven, Jr.
Illustrator: Unknown
Publisher: Random House
Used by permission of Random House Children's Books, a division of Random House, Inc. Copyright © 1956, 1984, by Bruce Bliven Jr.

are not limited to the juvenile population. Early war illustrations play heavily on these elements and display a minimum amount of blood loss on either warring side. Dust jackets for the popular "Boy Allies" series depict the protagonists engaged in battle, loading cannons, and leading assaults with no enemy in sight. Some series books have cover illustrations of young men posed in colorful military regalia with no hint of fighting. Several covers show characters involved with training and in other non aggressive duties.

In these early illustrations, there is even a limited amount of destruction of personal property. For the juvenile readers in the World War I era, respectability dictated that war was to be displayed with a reasonable level of wholesomeness. World War II differed in that regard, but only marginally. The enemy is at least inferred, usually at some distance, preferably in an airplane trailing a stream of smoke. The violence, though still largely bloodless, is apparent. There are casualties, illustrations of wounded men being pulled by their comrades to safety. There too are aerial dogfights with aircraft spitting forth tracers, evidence of actual gunfire. The depiction of the characters changes as well. Some of the freshness in the faces of the combatants had disappeared, replaced with the look of an older, more mature fighting man.

Realism had begun to creep into the dust jacket illustrations. The trend toward realism continued in the 1950s with the issuance of several sets of historical volumes. Among these educational offerings were the "Landmark Series" and "Signature Series" books. Although neither was a war series, each catalog contained a number of war books. Both display colorful dust jackets depicting romanticized characters and deeds but, in keeping with their historical intent, showing realism as well.

A particularly interesting pairing of the war and western genre is Nicholas Eggenhofer's illustration for "Signature's" *Story of General Custer*. The scene is overrun with horses, men, and fighting. The bluecoats are seen fighting for survival, with their legendary commander at center stage wielding his saber and standing tall. The Indians outfitted in feathered headdresses and armed with rifles and lances are waging war astride their painted war ponies. This is a fighting force to be reckoned with. As highly charged with romance as this scene appears, its realism and grim reality are evident too. The battle is fought up close and personal. For the Indians, avoiding serious injury appears improbable; for the soldiers, avoiding death is impossible. Eggenhofer is able to successfully complement the text while depicting heroic acts within the framework of war's horrifying aspects.

It is no simple act. In fact, it may be the most complex illustration to undertake, to engage the young reader in a war story without implying that war is its own glorification. If realism is the hallmark of western illustration, here too it is for the war illustration. Clearly, epics of war in a juvenile format are best depicted in a truthful light. Without an element of truth, the sacrifices in war are diminished and its lessons lost.

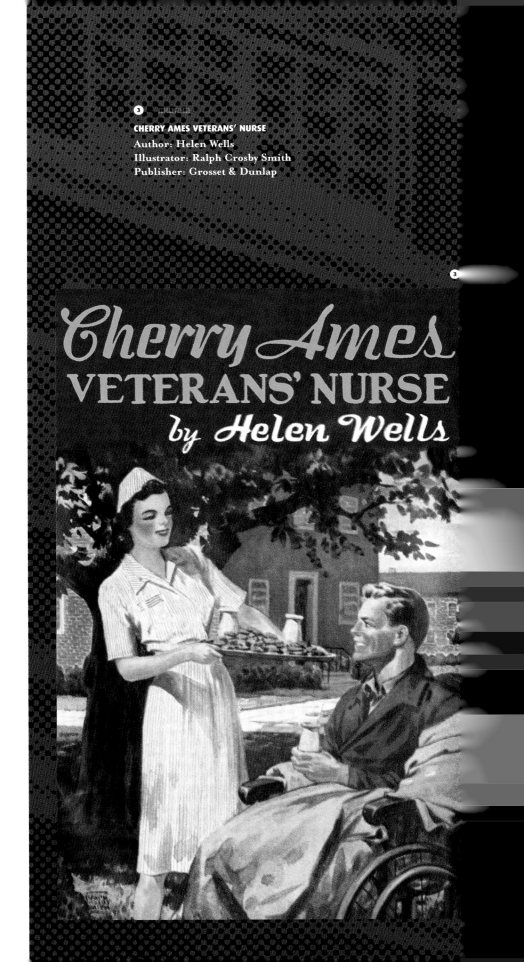

CHERRY AMES VETERANS' NURSE
Author: Helen Wells
Illustrator: Ralph Crosby Smith
Publisher: Grosset & Dunlap

Adventure stories carry a common theme; on some level, they all involve risk. The concept of risk is different for everyone, but a few standard scenarios exist: the risk that through an endeavor something of value may be lost, juxtaposed with the risk of having never endeavored at all; the risk inherent with each new experience — perhaps attending a new school or accepting a job offer; the risk in any journey or quest. The most common subject matter of storytelling — adventure and its associated risks is indeed broad enough to transcend the lines of all categories of reading material. A sense of adventure is uniquely human, but the adventure story is not. Often, members of the animal kingdom tell stories of adventure. But no matter whether they are told through man or beast, adventure stories offer unlimited opportunities for us to be involved in exciting and sometimes hazardous activities, perhaps preparing us in some small way for our own adventures to come.

Adventure stories for young people have always been plentiful. From the time that Stevenson and Twain were plying their craft with stories of pirates on the high seas and on the rivers of America, to the westerns and war epics produced by the Stratemeyer Syndicate, tales of adventure have enjoyed great success, even gaining classic status. One factor contributing to these early successes was the locale or setting of the story. The books often provided passage to strange lands that the young reader might never hope to visit. Topical events boosted the popularity of adventure stories as well. While thousands of men journeyed west and north in various gold rushes, young people left behind were conducting their own treasure hunting through the reading material of the day. With an increased emphasis on education and the opportunities it brought, juveniles began to purchase adventure stories that were occupationally oriented. Careers in engineering, communications, and transportation were the subjects of series books. The Stratemeyer Syndicate, ever ready to seize upon a trend in juvenile reading, was, as usual, among the leaders in producing titles of this kind. The Syndicate was fortunate in this regard for in its stable of writers was Howard Garis, the most prolific of all juvenile adventure authors.

Like a great many series book authors, Howard Garis began his career as a newspaperman. As a reporter for the Newark Evening News, he covered the police desk. He and his wife Lilian, who was a reporter at the same paper, were starting a family when Garis began writing magazine articles and a few juvenile books to augment the family income. His writing style brought him to the attention of Edward Stratemeyer who had recently formed his Syndicate. Stratemeyer offered Garis a standard Syndicate contract to provide writing services for a flat, per-book fee without future royalties. Garis initially disliked the contract, especially the uniform language stating that he was to surrender his name as author for the house pseudonym. Despite his misgivings, he entered into the agreement, an arrangement that endured for the next twenty-five years.

Garis soon enjoyed a role at the Syndicate far greater than any of the other contract writers, probably because of his prodigious output. His tireless energy rivaled Stratemeyer's and the two became close friends. He also retained a degree of independence from the Syndicate by continuing, at least part-time, to write for the Newark Evening News. Those part-time efforts one day evolved into his greatest contribution to the world of children's literature. At the Syndicate, Garis was writing for several series including "The Motor Boys" and "Baseball Joe." His style was exactly what the Syndicate ordered, fast-paced and exciting. He never solved a mystery or provided an escape from a cliffhanger before devising another to replace it. Action to hold the young readers' interest was the key. He understood the Syndicate's interest in wholesome adventures and answered its dictum for clear-cut heroes and villains, good always triumphing over evil that was seen through to the ultimate happy ending.

Within the Syndicate, he was allowed unsurpassed latitude in his storytelling. The Syndicate provided Garis with story outlines, as it did all contract writers. But the publisher allowed him to deviate from the outlines, so trusted were his writing instincts. His most well-known work for Stratemeyer was written under the pen name of Victor Appleton. These stories recount the adventures of a boy inventor named Tom Swift. Stratemeyer recognized that juveniles had a strong interest in the booming fields of science and technology. Drawing strongly on his instincts, he reasoned that a teenage inventor with an adventurous streak would prove a successful series hero. Further, he knew that his vision of the teenage wunderkind, Tom Swift, could be best brought to fruition in the hands of Howard Garis. Garis expressed his approach to the series in his usual vigorous style; he made the stories move with suspense and adventure and combined them with the latest in technological wizardry.

**❶** ᴄᴀᴘ

## THE BOBBSEY TWINS IN ESKIMO LAND

Author: Laura Lee Hope
Illustrator: Thelma Gooch
Publisher: Grosset & Dunlap
Reprinted with the permission of Pocket Books, a division of Simon & Schuster, Inc.  Copyright © 1936 by Simon & Schuster.  Bobbsey Twins™ is a registered trademark of Simon & Schuster, Inc.

**❷** ᴄᴀᴘ

## ROY BLAKELEY

Author: Percy Keese Fitzhugh
Illustrator: Howard L. Hastings
Publisher: Grosset & Dunlap

**❸** ᴄᴀᴘ

## WESTY MARTIN ON THE OLD INDIAN TRAIL

Author: Percy Keese Fitzhugh
Illustrator: Howard L. Hastings
Publisher: Grosset & Dunlap

**❹** ᴄᴀᴘ

## RUTH FIELDING AT SNOW CAMP

Author: Alice B. Emerson
Illustrator: Unknown
Publisher: Cupples & Leon

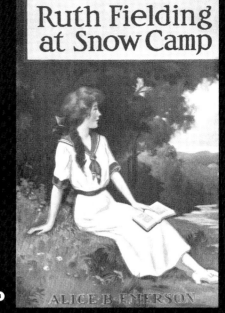

**❹**

**❺** ᴄᴀᴘ

## RUTH FIELDING IN THE FAR NORTH

Author: Alice B. Emerson
Illustrator: Clara M. Burd
Publisher: Cupples & Leon

**❸**

**❺**

# The Motor Girls
## On Cedar Lake

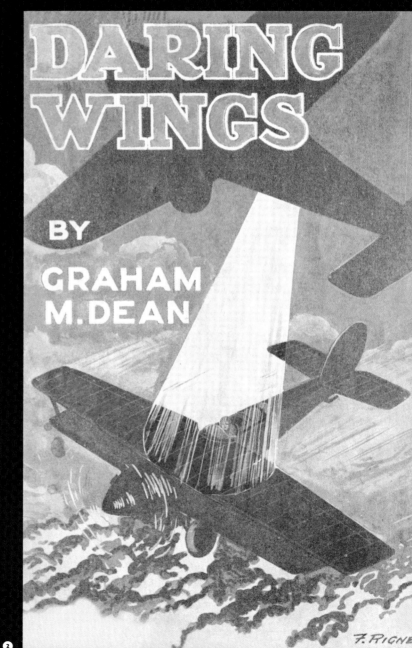

## DARING WINGS

### BY

### GRAHAM M. DEAN

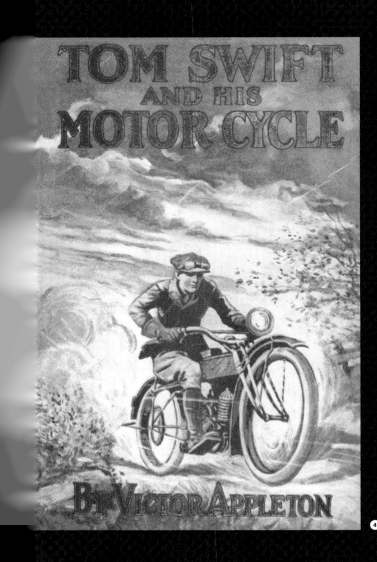

For example, he relates the story of an experimental electric plane that maroons Tom and his crew on a desert island during a test flight gone bad; he spins a tale of intrigue in Russia with the search for a lost platinum mine, and the freeing of an imprisoned man. Not to be forgotten is Tom's construction of a dirigible more than a thousand feet in length, which he uses to rescue his own family from a killer fire.

In general, the Tom Swift stories revolve around a crisis that could only be averted with a new invention or by vastly improving an existing contraption. Tom Swift, it seems, is a great one for thinking under pressure. The series has a number of continuing characters, including Tom's best friend Ned Newton; Eradicate "Rad" Sampson, general handyman and resident comic relief; and Tom's father, Barton Swift, a gifted inventor in his own right. Other characters come into play too but they all fill supporting roles to Tom and the machines.

Tom's machines are of all types and descriptions: flying machines such as the Sky Train, the Flying Boat, and the Air Glider; sea craft in the form of a motorboat, submarine, and the Ocean Airport; highly futuristic equipment like Electric Rifles, Photo Telephones, and the Television Detector — each indispensable when the chips are down and the day needs saving.

Tom is the master of machines in thirty-eight volumes spanning the years 1910-1935. Of the thirty-eight books comprising the series, Howard Garis is believed to have written as many as thirty-five. During the majority of its run, in terms of popularity and sales, the Tom Swift stories were the Syndicate's most successful. For Howard Garis, the end of the Swift series was merely a milestone, for he still had a character to write for, one of his own creation.

During the time when Garis was writing for the Syndicate on a full-time basis and contributing to the Newark Evening News part-time, he was asked to create a continuing character for the newspaper's children's section. Garis said he would give the request some thought. In doing so, he decided to depart from the standard children's reading fare of the day. He wanted to create a truly original character with an original premise.

One day, while on a walk and thinking about the project and its possible story options, he paused for a moment's rest. He became aware of a small animal cavorting nearby. The animal was a rabbit, and the more Garis studied the rabbit the more he realized how easily human characteristics might be applied to the creature and how other animals might figure into the storyline. He went home, collected his ideas, and developed an outline for the characters.

In typical Garis fashion, before the night ended, he had completed the first installment of a series that featured the adventures of a rabbit named Uncle Wiggily. Billed as the "bunny rabbit gentleman," Uncle Wiggily is a smart, kind, old fellow ever ready to assist his fellow creatures. Indeed, many of the stories involve a rescue of some sort by Uncle Wiggily. Longears, as he is also known, and his family live in a hollow stump bungalow, surrounded by a large cast of characters including Lulu Wibblewobble, the little duck girl, and Toodle and Noodle Flat-Tail, his beaver friends. Uncle Wiggily, when not

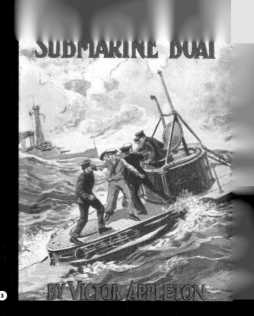

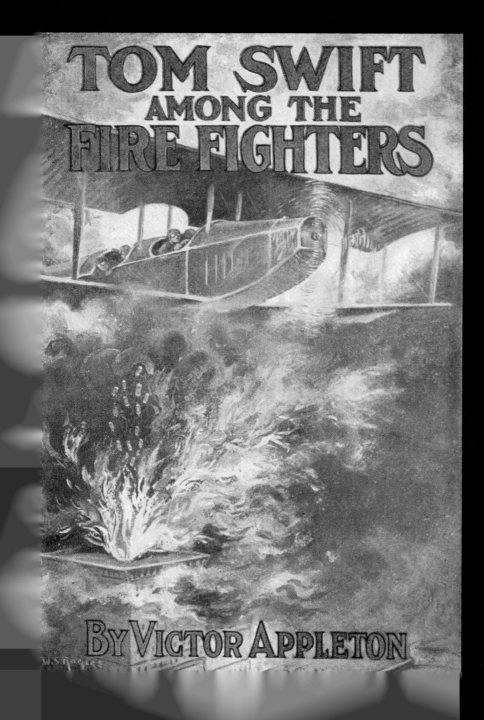

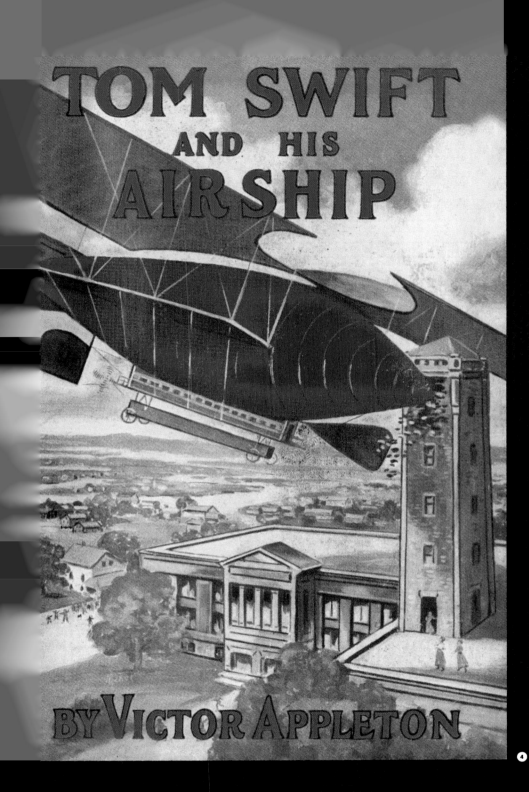

**④** 🔲🔲🔲🔲🔲

**TOM SWIFT AND HIS AIR SHIP**
Author: Victor Appleton
Illustrator: Rudolf Mencl
Publisher: Grosset & Dunlap
Reprinted with the permission of Pocket Books, a division of Simon & Schuster,
Inc. Copyright © 1910 by Simon & Schuster. Tom Swift™ is a registered trade-

**⑤** 🔲🔲🔲🔲🔲

**TOM SWIFT AND HIS GREAT SEARCHLIGHT**
Author: Victor Appleton
Illustrator: Richard Boehm
Publisher: Grosset & Dunlap
Reprinted with the permission of Pocket Books, a divi-
sion of Simon & Schuster, Inc. Copyright © 1912 by
Simon & Schuster. Tom Swift™ is a registered trade-
mark of Simon & Schuster, Inc.

**1**

**2**

**2**

helping his fellow creatures is busy saving his own hide from the villainous predators, Fuzzy Fox and Woozie Wolf.

The series was a smashing success from the start, beginning its run in the News as a six-times-a-week feature and eventually securing a nationwide audience through syndication. Such was the rabbit's popularity that when Garis devised a children's board game to merchandize his character, it became the most successful game of its era. Garis maintained his output of juvenile adventure books while somehow continuing to produce the Uncle Wiggily stories, which was no small task. The tales of the gentleman rabbit ran nationally for nearly fifty years. Books featuring the further adventures of Longears gained significant sales as well. Garis also made personal appearances to read his stories to children and even took to the radio to entertain his young fans. Even when Garis retired from his day-to-day writing assignments, he continued writing about his beloved rabbit. Although critics often dismissed his work as formulistic, no one could deny that Howard Garis fostered in his young readership a desire to read for entertainment and relaxation. Obviously, children loved Uncle

Wiggily, and through that wonderful rabbit, clearly Howard Garis loved them in return.

The most romantic of the adventure-based animal stories might well be those involving dogs. Authors long have immortalized man's best friend in tales of heroic service and faithful companionship. But Jack London approached this topic differently. In his classic *The Call of the Wild*, Buck, the pet of a wealthy family, is kidnapped and sold into a kind of slavery, hauling goods as a part of a sled dog team during the Gold Rush. Buck endures harsh treatment from his handlers. Within the hierarchy of the sled dog team, he must use violence to survive. Over the course of the story, Buck's domesticated nature is eroded as his relationships with humans begin to fail. Eventually, he returns to his primordial beast and the law of club and fang. *The Call of the Wild* is the story of an animal at home in both worlds, that of beast and human — with Buck ultimately choosing the animal kingdom; for even in its savagery, it implies a kind of justice, dictated by nature, that is not found among humans. London's stories, while they employ more sophisticated concepts than most adventure tales, are con-

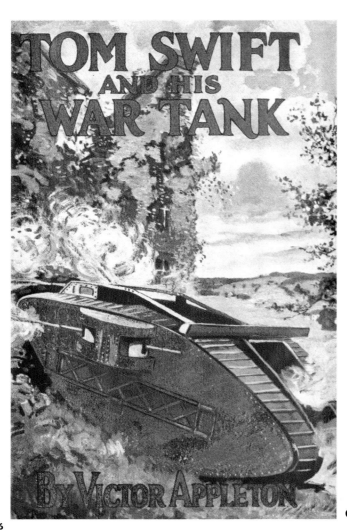

**❶** □□□□

**TOM SWIFT AND HIS WAR TANK**
Author: Victor Appleton
Illustrator: R. Emmett Owen
Publisher: Grosset & Dunlap
Reprinted with the permission of Pocket Books, a division of Simon & Schuster, Inc.  Copyright © 1918 by Simon & Schuster.  Tom Swift™ is a registered trademark of Simon & Schuster, Inc.

**❷** □□□□□

**TOM SWIFT AND HIS TELEVISION DETECTOR**
Author: Victor Appleton
Illustrator: Nat Falk
Publisher: Grosset & Dunlap
Reprinted with the permission of Pocket Books, a division of Simon & Schuster, Inc.  Copyright © 1933 by Simon & Schuster.  Tom Swift™ is a registered trademark of Simon & Schuster, Inc.

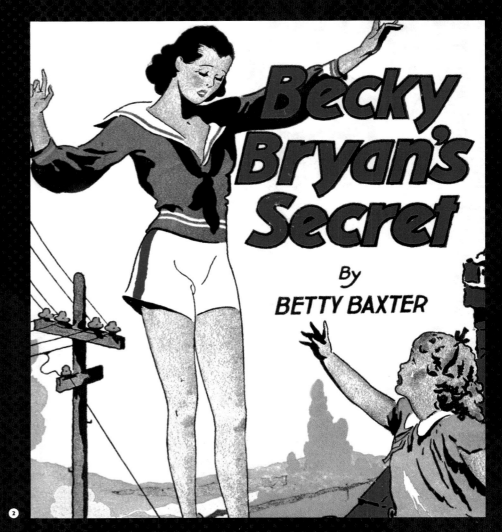

**2** 📖

**BECKY BRYAN'S SECRET**
Author: Betty Baxter
Illustrator: Unknown
Publisher: Goldsmith Publishing Co

**1** 📖📖

**CIRCLE 4 PATROL**
Author: Graham M. Dean
Illustrator: J. Clemens Gretter
Publisher: Goldsmith Publishing Co

sistently entertaining and full of excitement. Of course, a great many animal-based adventure stories are less violent than London's works, some of which are also considered classics. Among these were books written by E. B. White, including *Charlotte's Web* and *Stuart Little*, and the works of Thornton Burgess in his "Bedtime Story Book" series.

Two stories meant to appeal to the juvenile female reader are adventure stories associated with occupational pursuits. They were the "Cherry Ames" and "Vicki Barr" series, which began in 1943 and 1947, respectively, when career choices for women were limited. But the competency displayed in each title character was so formidable that the implication was clear that young women were capable of success in any field they might choose.

The "Cherry Ames" series follows the young woman's nursing career from her days as a student, through her service as a wartime nurse, to her postwar pursuits in a children's hospital, and in other nursing endeavors. Cherry's interest in nursing is the result of her view that it is a profession based on a higher calling of caring for others and helping those in need. For these efforts she is rewarded with the respect of her co-workers and with the knowledge that she makes a difference in the lives of her patients. In short, Cherry Ames has a passion for her work. Her adventures during World War II further speak to her character. She volunteers for dangerous missions and takes chances with her own safety in order to rescue and assist the wounded. In addition to these selfless acts, Cherry sends a portion of her service pay home to her mother; likewise, a portion of her wages is deducted to be invested in government-issued War Bonds. Later

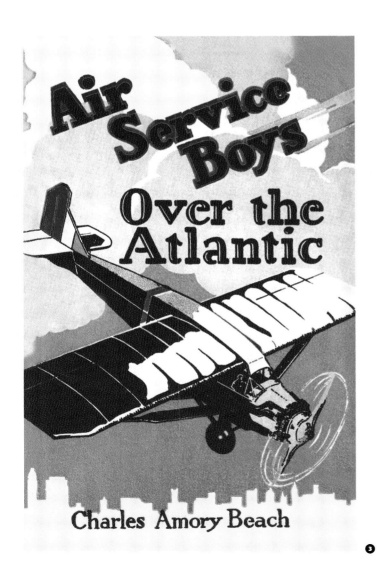

**❸** 📖📖

**AIR SERVICE BOYS OVER THE ATLANTIC**
Author: Charles Amory Beach
Illustrator: Walter S. Rogers
Publisher: Saalfield

**❹** 📖📖

**RANDY STARR AFTER AN AIR PRIZE**
Author: Eugene Martin
Illustrator: Radewald
Publisher: Saalfield

**❸**

**❹**

# FIVE LITTLE PEPPERS
## AND HOW THEY GREW
*Complete Authorized Edition*

**MARGARET SIDNEY**

①

"I'll eat this candy ball!"
snarled the bad chap.

③

"Oh Uncle Wiggily! Please wait a minute!" cried the girl.

②

**①**

**FIVE LITTLE PEPPERS AND HOW THEY GREW**
Author: Margaret Sidney
Illustrator: Pelagie Doane
Publisher: Grosset & Dunlap

**②**

**UNCLE WIGGILY'S STORY BOOK- INTERIOR**
Author: Howard R. Garis
Illustrator: Lansing Campbell
Publisher: A L Burt
Used by permission of Uncle Wiggily Classics.
Uncle Wiggily is a copyrighted property.

**③**

**UNCLE WIGGILY NEWSPAPER PANEL**
Author: Howard R. Garis
Illustrator: Lansing Campbell
Publisher: The Evening Leader
Used by permission of Uncle Wiggily
Classics.  Uncle Wiggily is a copyrighted
property.

**④**

**UNCLE WIGGILY STARTS OFF**
Author: Howard R. Garis
Illustrators: Mary and Wallace Stover
Publisher: Old Faithful Books
Used by permission of Uncle Wiggily
Classics.  Uncle Wiggily is a copyrighted
property.

**⑤**

**UNCLE WIGGILY AND GRANDDADDY LON**
Author: Howard R. Garis
Illustrators: Mary and Wallace St
Publisher: Old Faithful Books
Used by permission of Uncle Wig
Classics.  Uncle Wiggily is a copyri
property.

stories in the long-running series have Cherry involved in mystery-solving; her nursing activities are reduced to the subplot. Even so, Cherry remains true to her high standards of competency and helping the sick and those less fortunate.

Cherry Ames was the creation of author Helen Wells who modeled her character, at least partially, after her own interests in social issues. Wells firmly believed that people must invest themselves fully in their work, country, and fellow man. She was a lifelong volunteer for a number of causes and actively supported reforms to aid the underprivileged. At various times, she was employed as a social worker and as a teacher. And of course, she was a writer.

Wells's "Cherry Ames" series features a strong female protagonist who, in addition to her overall goodness, is a bit opinionated and prone to speak her mind with passion. Though her occupation is service-oriented, Cherry saw no reason to surrender her ambition or to curb her leadership skills. By design, Cherry Ames is no shrinking violet. In Cherry, author Wells provided her young readers a heroine with a realistic personality and a work ethic to aspire to.

During her career, Wells created several more strong female characters including Polly French, heroine of a series she wrote under the pen name Francine Lewis, and she created the character of Vicki Barr. Helen Wells left the "Cherry Ames" series for a time to pursue other interests; during her departure, the series continued under the authorship of Julie Tatham. A similar arrangement between the two authors took place with the "Vicki Barr" stories. Wells later returned to resume the writing for both series.

The "Ames" and "Barr" series did not suffer under Julie Tatham's interim writing. Her approach to character development and the strength of her female leads were similar to Wells's original concepts. This was in keeping with Tatham's style for her own creations, Trixie Beldon and Ginny Gordon, (both written under the pseudonym of Julie Campbell), which also portray strong, self-reliant characters.

The "Vicki Barr" series features the adventures of a flight attendant. Tatham placed the title character in the field of aviation to exploit the romance associated with flight. The series picks up with Vicki as she undergoes a training assignment. Vicki earns her wings in the first book, and in the course of the next fifteen stories she encounters a myriad of strange people, faces great peril, and rights a number of injustices. Throughout her career, working for Federal and Worldwide Airlines, Vicki plays an instrumental role in a probe into unscrupulous business practices, she intervenes in the lives of young people receiving unfair treatment, and she braves natural disasters. She becomes involved in a search for a missing person, investigates several thefts, and in a story reflecting the times, is aboard a hijacked flight.

There is something more to the "Vicki Barr" stories, something that reaches beyond the scope of the average juvenile adventure story. While the Cherry Ames character finds self-actuation in her career field, Vicki Barr's occupation offers her less fulfillment. As the series continues, Vicki Barr displays a growing discontentment for her work and even considers a career change

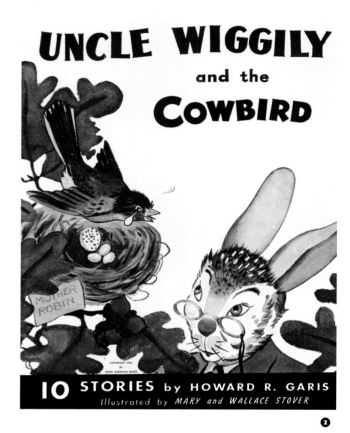

**UNCLE WIGGILY AND THE STARFISH**

Author: Howard R. Garis
Illustrators: Mary and Wallace Stover
Publisher: Old Faithful Books
Used by permission of Uncle Wiggily
Classics. Uncle Wiggily is a copyright-
ed property.

**UNCLE WIGGILY AND THE COWBIRD**
Author: Howard R. Garis
Illustrators: Mary and Wallace Stover
Publisher: Old Faithful Books
Used by permission of Uncle Wiggily Classics.
Uncle Wiggily is a copyrighted property.

**UNCLE WIGGILY AND THE PAPER BOAT**
Author: Howard R. Garis
Illustrators: Mary and Wallace Stover
Publisher: Old Faithful Books
Used by permission of Uncle Wiggily Classics.
Uncle Wiggily is a copyrighted property.

**UNCLE WIGGILY AND JACKIE AND PEETIE BOW WOW**
Author: Howard R. Garis
Illustrator: George Carlson
Publisher: Platt & Munk
Used by permission of Uncle Wiggily Classics.
Uncle Wiggily is a copyrighted property.

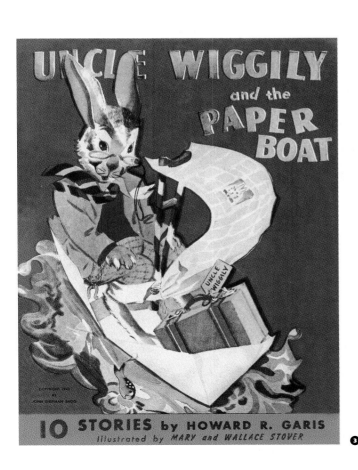

after she receives humiliating comments concerning her occupation. Eventually she decides to broaden her aviation pursuits and obtains a private pilot's license. Her work as a stewardess continues, but through personal ambition and training she secures for herself additional career options and thereby some peace of mind. This was interesting and realistic plotting. Few authors explored themes involving apprehension and self-doubt in their title characters. That Vicki Barr prevailed, improving her circumstances through hard work and determination, is a lesson in life for her juvenile readers.

To their credit, authors Wells and Tatham contributed to the juvenile adventure genre two of its most realistic characters in Ames and Barr. In addition to the high-flying adventures, the authors show that the drama of life itself holds adventure enough for anyone.

Illustrations accompanying adventure stories are extremely broad in nature. For stories of red-hot action, characters are often depicted in dangerous situations, sometimes on the very verge of some awesome calamity. Conversely, adventure tales involving soft cuddly creatures convey warmth and caring. Some illustrations depict no overt adventure at all but instead show the friendship between characters that are about to take on adventure within the books' covers. There too is the implied adventure through nature's landscape; the American West and the harshness of the North contain within their regional boundaries elements of high risk and adventure. And finally, adventure may be depicted in wholly man-made creations as well. In the early part of the part of the twentieth century, nothing held more romance and adventure than the fields of technology and motorized transportation.

It was a time for inventors and their inventions. The masses eagerly took advantage of new means of travel and conveniences. Time, it seemed, began to move a little more quickly. Juveniles in search of exciting reading material only required a glimpse of the latest Tom Swift

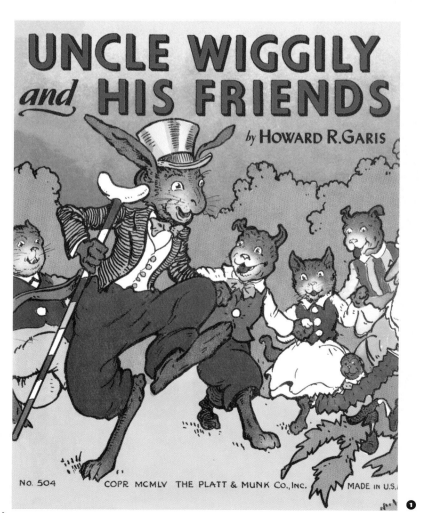

**❶** 📖📖📖

**UNCLE WIGGILY AND HIS FRIENDS**
Author: Howard R. Garis
Illustrator: George Carlson
Publisher: Platt & Munk
Used by permission of Uncle Wiggily Classics. Uncle Wiggily is a copyrighted property.

**❷** 📖📖📖

**THE ADVENTURES OF UNC' BILLY POSSUM**
Author: Thornton W. Burgess
Illustrator: Harrison Cady
Publisher: Grosset & Dunlap

**③** 🔲🔲🔲

**WIGGLE AND WAGGLE**

Author: Ethel M. Rice

Illustrator: Albert Kay

Publisher: Sam'l Gabriel Sons & Co

**④** 🔲🔲

**JUNEAU THE SLEIGH DOG**

Author: West Lathrop

Illustrator: Gahn Woods

Publisher: Grosset & Dunlap

**⑤** 🔲🔲🔲

**STUART LITTLE**

Author: E.B. White

Illustrator: Garth Williams

Publisher: Harper & Row

Used by permission of
HarperCollins Publishers.

④

③

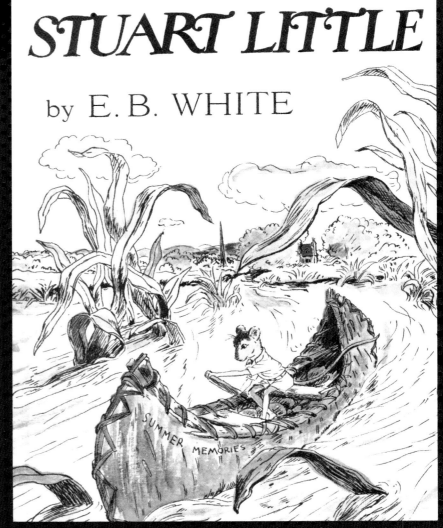

⑤

adventure story cover to pique their interest and ensure a sale. Such was the power of the times and the ability of the illustrators to capture that excitement and sense of adventure.

A number of illustrators applied their talents to the Swift dust jackets, among them Rudolf Mencl, H. Richard Boehm, and R. Emmett Owen. The jackets are action-packed affairs and depict daring rescues, destruction of property, and speed of movement. Nearly all contain a machine of some sort engaged in the act of tempting fate and taming the elements. Images of fire and the seas are common adversaries to Tom and his amazing inventions.

Walter S. Rogers, who later illustrated for the "Hardy Boys" series, was an early contributor. His work for the dust jacket *Tom Swift Among the Fire Fighters* is representative of many Swift jacket illustrations. The illustration depicts a burning building, presumably a high-rise, out of reach of conventional fire-fighting equipment. The top floors and the roof are awash in the blaze; the skies are dark and heavy with smoke. This fire is out of control. Out of the blackness emerges a biplane shown to be battling the horrific blaze by dropping a cargo of fire retardant materials. Our hero has mastered his machine and his own fear for such an undertaking. Here Walter S. Rogers successfully encompasses several exciting elements simultaneously: man over machine, man and machine over nature, as well as courage and service over self-interest and fear.

Illustrator Nat Falk also contributed to the Swift series. His illustration for *Tom Swift and His Television Detector* shows off the "gee whiz" aspects of the series. This dust jacket shows young Tom and his friend in their roadster at the base of a high stone wall. Using an ingenious television detector, they are able to see through the wall to a hulking, bearded figure armed with a knife who appears to be up to no good. The machine has enabled our lads to view a dangerous man with dangerous intentions. How might they act on this information? The answer comes quickly, as even now one of them advances with a club in hand to intervene in the situation. Here Falk gives us a scenario in which one man is thwarting another by using a machine. The outcome is uncertain, but clearly the parties are about to collide and be thrown into peril. The illustrator can offer no greater invitation to a potential reader than this.

Illustrating the Uncle Wiggily stories was a serious matter. The series' young audience was demanding in their depiction of Longears. Of course, he is friendly and lovable, but his adventures tend to put him in harm's way, and overly threatening illustrations of the old gentleman will not do. A little danger is acceptable, even warranted, but real danger is alarming and unnecessary. Often danger can be depicted in other ways — and without Uncle Wiggily's involvement — by merely showing one of his carnivorous adversaries in all its leering glory. The implication is enough.

Uncle Wiggily, as depicted by Mary and Wallace Stover, is a delightful combination. He is a nattily dressed gentleman rabbit complete with gold-rimmed spectacles and outfitted with a red, white, and blue crutch. The character has an air of dignity about him while maintaining his comic overtones.

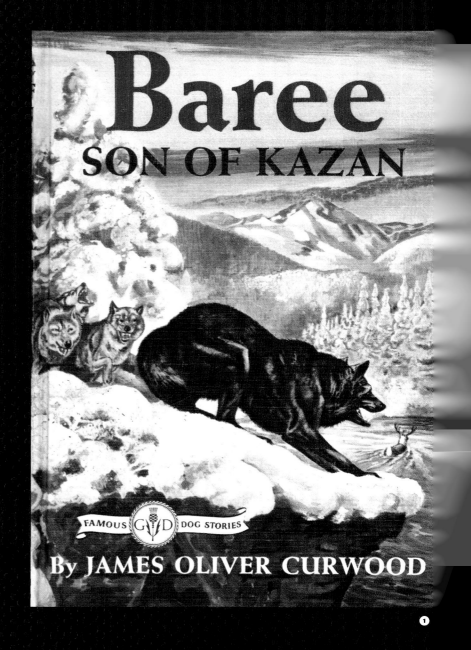

**BAREE SON OF KAZAN**
**Author: James Oliver Curwood**
**Illustrator: Unknown**
**Publisher: Grosset & Dunlap**

## LASSIE COME-HOME

### ERIC KNIGHT

**2** 📖

**THE RETURN OF SILVER CHIEF**
Author: Jack O'Brien
Illustrator: Kurt Wiese
Publisher: Grosset & Dunlap

**3** 📖📖

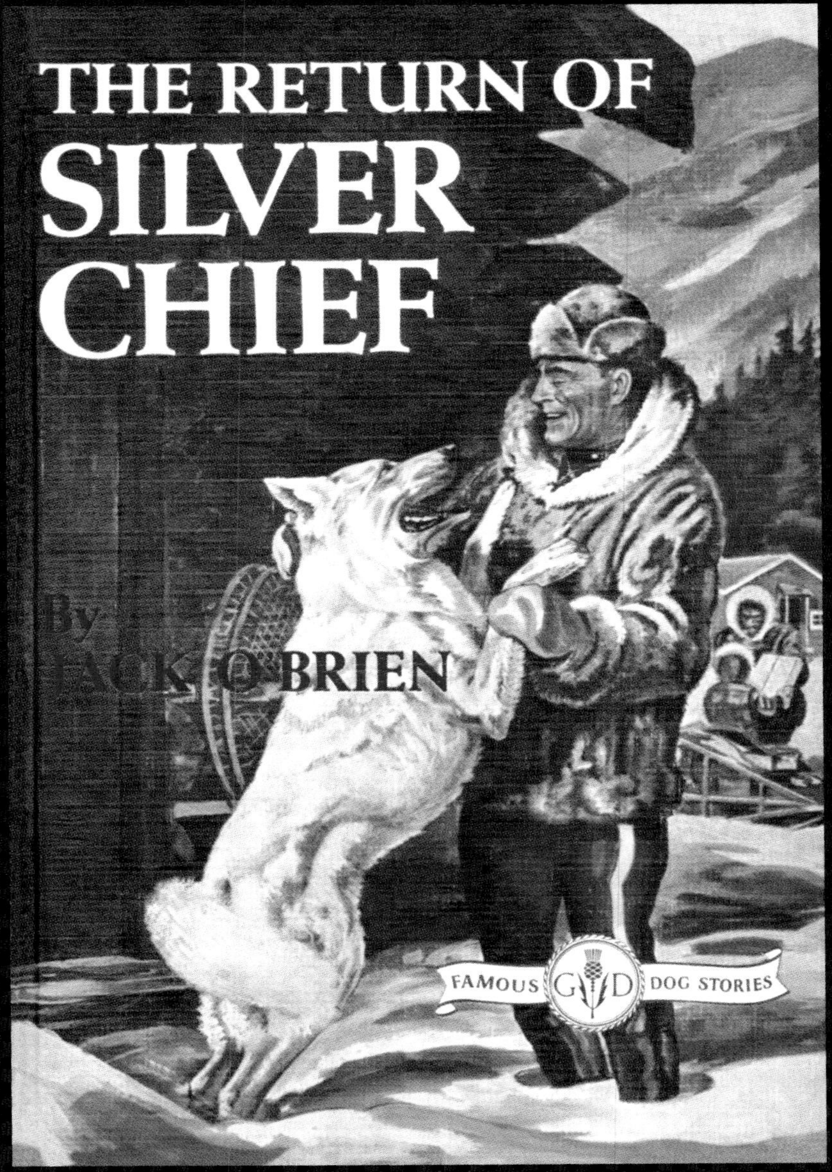

**LASSIE COME-HOME**
Author: Eric Knight
Illustrator: Gahn Woods
Publisher: Grosset & Dunlap

**4** 📖📖

**THE CALL OF THE WILD**
Author: Jack London
Illustrator: Unknown
Publisher: Grosset & Dunlap

FAMOUS **G/D** DOG STORIES

**3**

## THE RETURN OF SILVER CHIEF

By JACK O'BRIEN

FAMOUS **G/D** DOG STORIES

**2**

THE CALL OF THE WILD

JACK LONDON

## THE CALL OF THE WILD

### JACK LONDON

FAMOUS DOG STORIES

GROSSET & DUNLAP

FAMOUS **G/D** DOG STORIES

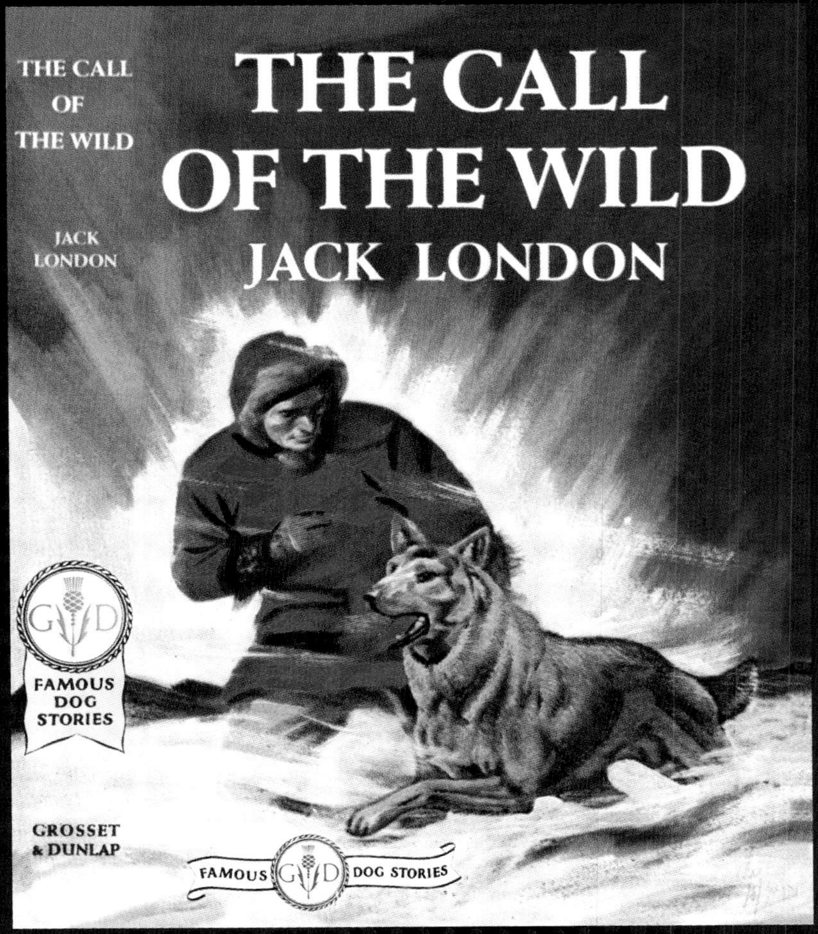

**4**

**BOMBA THE JUNGLE BOY AMONG THE SLAVES**

Author: Roy Rockwood
Illustrator: Howard L. Hastings
Publisher: Grosset & Dunlap
Reprinted with the permission of Pocket
Books, a division of Simon & Schuster,
Inc.  Copyright © 1929, 1953

**EAGLE SCOUT**

Author: Wilfred McCormick
Illustrator: Unknown
Publisher: Grosset & Dunlap

**SUE BARTON RURAL NURSE**

Author: Helen Dore Boylston
Illustrator: Major Felten
Publisher: Little, Brown, & Co
Used with permission by Little,
Brown, & Co

Often he looks directly at us, sometimes winking as if to say, "Come along. We're in this together." The Stovers accurately mirror in Uncle Wiggily the warmth and friendship that children feel for him.

Author E. B. White's first offering in the field of children's literature was a book entitled *Stuart Little*. White's choice of an artist was a young cartoonist for The New Yorker who had little previous experience in illustration. The book's incredible success launched Garth Williams's career in children and juvenile book illustration. Until that time, Williams's career path had been uncertain. With his father a cartoonist and his mother a painter of some renown, it seemed that the New Jersey farm boy would be destined for an artistic vocation. He found an interest in art early on and was given free rein to pursue the subject. Changes in his parents' employment required the family to move frequently. His formative years were spent in America, Canada, and England. While in England, his educational pursuits brought him to the field of mechanical drawing, which he undertook in hopes of one day entering into a career in architecture. But his interest in architecture waned when he found limited job opportunities.

Fortunately, Williams's artistic abilities were recognized, and he was offered a scholarship to study painting. He won quick praise from his instructors for his portrait work and soon moved on to study sculpture for which he showed an immediate aptitude as well. After graduation, he traveled Europe studying the works of the old masters. With war threatening, Williams returned to London and volunteered for duty with the British Red Cross. He became a casualty, receiving serious wounds during a German bombing raid, which forced him to leave the Red Cross. He returned to America and served as a consultant in private industry; among his projects was camouflage design. During those war years, he also worked in defense factories.

Just as World War II was ending, E.B. White chose Williams to illustrate *Stuart Little*. His illustrations for that book and for another White classic, *Charlotte's Web*, owe much to his early farm life. The creatures carry a certain nobility; they are depicted realistically, but also with great personality and decidedly human traits. His understanding and respect for

By Helen Dore Boylston

**❹** ▢▢▢

**SUE BARTON STAFF NURSE**
Author: Helen Dore Boylston
Illustrator: Major Felten
Publisher: Little, Brown, & Co
Used with permission by Little, Brown, & Co

**❺** ▢▢

**CHERRY AMES STUDENT NURSE**
Author: Helen Wells
Illustrator: Ralph Crosby Smith
Publisher: Grosset & Dunlap

❶ 　🖾🖾🖾

**CHERRY AMES SENIOR NURSE**
Author: Helen Wells
Illustrator: Ralph Crosby Smith
Publisher: Grosset & Dunlap

❷ 　🖾🖾🖾

**CHERRY AMES CLINIC NURSE**
Author: Julie Tatham
Illustrator: Unknown
Publisher: Grosset & Dunlap

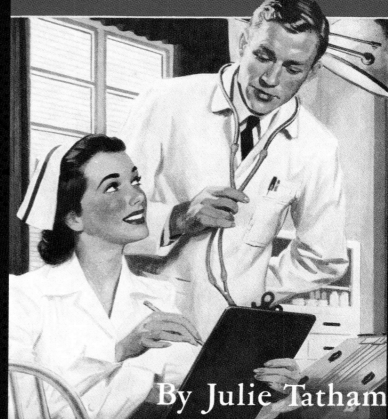

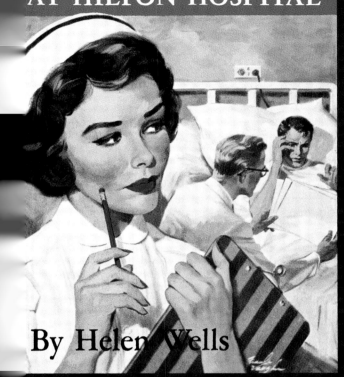

# Cherry Ames
## AT HILTON HOSPITAL

By Helen Wells

# Cherry Ames
## DEPARTMENT STORE NURSE

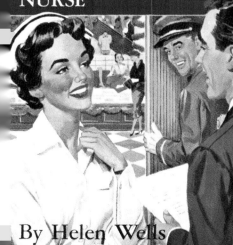

By Helen Wells

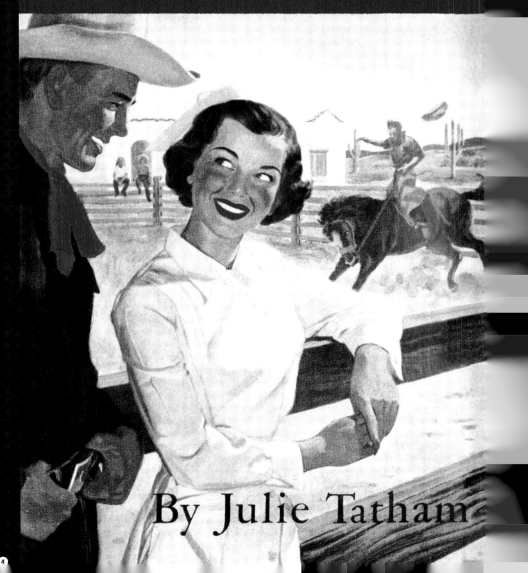

# Cherry Ames
## DUDE RANCH NURSE

By Julie Tatham

animals is apparent. That he was a lover of literature further complements his efforts as an illustrator. His work is understated, subtle, and a perfect match for White's prose.

By the early 1950s, Williams was offered and accepted the prestigious assignment of illustrating the Laura Ingalls Wilder books. It was a monumental effort yielding hundreds of illustrations. The drawings were to become that series definitive illustrations, gaining a classic status of their own.

Williams's artistic endeavors, it would seem, were unlimited. To his successes in painting, sculpting, and illustrating, he added writing. One of his works drew harsh criticism and was even banned in some areas of the South. It was a children's book called *The Rabbits' Wedding* concerning the marriage of two rabbits, one of which was white and the other black. The controversy stemmed from the perception that the book was promoting racial integration. Williams, who also illustrated his text, explained that he had chosen to depict the rabbits as black and white in order to help the reader keep track of the characters. As is often the case with banned books, *The Rabbits' Wedding* was a lasting success, a creation more powerful than the effort to silence the author's voice.

Garth Williams was without question a man of many talents, though it is for his illustrations that he is best remembered. His approach to his work was simple. He understood the influence of the illustration and its role in accompanying and enhancing the text. He knew the subjects of his illustrations, and he knew and respected his young audience.

Dust jacket illustrations for the occupationally based adventure books was, in the first few volumes of a series, a little more structured and formalistic than other jacket art. To effectively introduce the title characters and to visually establish their careers, the artist often found it necessary to depict the character in portrait and in uniform. The Cherry Ames and Vicki Barr covers illustrate this formula. We see the attractive smiling faces of our new heroines outfitted in nursing whites and in flying blues; each wears a cap indicating her profession. Extraneous characters or events do not encumber the illustrations. Over the course of the "Ames" series, Cherry, for the most part, continues to be seen in uniform, posing something of a challenge for the illustrator because it limited his color palette. To augment color in the Ames illustrations, artists used several backgrounds. Among these, the outdoor settings are highly effective, especially those displaying fall colors. In her portraits, Cherry has a rosy, almost flush complexion. The starched white of her ever-present nurse's cap deepens and enriches her brunette locks. She appears comfortable in her professional environment, suggesting a competency in her work. She is generally smiling, but when patients are present, she is shown thoughtful and concerned too. She is depicted as the girl-next-door with a mission. Ralph Crosby Smith and Frank Vaughn provided many of the early Ames illustrations. Their skills were such that they were able to successfully depict the title character as a positive, vibrant role model whose very career is cause for adventure.

Vicki Barr is depicted somewhat differently. After her occupation is estab-

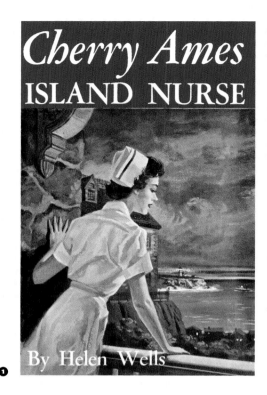

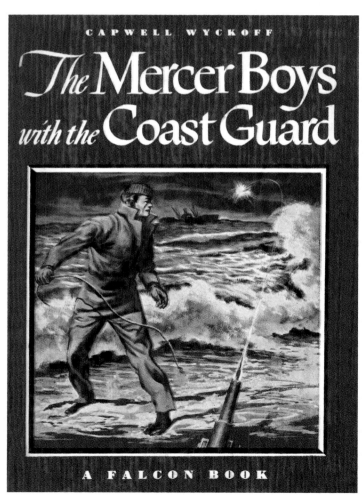

**1** 🔲🔲🔲

**CHERRY AMES ISLAND NURSE**
Author: Helen Wells
Illustrator: Unknown
Publisher: Grosset & Dunlap

**2** 🔲

**THE MERCER BOYS WITH THE COAST GUARD**
Author: Capwell Wyckoff
Illustrator: Chris Schaare
Publisher: World Publishing Co

CAPWELL WYCKOFF

# The Mercer Boys at Woodcrest

A FALCON BOOK

**3**

# The Story of the SECRET SERVICE

## FERDINAND KUHN

Foreword by U. E. Baughman,
Chief, U. S. Secret Service

*Landmark* BOOKS

75

**4**

**3** 📖

**THE MERCER BOYS AT WOODCREST**
Author: Capwell Wyckoff
Illustrator: Chris Schaare
Publisher: World Publishing Co

**4** 📖📖

**THE STORY OF THE SECRET SERVICE**
Author: Ferdinand Kuhn
Illustrator: Mal Singer
Publisher: Random House
Used by permission of Random House Children's
Books, a division of Random House, Inc.
Copyright © 1957 by Ferdinand Kuhn.

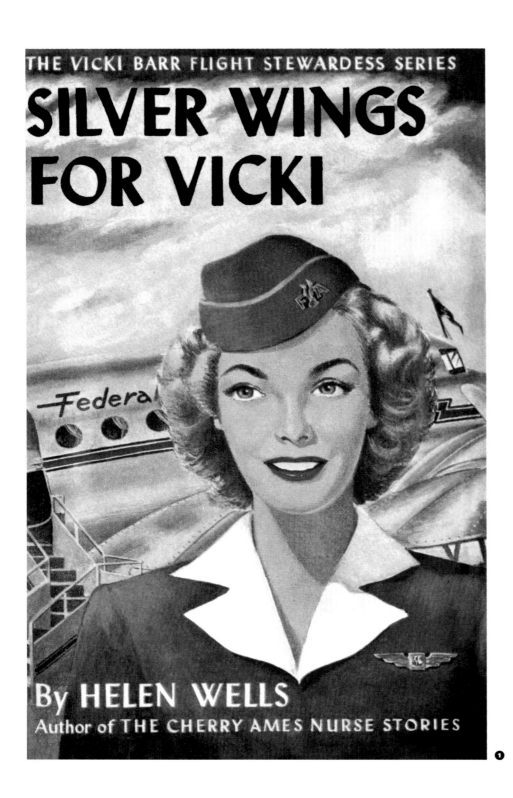

THE VICKI BARR FLIGHT STEWARDESS SERIES

# SILVER WINGS FOR VICKI

By HELEN WELLS
Author of THE CHERRY AMES NURSE STORIES

**❶**

THE VICKI BARR AIR STEWARDESS SERIES

# THE MYSTERY OF THE VANISHING LADY

By HELEN WELLS
Co-Author of THE CHERRY AMES Nurse Stories

**❷**

**❶** 🔲🔲

**SILVER WINGS FOR VICKI**
Author: Helen Wells
Illustrator: Unknown
Publisher: Grosset & Dunlap

**❷** 🔲🔲

**THE MYSTERY OF THE VANISHING LADY**
Author: Helen Wells
Illustrator: Unknown
Publisher: Grosset & Dunlap

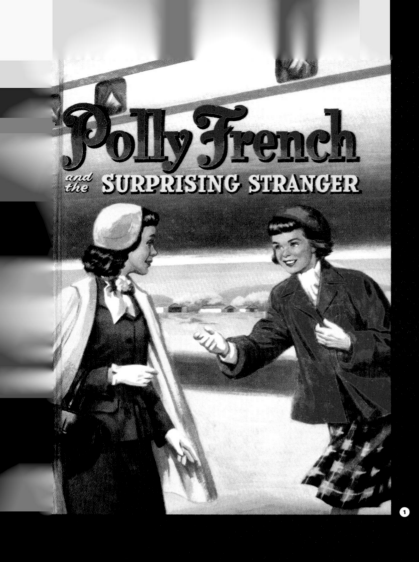

**1** 📖

**POLLY FRENCH AND THE SURPRISING STRANGER**
Author: Francine Lewis
Illustrator: Nina Albright
Publisher: Whitman
Used by permission. Golden Books
Publishing Company, Inc. Copyright
© 1956. 1984. All rights reserved.

**2** 📖

**DONNA PARKER SPECIAL AGENT**
Author: Marcia Martin
Illustrator: Jon Nielson
Publisher: Whitman
Used by permission. Golden Books
Publishing Company, Inc. Copyright
© 1957. 1985. All rights reserved.

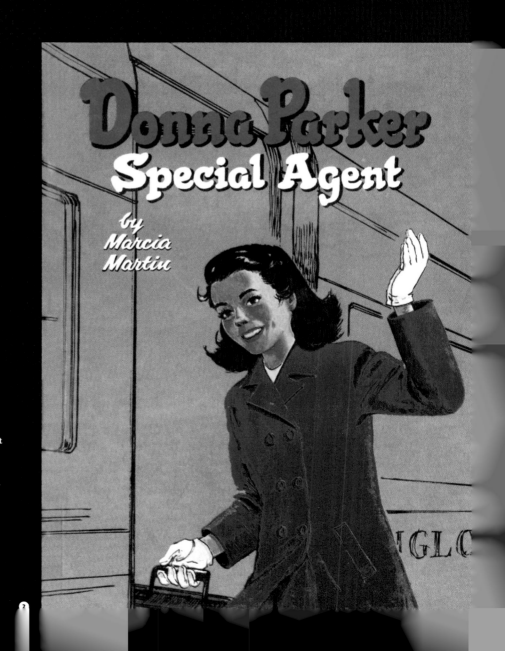

**3** 📖📖

**THE BOBBSEY TWINS ON BLUEBERRY ISLAND**
Author: Laura Lee Hope
Illustrator: Unknown
Publisher: Grosset & Dunlap
Reprinted with the permission of Pocket
Books, a division of Simon & Schuster,
inc. Copyright © 1917, 1945, 1959 by
Simon & Schuster. Bobbsey Twins™ is a
registered trademark of Simon &
Schuster, Inc.

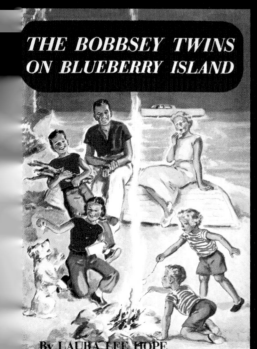

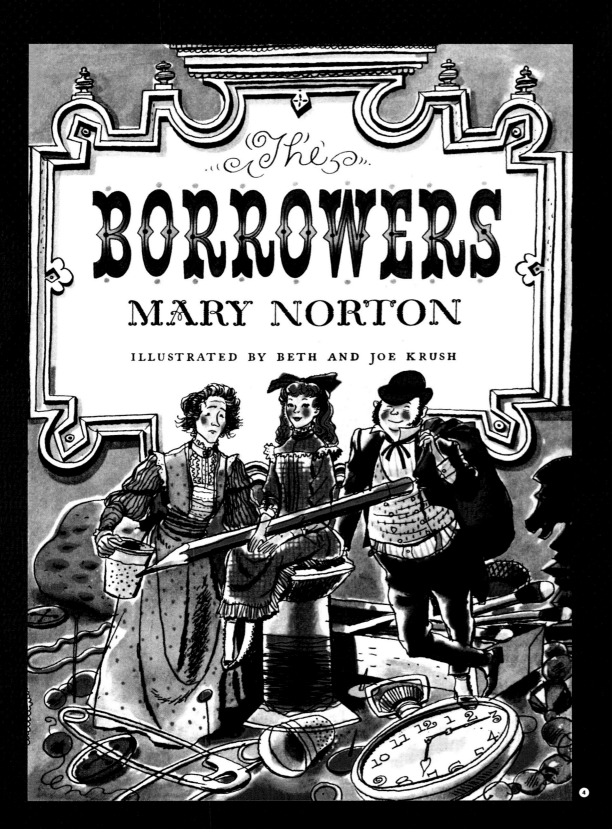

**5**

**4**

lished through the initial illustrations, Vicki often appears in civilian attire. A young woman with an active lifestyle, she often finds herself in dangerous situations. The Vicki illustrations display a relaxing of the formula commonly associated with the occupational series.

The first covers featuring attractive yet staid blues give way to an increasingly colorful dust jacket. The illustration for *Peril Over the Airport* shows this trend. Although our heroine is piloting a small plane, her attention is not on the task at hand. Instead, she is looking at another aircraft, one that appears to be drawing dangerously close. This aircraft is coming from behind and above Barr's plane; the pilot's exact interests are unclear, but that he is undertaking a maneuver of this sort speaks to his dangerous intent. Further, that this rogue pilot is up to no good is evident by his attempt to shield his identity. The pilot appears to be masked, and the plane carries no identification numbers. The illustration features the use of bold colors. Barr is in profile. Her skin tone is decidedly rosy, the color of her hair golden. She is wearing a blue neckerchief above her brown flight jacket. She is well dressed and attractive, but our interest in her appearance is fleeting because the drama in the scene is underscored by the aircrafts, which are alive with color. Barr's plane, seen only in part, is a bright but neutral yellow. The enemy's aircraft is red. Behind his cockpit, a cabin window is darkened, and a few narrow, black stripes appear on the fuselage. The plane itself seems almost menacing, as if the machine were capable of aggressive behavior. In this illustration, adventure and risk are as one. For Vicki Barr, what lies ahead is a daunting task, for she must conquer both man and machine to win the day.

The use of strong colors for the series' dust jacket illustrations continues with *The Ghost at the Waterfall*. The background features a full moon winter's night with mountains in the distance. Closer there is a frozen waterfall, and nearby is a small cabin with its windows illuminated. It would be a tranquil scene except for the two figures in the foreground that apparently are planning what may be an unwelcome visit to the cabin. One of those figures is our Vicki, outfitted in a long yellow winter coat trimmed with white fur. She is gesturing toward the cabin, pointing with her dark gloves, which are clearly defined against the background of a waterfall. While Vicki is easily identifiable, her companion is not. We know him only by his profession, for he is attired in the uniform of the Royal Canadian Mounted Police. Although Vicki is at the center of the illustration, the Mountie, due to the blazing red of his coat, draws our attention. His large frame is bent slightly forward giving the impression that he is poised for action and ready to enter the fray. Further, the illustration is noteworthy for the appearance of a handgun, rather unusual in juvenile series dust jacket illustrations. The Mountie has drawn his service revolver and is pointing it in the general direction of the cabin. Just as Vicki's gesture is made against the icy waterfall, the revolver is defined against Vicki's yellow coat. There is no question that something exciting and dangerous is about to happen. One only needs to pick up the book and read it to find out.

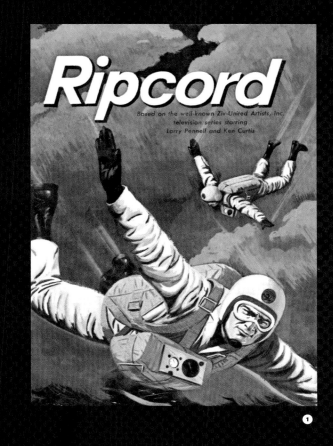

📖 
**RIPCORD**
Author: D.S. Halacy, Jr.
Illustrators: Al Andersen and Robert D. Smith
Publisher: Whitman

📖📖
**WAIT TILL THE MOON IS FULL**
Author: Margaret Wise Brown
Illustrator: Garth Williams
Publisher: Harper & Brothers
Used by permission of HarperCollins Publishers.

**❸** 📖
**VOYAGE TO THE BOTTOM OF THE SEA**
Author: Raymond F. Jones
Illustrator: Leon Jason Studios
Publisher: Whitman

**❹** 📖📖
**SEA HUNT**
Author: Cole Fannin
Illustrator: Al Andersen
Publisher: Whitman

**❺** 📖📖
**CURIOUS GEORGE FLIES A KITE**
Author: Margret Rey
Illustrator: H.A. Rey
Publisher: Houghton Mifflin Co

**4**

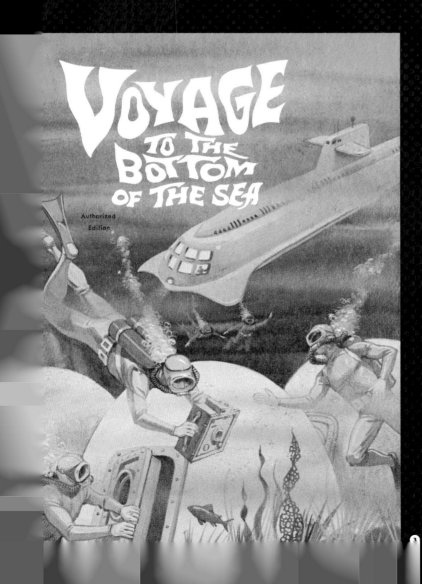

**3**

**5**

Ever since man first gazed upon the heavens and dreamed of travel beyond his home planet, he has developed stories of how it might be accomplished. From the time he stood at the shore of some vast ocean, man has imagined exploring its depths and has related his musings to others of a similar interest. He has also garnered inspiration from his earth and created tales of exploration into foreboding jungles and down mysterious rivers.

This subject matter served as the genesis for the science-fiction story. It was a genre that was unencumbered by the impossible, where man had his best chance of conquering land, sea, and space. But for all its enthusiasm and hopefulness, science fiction from its earliest times displayed a self-conscious nature. The writers wondered if advances in the scientific field would indeed improve man's way of life or if these advances might go unchecked and even accelerate his destruction. These weighty issues coupled with stories of adventure and fantasy gave science fiction a broad base.

While science fiction is rooted in the dreams of man, it is also a genre closely linked to its times. For as technology approaches territory set forth within the pages of science-based stories, the stories must forge ahead always beyond the grasp of the present day. One might conclude that the works of science-fiction writers are highly accurate indicators of the times in which they lived, as their stories of future times were often rooted in the concerns of the present.

In the development of science fiction, two writers were responsible for its entry into serious literary consideration — Jules Verne, widely considered the father of science fiction, and H. G. Wells who brought it into the twentieth century.

Jules Verne's formal education was in law, but his interest was in writing. He enjoyed moderate writing success in the latter until his work, *Five Weeks in a Balloon*, was published to strong reviews and even greater popular acclaim. From the success of this story, Verne seemed to have found his niche, which he soon developed to great success. His formula brought together the latest in scientific information and thought with

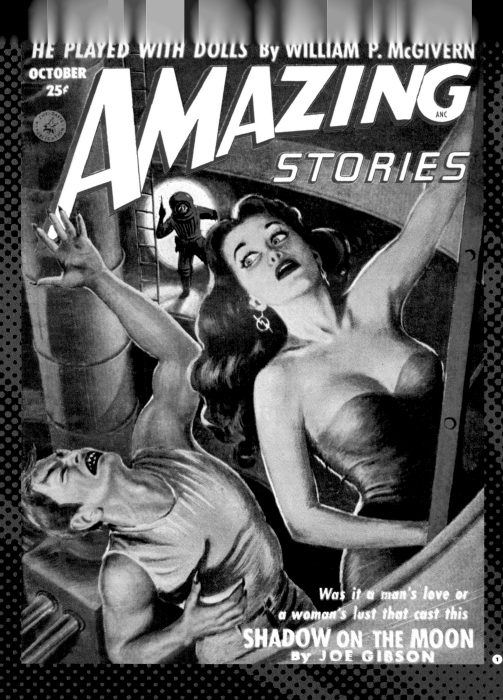

HE PLAYED WITH DOLLS By WILLIAM P. McGIVERN

OCTOBER 25¢

# AMAZING
## STORIES
ANC

Was it a man's love or a woman's lust that cast this
### SHADOW ON THE MOON
By JOE GIBSON

**1**

AMAZING STORIES MAGAZINE
**Author:** Cover story by Joe Gibson
**Illustrator:** Walter Popp
**Publisher:** Ziff-Davis Publishing Co

**2**

TREACHERY IN OUTER SPACE
**Author:** Carey Rockwell
**Illustrator:** Vaughn
**Publisher:** Grosset & Dunlap

**3**

AMAZING STORIES MAGAZINE
**Author:** Cover story by John Bloodstone
**Illustrator:** Walter Popp
**Publisher:** Ziff-Davis Publishing Co

TOM CORBETT
# TREACHERY
# IN OUTER SPACE

By CAREY ROCKWELL
WILLY LEY Technical Adviser

**2**

**4**

RIP FOSTER RIDES THE GRAY PLANET
**Author:** Blake Savage
**Illustrator:** E. Deane Cate
**Publisher:** Whitman
Used by permission.  Golden Books
Publishing Company, Inc.  Copyright © 1952.
All rights reserved.

**5**

THE REVOLT ON VENUS
**Author:** Carey Rockwell
**Illustrator:** Vaughn
**Publisher:** Grosset & Dunlap

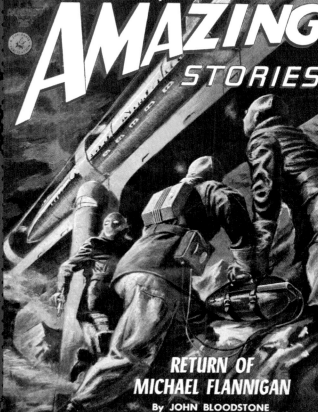

THE WINGED PERIL By Robert Moore Williams
# AMAZING
## STORIES

### RETURN OF
### MICHAEL FLANNIGAN
By JOHN BLOODSTONE

**3**

topical issues of the day. In some instances, the development of the characters was sacrificed for the sake of science and action, but his readers barely seemed to notice or dwell upon this criticism. This was a form of writing that was not only exciting, but also successfully disseminated scientific information that was once thought to be dreary and overly academic.

Verne's literary triumphs include *Journey to the Center of the Earth*, a tale of three adventurers who locate a passageway to the earth's core through a dormant volcano. Their perilous journey leads them to encounters with previously unknown creatures and the discovery of unusual geologic formations. In *20,000 Leagues Under the Sea*, an expedition is mounted to investigate the existence of an enormous sea creature rumored to be sinking cargo ships. The expedition meets with disaster when the creature — actually a submarine — sinks their ship as well. Three survivors are rescued by the submarine and become the guests/prisoners of Nemo, captain of the Nautilus. Their journeys together are filled with undersea adventure.

Verne's works were not solely earthbound; *Off on a Comet* and *From the Earth to the Moon* are stories of space travel and moon shots. Perhaps the most remarkable aspect of Verne's work was his uncanny ability to predict future technology. Not only did his visions of modern submarines, rocketry, and space travel reach fruition, but they did so much in the way he described them, well in advance of the twentieth century.

For Herbert George Wells, science had been a vocation for several years prior to the publication of his first novel. Educated at the Normal School of Science in London, he had gained employment as a science teacher and as an aide to scientist and lecturer Thomas Huxley. Eventually he turned to journalism, and, while in pursuit of that career, he penned his first book, *The Time Machine*, a tremendously important and successful initial offering. It tells the story of a young man who travels by machine through time to the distant future where he discovers society in an advanced state of decay. With the promise of the future shattered, the young man finds himself in a struggle to return to his own time.

In *The War of the Worlds*, Wells added a full measure of horror to his science-oriented tale. The story concerns the landing of Martian spaceships near London. Through the expert pacing of the narrative, the wonder of seeing visitors from another planet gives way to the acceptance that this is not a visit but an invasion; further, the aliens have intentions far more horrific than were initially imagined.

Wells's novel *The Invisible Man* is a study in science gone wrong. This tale follows a scientist who developed a treatment to make living organisms invisible. He subjects himself to a test of the formula and finds success beyond his expectations. He soon discovers that the price of his success is high, for a side effect of the formula is the inability to return to a visible state. His mental condition deteriorates and his behavior turns violent. Finally, instead of gaining notoriety for his remarkable discovery, he is

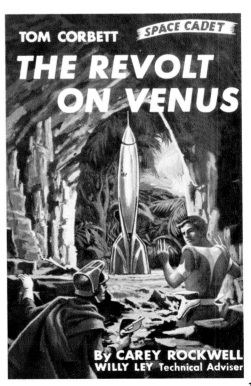

❹

❺

hunted by a group of townspeople for the crimes he committed against humanity. The author's strong skills in the area of character development were never more apparent and useful than in *The Invisible Man*.

Perhaps Wells's most significant contribution to the science-fiction genre was the level of social conscience he inserted into his text. He explored issues of class struggle and the increasing role of science in society. His vision of the latter was both positive and progressive while cautious of the terrible effects of science misused, particularly in the area of the development of advanced weaponry. The issues he raised in his work were valid, and they added realism to the novels. In his highly imaginative works, H.G. Wells seamlessly combined science, adventure, and his own brand of social commentary.

After the turn of the century, the works of Verne and Wells were available in the United States, but for a steady source of reading material the American enthusiast had to purchase science-fiction in magazine form often accompanied by tales of adventure. The magazines, particularly in their infancy, were not considered to have much literary value, as the technical aspects of the stories seemed to be paramount. Consequently, the magazines did not appeal to a mass readership. Still, science-fiction devotees proved to be a stubborn lot, and the magazines continued to stay in business.

Among these offerings was Amazing Stories, founded by Hugo Gernsback and one of the first magazines fully devoted to science fiction. In the juvenile trade, Edward Stratemeyer recognized the potential of the subject matter and created his enormously successful "Tom Swift" series. But the Tom Swift books did not give themselves entirely to science fiction; they were instead adventure stories with a focus on invention. The Stratemeyer Syndicate's actual entry into the science-fiction field did not begin for another two decades. If in that intervening time the juvenile readership had an interest in science fiction, they too would have to turn to magazines for their reading material. But in the years just prior to, during, and after World War II, current events formed the foundation of juvenile science fiction.

The rocket, a centuries old device, had primarily been used for amusement in fireworks displays and, with qualified success, nations had used it in time of war. However, the rocket, in the short span of the first half of the twentieth century, had evolved to a point that it began to alter the course of history. Indeed it was rocketry that produced the space age. Pioneers in rocketry such as Robert Goddard recognized the scientific uses of the rocket and conducted experiments to test his theories. It was Goddard who conducted the first launch of a liquid-fueled rocket. The use of liquid fuel proved to be a dramatic advance in increasing a rocket's altitude. Among Goddard's many achievements were the development of increased rocket speeds and the improvement of a rocket's maneuverability and steering.

Another leading engineer who advanced Goddard's findings joined the U.S. Space Program in an unusual way. Wernher von Braun was the director of the German Rocket Research Center on the Baltic Sea during World War II. His responsibilities included the development of the V-2 guided missile that terrorized England during the latter stages of the war. At the close of the war, von Braun surrendered to American troops and was brought to the States to serve as a consultant along with a number of other German engineers to aid the U.S. Army's rocketry program. His

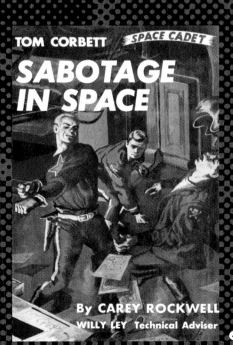

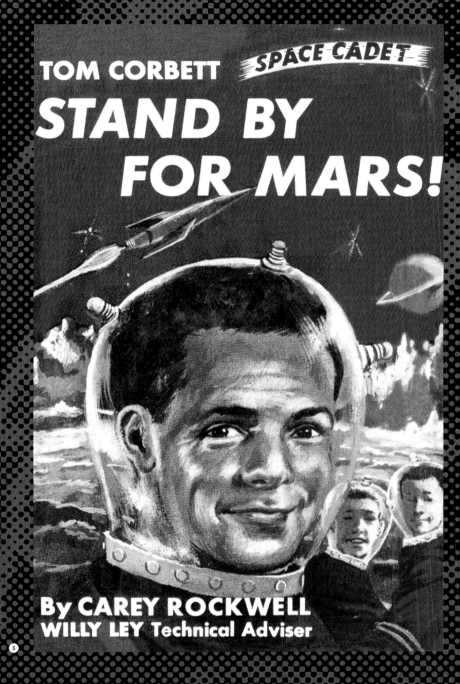

**THE SPACE PIONEERS**

Author: Carey Rockwell

Illustrator: Vaughn

Publisher: Grosset & Dunlap

**THE ROBOT ROCKET**

Author: Carey Rockwell

Illustrator: Vaughn

Publisher: Grosset & Dunlap

**DANGER IN DEEP SPACE**

Author: Carey Rockwell

Illustrator: Vaughn

Publisher: Grosset & Dunlap

**SABOTAGE IN SPACE**

Author: Carey Rockwell

Illustrator: Vaughn

Publisher: Grosset & Dunlap

**STAND BY FOR MARS!**

Author: Carey Rockwell

Illustrator: Vaughn

Publisher: Grosset & Dunlap

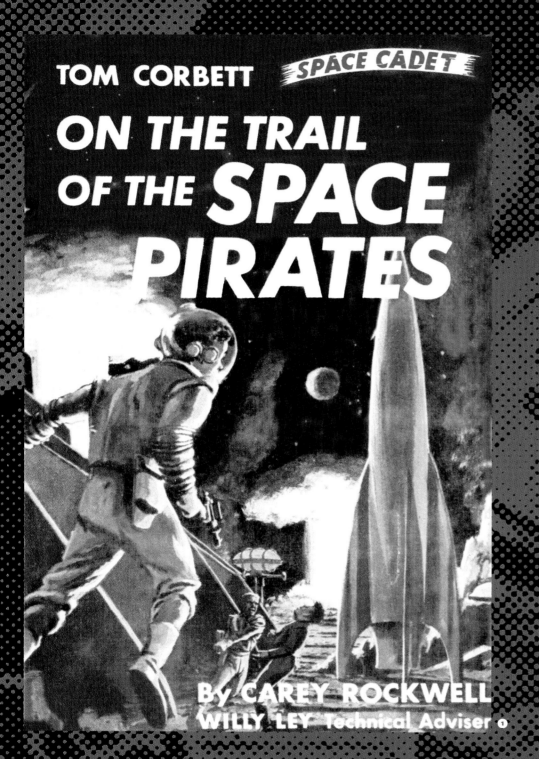

TOM CORBETT **SPACE CADET**

# ON THE TRAIL OF THE SPACE PIRATES

By CAREY ROCKWELL

WILLY LEY Technical Adviser ❶

**THE SCARLET LAKE MYSTERY**
Author: John Blaine
Illustrator: Unknown
Publisher: Grosset & Dunlap
Used by permission of Estate of
Harold L Goodwin and the John
Blaine/Rick Brant Trust.

**TOM SWIFT AND HIS OUTPOST IN SPACE**
Author: Victor Appleton II
Illustrator: Graham Kaye
Publisher: Grosset & Dunlap
Reprinted with the permission of Pocket
Books, a division of Simon & Schuster,
Inc. Copyright © 1955 by Simon &
Schuster. Tom Swift Jr™ is a registered
trademark of Simon & Schuster, Inc.

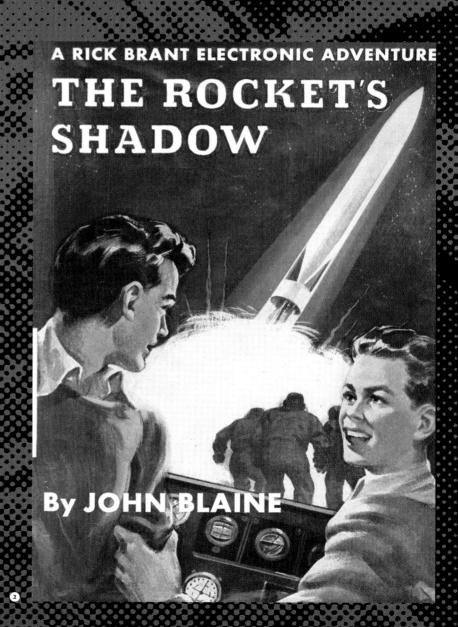

A RICK BRANT ELECTRONIC ADVENTURE

# THE ROCKET'S SHADOW

By JOHN BLAINE

**ON THE TRAIL OF THE SPACE PIRATES**
Author: Carey Rockwell
Illustrator: Vaughn
Publisher: Grosset & Dunlap

**THE ROCKET'S SHADOW**
Author: John Blaine
Illustrator: Elmer Wexler
Publisher: Grosset & Dunlap
Used by permission of Estate of Harold L
Goodwin and the John Blaine/Rick Brant
Trust.

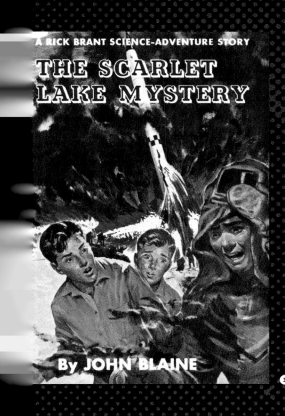

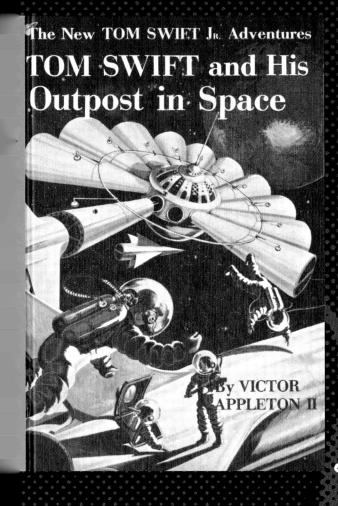

formidable abilities soon propelled him to a leadership position. He carried that leadership role with him to nearly every important U.S. rocket and space program from the 1940s to the 1970s. Among his many credits were the development of the Redstone rocket and later the Saturn rocket employed in the first moon landing.

World War II accelerated scientific research and development in many fields. The overwhelming concern was to finish that which was under development and implement it successfully before the enemy was able to implement its own project. It was a worldwide scientific competition, and nowhere was it more intense than in the rush to acquire the ultimate in weapons: the nuclear device. When Albert Einstein voiced his concerns about nuclear weaponry in the hands of the German military, a California physics professor listened and agreed. J. Robert Oppenheimer joined the Manhattan Project to develop such a weapon in advance of the Nazi regime. Oppenheimer's leadership in the Project produced results with the construction of two nuclear devices that ended World War II. The world had entered the Nuclear Age.

In short order, the Soviet Union had an atomic device of its own. The earth seemed to be an increasingly dangerous place to live. Students practiced bomb drills, and bomb shelters were erected in preparedness for the impending blast. There was a shared national fear. The Cold War was upon us.

The arms race and the space race between competing U.S. and Soviet programs captivated the world. In America every school age child, as a part of the science and current events curricula, studied exploration of space and the dangers of nuclear war. Astronauts attained the celebrity status previously bestowed upon movie stars and sports heroes. Scientists and engineers like Goddard, von Braun, and Oppenheimer did not gain celebrity of the same kind, but their significant contributions to the winning of the space race and for assisting in the ending of World War II were well recognized. Science was a respected field and was even considered an inspired calling. For these reasons, it seems likely, in retrospect, that juvenile reading material would carry the banner of fictional adventures in science, and would serve up tales of young Space Age heroes at a time when the earth was in desperate need of saving.

Harriet Adams had by now been at the helm of the Stratemeyer Syndicate for more than twenty years; she had guided her father's company through the Great Depression and in doing so had made the company her own. During the war years, she had scaled back the number of series books to a few tried-and-true titles, and now she looked to expand the company's presence in the market once again. She recognized the expanding role of science in modern life, from home conveniences to world affairs. It was the Nuclear Age on the verge of becoming the Space Age. Obviously, something was afoot in the scientific field, and there were stories to be told.

Adams was aware of several other successful science-based series and decided that the Syndicate should offer its own titles as well. The Syndicate, though not producing as many books as in the past, was still a formidable fiction machine capable of creating the "breeder," or instant series, of three or more titles to get a new collection up and running. For her new series title character, she looked to one of her father's most successful creations, Tom Swift.

Swift had embodied adventure and technological wizardry but, alas, he belonged to an earlier generation. To modernize an old hero did not seem feasible, as juveniles demanded their own heroes suited to their own youthful sensibilities. The solution was simple and inspired. Tom Swift became a father; his son, Tom Swift, Jr., was made the title character of the new series. Thereby, with instant name recognition, a new and improved teenage science-fiction hero was born.

Tom Swift Jr. is something of a chip off the old block; he has free rein in pursuing his adventures and suffers little in the way of monetary restraint. Like his famous father, who also has a role in the series, Tom Jr. is an inventor. In both series, the invention is a prominent element of the story. In each new book, the likelihood that Tom had recently developed, or is currently developing, an invention precisely suited to saving the day is a lucky and, of course, fortunate occurrence. While much of his father's focus had been on improving existing technology, Tom Jr.'s work proves to be more progressive and knows no bounds.

From the home of Swift Enterprises at Shopton, Tom Swift Jr.'s science-based adventures begin with the design and construction of the Sky Queen, the ultimate flying laboratory. Among his future inventions would be the atomic spacecraft Titan, the cycloplane Drumhawk, and his underwater helicopter, the Ocean Arrow. Often the test piloting of these new crafts offers adventure and hazard of its own, adding much to the subplot. At Swift Enterprises is a top-drawer engineering staff with whom young Tom is on equal footing. Some of these engineers appear in the stories and at times play even larger roles, but Tom's principal sidekick and closest friend is Bud Barclay. Barclay is a strong, handsome, and able-bodied copilot suited for action and daring rescues. Sometimes he is in need of rescue himself, but always he is in awe of Tom's amazing scientific knowledge, an attribute which, overall, serves as an excellent credential for a sidekick.

For awe bordering on reverence, however, no character surpasses Charles "Chow" Winkler. Swift Enterprises employs Winkler as an expedition cook. His real job is to provide the books' comic relief. The text often reminds us that Winkler hails from Texas, a point brought home in the dialogue by the balding ranch cook's declarations, which begin with expressions such as, "Brand my sagebrush stew..." and "Brand my flyin' flapjacks..." Beyond comic relief, Winkler's strength lies in his Everyman's bewilderment of all things scientific, allowing us to feel, by merely following the storyline, a certain camaraderie with those in the know. Further, Winkler's astonishment over young Tom's innovations adds to Tom's emerging legend.

In addition to Tom Sr. and Mrs. Swift, the family also includes Sandra, or Sandy, the blond, blue-eyed sister who is a year younger than Tom. Sandy's best friend is a pretty, dark-haired, girl named Phyllis Newton. Phyllis and Tom often attend parties and other social engagements together, as did Sandy and Bud. Of course, at the very heart of this group of characters is Tom Jr., the tall, clean-cut, blue-eyed, eighteen-year-old inventor. He is an honest and decent young man who studies and works in the scientific field for the advancement of man. Respect for Tom's work is

international; at important conferences he and his father are invited to lecture on science-related issues. It is in the name of science that his many adventures begin. Generally he is engaged in research or development when he uncovers the work of rogue elements in the scientific community. These are usually foreign scientists misusing their field in an effort to obtain power and wealth. Tom, backed by a supportive family, friends, assistants, and a Texas cook, does battle with these nefarious characters.

He embarks upon a host of adventures including foiling modern day pirates on the high seas. He works on colonizing the moon and leads expeditions into deepest Africa in pursuit of advancements in atomic energy. Within the rain forest, Tom discovers ancient artifacts of visitors from other planets, frustrates a criminal's destruction of an important government laboratory, and fights to recover precious sunken cargo from the ocean's depths. With calm demeanor and scientific know-how he is able to design and construct an amazing assortment of inventions to overcome the forces of nature and the evils of man.

The Syndicate pseudonym for the author of the original "Tom Swift" series was Victor Appleton. If the fictional Tom Swift was to bestow the

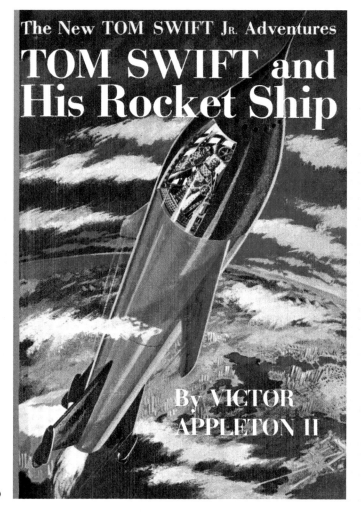

heroic family legacy to his son Tom Swift, Jr., then it was only fair that the author of the new series should be the son of the original series author. So it was that the "Tom Swift Jr." series was written under the pseudonym of Victor Appleton II. As always, writing for the Syndicate meant entering into an agreement stating that the author be paid a flat fee without future royalties. In the Stratemeyer tradition, the ghostwriter was issued series guidelines and story outlines from which he would write the book.

A number of writers contributed to the series, but the principal author was James Duncan Lawrence. Lawrence was a perfect match for the work. He had a mixed background; though formally educated in engineering, he was a successful radio scriptwriter when the Tom Swift, Jr. writing opportunity became available. He took his author's role seriously, endeavoring to place as much real science as possible into each volume. His engineering background enhanced the technical aspects of the writing, and to further that effort he regularly communicated with scientists and engineers in order that the writing and storylines remain rooted in reality. His work in radio served the series with economical, fast-paced writing.

The Syndicate, realizing the value of his work, promoted Lawrence to an editor's position. In addition to his editorial duties, he continued to write for the "Tom Swift, Jr." series and for other series as well. His contributions included the authorship of several "Hardy Boys" and "Nancy Drew" titles. Eventually he left the Syndicate to resume his freelance career, but not before leaving a lasting mark on the juvenile science-fiction field.

"Tom Corbett, Space Cadet" was a science-fiction series born of another medium. The original stories were produced for radio; later the series moved to television where it was eventually aired by the three major networks. Each program began with a countdown to zero followed by the ignition of a rocket launch, and from that dramatic beginning the space adventure unfolded.

The book series was issued as a kind of spin-off to those broadcasts. Authorship of the series was credited to Carey Rockwell, a Grosset & Dunlap pen name. Below that pseudonym was the acknowledged technical adviser to the series, Willy Ley. Ley's contributions were significant. He believed that science fiction, particularly for young people, was greatly enhanced by infusing the stories with real science. Working from that point of view, his recommendations directed the stories into areas with sound scientific footing and provided the reader with a degree of instruction veiled in entertainment.

Ley knew the subject matter well. A respected German rocket scientist, he founded the German Society for Rocket Research to further progress in liquid-fueled rocket experimentation. The Society was an international organization drawing upon the greatest minds in the field of rocketry; among its members was Wernher von Braun. When the emerging Nazi regime looked to the scientists and engineers in the rocketry field for assistance in its effort to make war, Ley dissented and left Germany for the United States. Here, he embarked upon a science-based writing career. His work was published in a host of magazines and books, and he served as a technical advisor to several noted movie and television producers. It was his work in television that brought him to the "Corbett" series, and it was there that he supplied just the right amount of technical expertise to ignite the readers' imagination, sending them into the future where adventure was found among the stars.

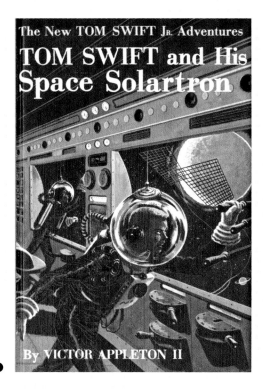

**❶**

**❷**

## The New TOM SWIFT Jr. Adventures

# TOM SWIFT and His Flying Lab

### By VICTOR APPLETON II

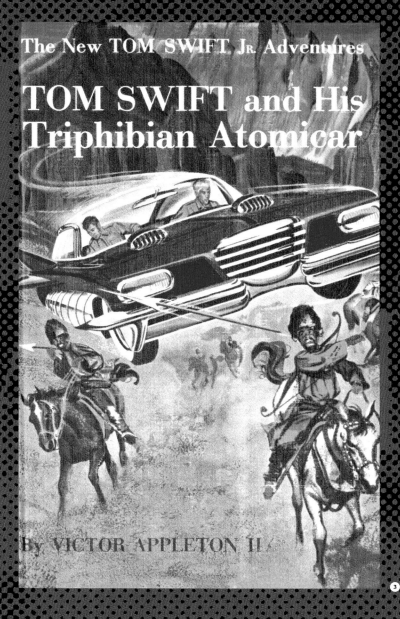

## The New TOM SWIFT Jr. Adventures

# TOM SWIFT and His Triphibian Atomicar

### BY VICTOR APPLETON II

The "Tom Corbett" series takes place circa 2350 and follows the adventures of three cadets enrolled in the Space Academy, a Space Age institution of higher learning. The cadets, young men in their late teens and early twenties, serve in the Solar Guard from which their many adventures stem. Handsome, curly-haired Tom Corbett is the leader of his three-man Polaris unit, which also includes the Venus colonial named Astro, and the cocky and brash Roger Manning. The cadet team takes on a variety of assignments in hopes of graduating the program and becoming full-fledged officers. Their adventures in space include struggle for control of interplanetary shipping lanes against space pirates and daring rescues to save comrades on the verge of being hurtled into the sun. It is an action-packed series to be sure, but it has other merits as well.

The personal dynamics within the cadet unit often serve as a potent subplot to the stories. This is where Corbett's leadership skills are called upon, where he holds the group together against outside forces to accomplish the unit's goals. The series, like all great science stories, has a language of its own, with terms such as "slidewalks" for moving sidewalks and "rocket juice," a term for adult beverages. There are original series phrases such as exclamations on the order of, "By the rings of Saturn!," which was considered to be harsh language. Additionally, it is a series complemented by marvelously complex futuristic machinery, with large helpings of the can-do spirit of the Space Age.

Originally, the banner above the title proclaimed them to be electronic adventures; later they were billed as science adventures, but for

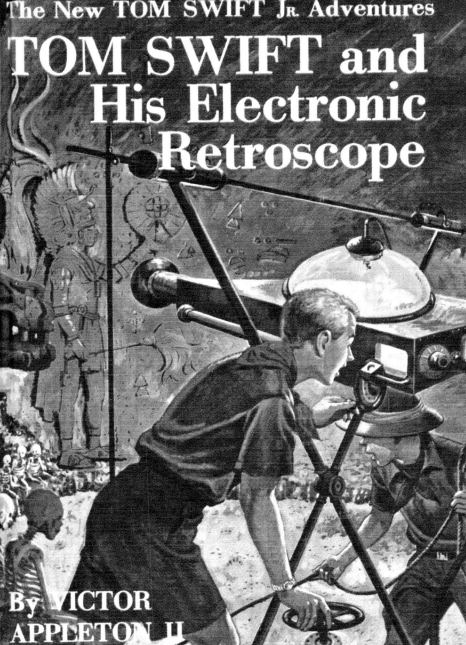

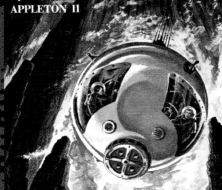

the readers of the "Rick Brant" series there was little doubt that the stories and the writing were the best in the juvenile science-fiction field.

The series followed teenager Rick Brant as he embarks on science-related adventures around the globe. For Brant, science in all its many fields had long been a way of life. His family home is off the New Jersey coast on Spindrift Island, which also serves as home to a small community of scientists and engineers. Spindrift is in essence a self-contained scientific compound. The island is large enough to accommodate modern laboratories, a rocket launch site, and a small landing strip from which Brant pilots his own plane, a Piper Cub. There are boat docks, a farm, an orchard, and a large wooded parcel of land. A narrow strip of tidal flats separates the island from the mainland. The island is the kind of place that juvenile dreams are made of. Unlimited in its freedom and set in an atmosphere of discovery, it is an excellent site from which to launch adventures.

Though the ever resourceful and courageous Brant is fully capable of undertaking his own enterprises, he does have the standard issue sidekick. Donald Scott or "Scotty" is such a character with some noteworthy improvements. Scotty, though close to Brant in age, is a veteran of the U.S. Marine Corps with combat experience. That Scotty's character is allowed such heroic credentials of his own is unusual. Scotty does not fawn over Brant's intellect or accomplishments, for he possesses strengths of his own. To be sure, Brant is the lead character, but his pairing with Scotty is more like a partnership. Another character along for the adventures is Brant's friend, Chahda, an Indian boy who had been rescued from a life of begging on the streets of Bombay.

The entire Brant family is prominently featured in the series as well. Rick's father, Hartson, is a respected engineer and electronic scientist. The relationship between father and son is affectionate and respectful. There is also a sense of equality and camaraderie between them. Rick's mother, though playing a smaller role in the series, is portrayed as an intelligent and hardworking person who cares deeply for her family. A year younger than Rick, "Barby" Brant is the pretty, athletic, little sister who figures in a number of the adventures in which she is cast in a helpful, positive light. Among the series other supporting characters are the Spindrift scientists, Professor Zircon and Professor Weiss.

Young Brant's adventures touch upon the major fields of scientific study: land, sea, and space. Themes involving elements of crime and international intrigue are stirred into the mix as well and, interestingly, so are several topics generally considered to be a bit high-minded for a juvenile readership, such as a realistic examination of the relationship between Cold War extremists and nonextremists. Overall, it is the cause of science and high adventure that is served when Rick, Scotty, and crew take on a menacing group of adversaries bent on destroying their mission to Tibet. So too is it served when they investigate sabotage at a Nevada rocket launch site and when they employ their latest invention, the "Submobile," to explore the depths of the sea in search of a lost civilization only to be confronted by murderous treachery born out of greed.

The "Rick Brant" series isn't the standard juvenile offering; never is the science watered down or the adventure overly contrived. Because of its realistic nature and the strength of the plotting and subplotting, the series enjoyed a long successful run of more than twenty years.

For an explanation of the success of the "Rick Brant" series, one need look no further than the author, John Blaine. Blaine was the pseudonym of Harold L. Goodwin, whose career was intertwined with some of the greatest scientific developments, events, and institutions of the twentieth century. Goodwin's education and early work experience was in the field of radio. The radio business in the first half of the century required employees to perform a number of tasks; as a jack-of-all-trades at several stations, Goodwin gained experience as an announcer, program director, and, most importantly, as a writer. From writing radio copy he developed a strong, concise style brimming with content. He began writing copy for an advertising agency while supplementing his income with freelance writing assignments. When his country went to war, Goodwin enlisted in the

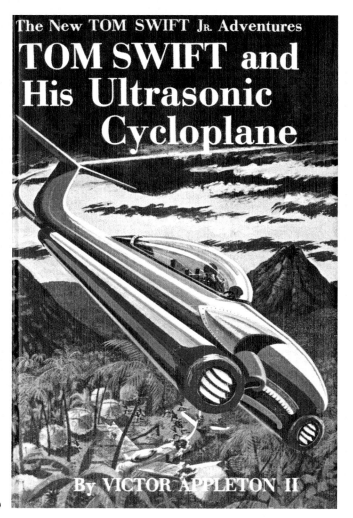

❶

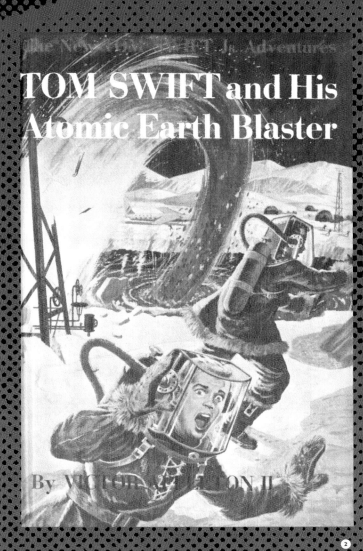

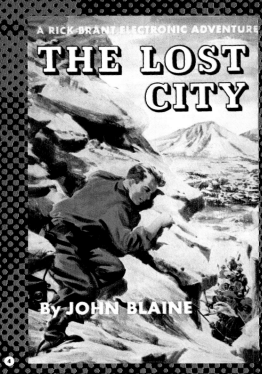

A RICK BRANT ELECTRONIC ADVENTURE

# THE LOST CITY

By JOHN BLAINE

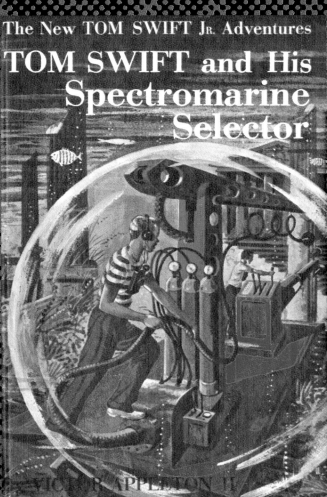

The New TOM SWIFT Jr. Adventures

# TOM SWIFT and His Spectromarine Selector

RICK BRANT SCIENCE-ADVENTURE STORY

# THE CAVES OF FEAR

By JOHN BLAINE

**1.**

**TOM SWIFT AND HIS ULTRASONIC CYCLOPLANE**
Author: Victor Appleton II
Illustrator: Graham Kaye
Publisher: Grosset & Dunlap
Reprinted with the permission of Pocket Books, a division of Simon & Schuster, Inc. Copyright © 1957 by Simon & Schuster. Tom Swift Jr™ is a registered trademark of Simon & Schuster, Inc.

**2.**

**TOM SWIFT AND HIS ATOMIC EARTH BLASTER**
Author: Victor Appleton II
Illustrator: Graham Kaye
Publisher: Grosset & Dunlap
Reprinted with the permission of Pocket Books, a division of Simon & Schuster, Inc. Copyright © 1954 by Simon & Schuster. Tom Swift Jr™ is a registered trademark of Simon & Schuster, Inc.

**3.**

**THE CAVES OF FEAR**
Author: John Blaine
Illustrator: Unknown
Publisher: Grosset & Dunlap
Used by permission of Estate of Harold L Goodwin and the John Blain/Rick Brant Trust.

**4.**

**THE LOST CITY**
Author: John Blaine
Illustrator: Howard Connolly
Publisher: Grosset & Dunlap
Used by permission of Estate of Harold L. Goodwin and the John Blaine/Rick Brant Trust.

**5.**

**TOM SWIFT AND HIS SPECTROMARINE SELECTOR**
Author: Victor Appleton II
Illustrator: Graham Kaye
Publisher: Grosset & Dunlap
Reprinted with the permission of Pocket Books, a division of Simon & Schuster, Inc. Copyright © 1960 by Simon & Schuster. Tom Swift Jr™ is a registered trademark of Simon & Schuster, Inc.

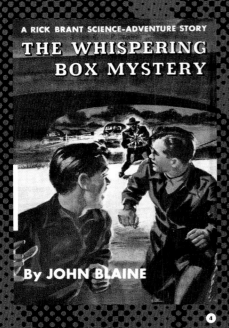

A RICK BRANT SCIENCE-ADVENTURE STORY

# THE WHISPERING BOX MYSTERY

By JOHN BLAINE

**THE WHISPERING BOX MYSTERY**
Author: John Blaine
Illustrator: Howard Connolly
Publisher: Grosset & Dunlap
Used by permission of Estate of
Harold L Goodwin and the John
Blaine/Rick Brant Trust.

**TOM SWIFT AND HIS JETMARINE**
Author: Victor Appleton II
Illustrator: Graham Kaye
Publisher: Grosset & Dunlap
Reprinted with the permission of
Pocket Books, a division of Simon &
Schuster, Inc. Copyright © 1954 by
Simon & Schuster. Tom Swift Jr™ is
a registered trademark of Simon &
Schuster, Inc.

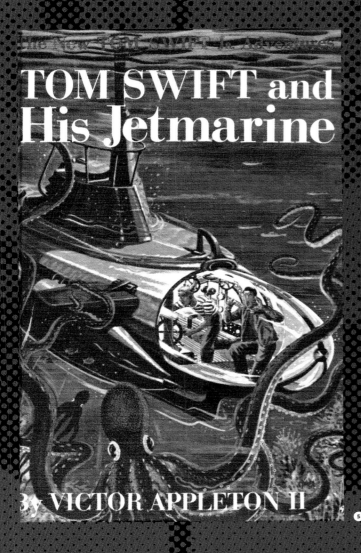

The New TOM SWIFT Jr. Adventures

# TOM SWIFT and His Jetmarine

By VICTOR APPLETON II

Marine Corps and saw action in the South Pacific as a combat correspondent. His extensive wartime travels began a lifetime of globe-trotting, which added depth to his adventure stories. At the war's end, he resumed his freelance writing career. It was his literary agent who suggested that he give juvenile series writing a try.

Goodwin invited his longtime friend and fellow writer, Peter Harkins, to collaborate with him. Harkins agreed and the pair decided to work under a pen name, choosing the moniker of John Blaine, after a character in an earlier Goodwin novel. After devising an outline for the series, which included a list of characters, their various attributes, and the island home base for adventures to come, they began writing the first Rick Brant book entitled *The Rocket's Shadow*. The writing team of Goodwin and Harkins found its style quickly with promising results. Following the publication of the first three installments of the series, Harkins declined further involvement. Goodwin would now work alone.

Like most writers, Goodwin inserted his own experiences into his work. Scotty's fictional wartime service was born out of Goodwin's actual experiences in fierce combat situations in the South Pacific. Likewise, Rick Brant was Goodwin's alter ego, which added perspective and believability to the character. Once the series had an established audience, Goodwin was able to write the Brant stories while pursuing other occupational interests. In no way did these interests interfere with his series writing; on the contrary, they only proved to enhance his future offerings.

Beginning with his employment in the U.S. Foreign Service, Goodwin's resume told the tale of his involvement in a variety of organizations and missions on the cutting edge of science and exploration. These organizations included the Federal Civil Defense Administration where he served as director of atomic test operations, a position in which Goodwin conceived, planned, designed, and implemented "Operation Doorstep." Operation Doorstep was the best known of the Nevada test site blasts. The test, in part, involved the detonation of a nuclear device in proximity to dressed mannequins, automobiles, wood frame houses, and other structures. The test demonstrated the impact of a nuclear blast and its associated thermal effects. The test was open to members of the press and was filmed. The motion pictures and still photographs of the test offered Americans their first, and perhaps most lasting, image of the destructive power of nuclear weapons.

While Goodwin was with the U. S. Information Agency, where he worked with Edward R. Murrow and served as science advisor, he participated in "Operation Deepfreeze," a project that brought the scientific efforts of more than sixty countries into a unified team to establish bases on Antarctica for research purposes.

At the National Aeronautics and Space Administration, he served as a Presidential Appointee of John F. Kennedy. Goodwin foresaw the onslaught of media attention on the Mercury astronauts and its impact on the space program. He designed a plan for managing press activities with the space team, which was implemented to great success.

Goodwin made significant contributions to a host of other organizations and societies, among them the National Oceanic and Atmospheric Administration, the National Marine Education Association, and the World Aquaculture Society. Through his work in these organizations, he traveled the world, visiting all seven continents. He visited India, Egypt, Nigeria, and Iran. He traveled extensively

The New TOM SWIFT Jr. Adventures

TOM SWIFT and His Aquatomic Tracker

VICTOR APPLETON II

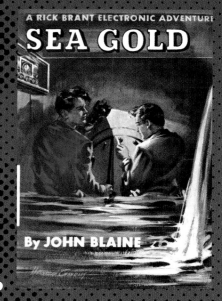

A RICK BRANT ELECTRONIC ADVENTURE

SEA GOLD

By JOHN BLAINE

**①**

**TOM SWIFT AND HIS AQUATOMIC TRACKER**
Author: Victor Appleton II
Illustrator: Edward Moritz
Publisher: Grosset & Dunlap
Reprinted with the permission of Pocket Books, a division of Simon & Schuster, Inc. Copyright © 1964 by Simon & Schuster. Tom Swift Jr™ is a registered trademark of Simon & Schuster, Inc.

**②**

**SEA GOLD**
Author: John Blaine
Illustrator: Howard Connolly
Publisher: Grosset & Dunlap
Used by permission of Estate of Harold L Goodwin and the John Blaine/Rick Brant Trust.

**③**

**SMUGGLERS' REEF**
Author: John Blaine
Illustrator: Unknown
Publisher: Grosset & Dunlap
Used by permission of Estate of Harold L Goodwin and the John Blaine/Rick Brant Trust.

**④**

**THE WAILING OCTOPUS**
Author: John Blaine
Illustrator: Unknown
Publisher: Grosset & Dunlap
Used by permission of Estate of Harold L Goodwin and the John Blaine/Rick Brant Trust.

**⑤**

**THE PHANTOM SHARK**
Author: John Blaine
Illustrator: Unknown
Publisher: Grosset & Dunlap
Used by permission of Estate of Harold L Goodwin and the John Blaine/Rick Brant Trust.

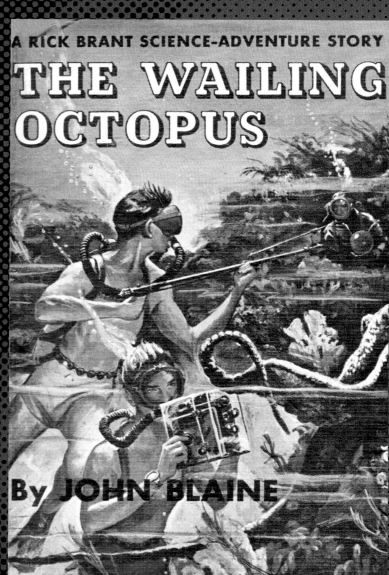

A RICK BRANT SCIENCE-ADVENTURE STORY

THE WAILING OCTOPUS

By JOHN BLAINE

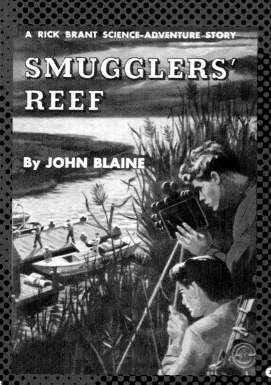

A RICK BRANT SCIENCE-ADVENTURE STORY

SMUGGLERS' REEF

By JOHN BLAINE

throughout Europe and in the Scandinavian countries. He didn't miss much; with his writer's eye for detail, he used his travel experiences as the backdrop for his stories and shared with his readers insights into faraway locales. Those experiences were coupled with the latest in scientific fact and theory, which he derived from his varied occupational pursuits. Even his personal life figured into his writing when his hobby of scuba diving was shared with his juvenile audience.

That Goodwin, for all his notable achievements, found time to write for or, for that matter, had an interest in a young audience was remarkable. He viewed the writing as a form of relaxation, but genuine interest and respect for young people was evident in each volume of his "Brant" series. He sometimes offered for consideration a viewpoint or moral question without having steeped it in heavy-handed morality as many juvenile series writers had done, and this was not lost on his readers. That he thought the work of science was important and that he chose to share its accomplishments and his own formidable gifts with young people is a testimony to the value he placed in each.

Science-fiction illustrations have a wide range of styles. Because the future cannot be accurately foreseen, illustrators have great latitude in their creations. Elements of fantasy are well established in the field of science-fiction illustration with the elaborate depiction of alien lands and alien beings. Fantasy illustrations also have erotic components to them,

particularly when featuring men and women of the future with disproportionate physical characteristics clad in small, tight fashions apparently suited to some form of futuristic warfare. Horror is another accepted form of science-fiction illustration. It is often depicted through invading aliens, monstrous sea creatures, and in the laboratory where man's own creations have gone awry.

In the second half of the twentieth century, most illustrations with strong fantasy and horror themes were considered inappropriate for juvenile literature. Instead, illustrators of juvenile science-fiction series books balanced aspects of high adventure with science, forming an acceptable expression of the subject matter. The science-adventure illustration was precisely what the juvenile market required, dramatic, action-packed science-based studies, tame enough so as not to raise the ire of parents.

The juvenile science-adventure illustration had at its roots the style featured in the science-fiction pulps of the day. Perhaps foremost of the pulps was the publication Amazing Stories. It was a magazine wholly different from juvenile series work. It contained no continuing characters or series-style heroes; instead it was a collection of short stories and novelettes. Despite these contrasts, there was a similarity in the intent of the cover illustrations, which was to catch the eye of the newsstand patron.

Walter Popp's illustration for the August 1952 edition is representative of the strength of the covers. The bold, white lettering dramatically edged in red comprises the banner reading Amazing Stories. Beneath it unfolds a story in a picture. Under cover of darkness, against a mountainous terrain, three men gather beneath a passenger transport facility. The facility is enclosed in a kind of clear tube; vertical columns support the tube as it spans the valley below. Within the tube, a bullet-shaped passenger transport resembling a train speeds toward its destination. The transport's cabins are illuminated, and we see silhouettes of its precious human cargo who are unaware of the events taking place on the valley floor. The three men, if indeed they are human, are attired in heavy clothing and wear hoods obscuring their faces. The hoods might have eye openings, but from the only man turned in our general direction we can gather little information as the opening emits only light. This same man carries in his gloved hand a pistol; his posture appears defensive as he looks back down the mountain, presumably to ascertain if his group is being followed. The remaining two carry a bulbous apparatus wired to a pack that one of the men has fastened to his belt. The men with the apparatus are looking upon the facility, one at the transport, the other at the support column.

Like all good science-fiction illustrations, this cover asks more questions than it answers. Chiefly, what is the intent of these men; is it sabotage or are they fugitives on the lam? Are they attired to conceal their identity or as protection against the harsh mountainous environment? Because the transport is traveling within a tube, one wonders about the outside atmospheric conditions. Finally, is the scene we are viewing even upon our own earth? These questions are too numerous and complex to answer while

THE PHANTOM SHARK

A RICK BRANT SCIENCE-ADVENTURE STORY

THE PHANTOM SHARK

JOHN BLAINE

A RICK BRANT ELECTRONIC ADVENTURE

By JOHN BLAINE

GROSSET & DUNLAP 6

5

browsing at the newsstand. We must purchase a copy and invest a little time reading to be rewarded with the solution.

The "Tom Corbett" series features pure space adventure in its dust jacket illustrations. The scenes are placed against the background of a dark and infinite space dotted with quasars, asteroids, and a planet or two to break up the stark nothingness. The ever-present rockets are depicted in several scenarios, standing stately and virile upon the launch pad, spitting fire as they blaze across the heavens in flight, and in horrific catastrophic collisions in deepest space. When the action takes place in a controlled atmosphere, the illustrations are rich and colorful, the electronic equipment futuristic beyond any recognizable implementation. Corbett and his pals are pictured in their space suits and often seen doing battle with space outlaws. Generally, the illustrations do not show space exploration in an inviting light. The scenes are fraught with danger and are not set upon the friendly confines of our own earth, but that only served to make the exploits of Tom Corbett and his fellow space cadets that much more heroic.

The stories and the locales of the "Rick Brant" series are more varied than those of the "Corbett" series. As a result, the illustrators, among them Elmer Wexler and Howard Connolly, had a wide range of topics and backdrops from which to design the dust jackets. The illustrators took full advantage of their opportunities producing strong, exciting illustrations. Brant traveled the world, and so it is portrayed with action scenes set upon tropical islands, Asian mountain ranges, as well as on and under the high seas. The action sometimes stems from the locale itself with a depiction of light aircraft skirting an erupting volcano or the danger associated with extreme deep-sea exploration.

The illustrations involved man-made peril as well. The jacket for *The Scarlet Lake Mystery* is such a work. The title's red lettering is spectacularly set against a huge plume of black smoke produced from an immense fireball. The fireball is engulfing a large white rocket, which is leaning and about to collapse. Nearby, in silhouette, a team of firefighters struggles to contain the blaze. Their efforts seem impotent against the inferno. With these elements the illustration could stand alone, but they serve only as a background for the action involving our heroes. In the foreground, we see that the fire might have claimed a casualty. To what degree is impossible to know, but the victim, dressed in protective clothing, is clearly registering the horror of his situation. Though we can't see the flames, smoke is coming from his suit. Is he in a panic, on fire, or both? At his side are Rick and Scotty, their faces showing surprise and concern. We know from reading past adventures that their surprise is a momentary reaction, that in an instant they will throw themselves into harm's way to assist the man. We want to know what happens next and how it all got started. Powerful illustrations of this kind are typical of the "Brant" series. Though some covers exhibited greater subtlety, they are no less engaging to a reader in search of science-based adventures.

The illustrations do not express much in the way of danger, doom, and destruction. They are bright and carry a sort of "gee whiz" approach to the juvenile science-fiction genre. They are the work of several illustrators including Charles Brey and Edward Moritz. However, the original illustrator Graham Kaye best exemplified the design and style of the "Tom Swift Jr." series.

The dust jackets feature a dizzying assortment of futuristic machines. There is every-

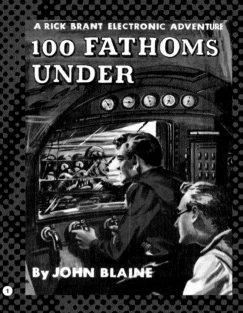

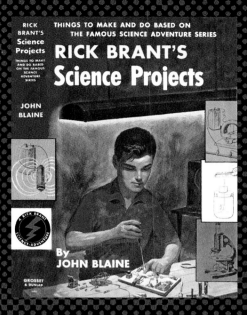

thing imaginable including a "souped-up" flying automobile complete with fins — which, as it happens, is perfect for cruising the skies in avoidance of a horde of spear-wielding tribesmen. There too are shiny rockets outfitted with control panels of multicolored lights and large windows that offer splendid views of the vast expanse of space.

The illustrations, of course, focus on the adventures of Tom, Jr. and sidekick Bud Barclay. Tom is depicted as a well-centered lad in control. The adventures are obviously harder on Bud, who is generally shown under severe mental strain, gesturing wildly, his mouth agape. The boys are usually dressed for the occasion, whether it is a walk in space, handling hazardous substances, or an excursion deep into the rain forest. Among the many elements that contribute to the success of the illustrations is a sense that Tom and Bud are embarking upon adventures of some importance. There are also elements of comedy, particularly in Bud, but never silliness. And the illustrations show that science could be fun.

Kaye's dust jacket for *Tom Swift and His Outpost in Space* is such an illustration. It shows the convergence of a number of spacecraft high among the stars. A spacewalk is underway with two boys floating along, free of gravity; another stands on the deck of one of the ships, while yet another boy emerges from a hatchway below him. This is obviously an important mission, but it looks like fun too. In fact, it appears that for the participants, space and its weightlessness is the greatest playground this side of the Crab Nebula. The illustration so stimulates the imagination that at first we don't even notice our own earth occupying a large portion of the right corner of the jacket. We may suspect that the boys, in the midst of their space party, haven't paid much attention either. But just in case they get a little lonesome for their home planet, there it is spinning above them providing them a clear view of their North American home.

There are illustrations filled with drama too. One such illustration, again the work of Kaye, is from *Tom Swift and His Jetmarine*. Though the setting takes place under water, the boldness of the illustration's few colors add to its success. The light green water at the jacket's top quickly yields to the deep blue of the ocean's depth. Fish of red and green glide around the obstacle that is Tom's undersea vessel. The bow of the ship is manufactured from a clear material, which offers her crew an unparalleled view of the underwater environment. The darkness of the ocean makes the sub's interior lighting seem all the brighter and allows us, the viewer, a peek inside. Here we find Tom: cool, collected, in command, and at the wheel. Crewmember Bud, openmouthed, wide-eyed, with his arms aflutter, does his part for the illustration by conveying the seriousness of the evolving situation. The object of his dismay, understandably, is a giant octopus, which has seized the Jetmarine. This is a creature in the midst of a predatory act; even with a firm hold upon the vessel's bow it reaches its remaining arms to further encumber the ship. The coldness of its stare seems to offer little hope for those who are caught in its grasp. Interestingly, the schools of fish passing by don't appear fearful of the situation or to care little about the underwater turbulence that must be generated by such a struggle. Perhaps it is because for those in the savage deep-sea environment, life and death struggles are business as usual. So too is it business as usual for two enterprising young men on the verge of yet another science-fiction adventure. And here again is another illustration that serves as an invitation to join them.

Public education in the United States, from its very inception, has been the subject of intense scrutiny and debate. It's an area that has had little in the way of common ground for its opposing groups; even the value of an education has been disputed. Many educational decisions of historical proportions have involved, even defined, each branch of government, and have cut across racial, cultural, and economic lines. In the century just past, public education endured its first great challenges.

By the opening of the twentieth century, the structure of the public school system was well established. Education and its funding through taxation were a function of each state, organized and administered at the local level. There was the notion that maintaining a strong and lasting democracy required an educated electorate capable of comprehending information of a complex, often conflicting nature. Because public education was considered vital to democracy, it was offered free of charge. Attendance at the elementary school level had become compulsory. The generally accepted purpose of an education was to offer instruction in reading, writing, mathematics, and social studies in the interest of producing productive citizens and as a means to encourage independence and self-fulfillment. As a result of the Industrial Revolution, the nation's labor force was in need of greater education and improved technical skills. Soon the needs of industry would be coupled with a great wave of immigration to press the limits of the public school system.

Administrators could not accurately project and plan for the number of new students who entered the United States through immigration. This problem was not limited to a disproportionate student-teacher ratio. The new pupils had a number of special needs. For many, English was not a first language. Great numbers experienced conditions of poverty resulting in unmet health and nutrition needs. Parental assistance in academic areas was often nonexistent due to the parents' own limited education or lack of English skills. But what immigrant parents could offer their children was support and encouragement. Despite their great challenges, children learned the fundamentals of an elementary education and quickly realized the benefits of this education. But few continued their studies beyond the elementary level.

Indirectly, a piece of legislation changed that. Child labor laws drove the underage labor force from the workplace into an area of supervision that was the public school system. More laws followed including one requiring children to attend school to a designated minimum age. No one could have imagined the empowering effect these laws would have on education or the degree of empowerment that an education would have on the individual, the family, the community, and the nation.

At the turn of the century, most public schools offered physical education of one sort or another. For some schools, P.E. was little more than an organized playtime designed to reduce monotony and enhance alertness for classroom activities. Other schools placed a greater emphasis on physical education with a program tailored to the classical movements of the human form and instruction focusing on physical grace and agility. Few school districts viewed physical education classes as a means to ready children for active and healthy adult lifestyles. There were, after all, plenty of opportunities to stay in shape over the course of a hard day's work. That was a belief that would change quickly.

Such was the rapid growth of technology that fears arose that labor-saving machinery would actually toil at the expense of man, reducing his muscle mass and stamina. It reduced him in other ways as well. The technological onslaught not only restricted his movements, but in the case of the new assembly lines, it lessened his cognitive skills as well. Workplace stress was on the rise. These were problems symptomatic of the new age, and they were recognized as such. It was only the second decade of the twentieth century.

Advances in science and industry progressed at a dizzying pace throughout the century and touched nearly every American. Modern conveniences thoroughly changed life at home. Refrigerators and freezers altered how food was stored and offered options in preparation. Washing machines and new fabrics reduced the laborious tasks associated with washday. And then it happened. The age of television began.

Television, almost from its inception, was vilified for its unhealthy impact on the lives of children and youth. It couldn't have been more popular. Parents and educators realized its influence early on, both academically and in the physical stature of the students. It was television, they said, that curtailed study and playtime. Television was an easy target for rhetoric concerning the ills of the nation's youth, but accurate testing was not available to convince and mobilize the public into action regarding fitness. In 1962, the physical fitness problem was finally quantified with the publication of a fifteen-year, government-sponsored study that examined physical conditioning of American youths. The results of the study were compared to studies using the same performance tests in other countries. The test scores were alarming. They showed that American youths were no physical match to their European counterparts. It wasn't even close. While 42 percent of American youth successful passed the fitness tests, 91 percent of the Europeans passed the same tests.

The text of the study presented an examination of the results and supplied

137

**❹**

83

**❸**

**Seeing the Newsreel**

What newsreel interested Jack most?

It was Safety Week in the city schools.
A man had taken a motion picture of a
fire drill at the Pullman School. Jack
was a patrol boy in the fire drill. He was
proud to be a patrol boy.

The man who took the picture told the
children when the newsreel would be
shown at a near-by theater. Jack could
hardly wait to see his picture in the fire
drill.

127

**❺**

**1** 📖

**ON THE WAY TO STORYLAND**
Authors: Gerald Yoakam, Kathleen Hester,
Louise Abney
Illustrators: Milo Winter, Ester Friend, et al
Publisher: Laidlaw Brothers

**2** 📖

**NUMBERS WE NEED WORKBOOK**
Authors: William A. Brownell, Fred Weaver
Illustrators: Hazel Hoecker, A and J Jousset
Publisher: Ginn & Co

**4** 📖

**SUSAN AND TOM- INTERIOR**
Authors: Paul R. Hanna, G.A. Hoyt
Illustrator: Ruth Steed
Publisher: Scott, Foresman & Co

**3** 📖

**OUR GOOD NEIGHBORS- INTERIOR**
Authorss: William H. Burton, Clara Belle
Baker, Grace K. Kemp
Illustrators: Naylor, Hartsock, Maltman, Funk
Publisher: Bobbs-Merrill Co

"That fire nearly burned my house," said
the chief to a fireman. "Those boxes were
burning right beside my house."

"Yes, you are lucky to have your house
left," said the fireman.

"We have a good fire chief and fireman
in Pine Square," said the chief, looking
toward Don and Peggy.

"The fire chief is looking our way," said
Don. "Why does he look?"

"Oh, I know," said Peggy. "He is the man
that we met on the sidewalk today."

8

further documentation underscoring the causes of the fitness problem. It found that many young people were overweight, with a growing number headed toward obesity. Diet or eating disorders, the study found, were not the principal causes of overweight; instead, the blame was focused on inactivity. Modern conveniences and television were named as contributing factors. The study confirmed the concerns already held by educators and parents. When confronted with the results, officials and policymakers accepted that action was clearly warranted.

As a starting point in resolving the fitness issue, officials again turned to the report. It indicated that physical fitness programs in public schools carried far greater emphasis in Europe than in the U.S. Further, it was found that after-school sports programs were better developed and attracted greater participation in countries outside the U.S. The President's Council on Youth Fitness provided leadership, and Americans became aware that health and fitness were as important to the nation as they were to the individual. Funding for sports and fitness programs increased. Physical education programs became goal oriented and intramural sports programs enhanced participation in team sports. The activity associated with these athletic endeavors carried benefits beyond the fitness objective.

"Hop in the car," said Grandfather.

"Hop, hop, hop.

Hop in the big red car."

"Here I go," said Susan.

"Here I go in the big red car.

Here I go to get a baby chicken.

A little yellow baby chicken."

The programs resulted in a greater appreciation for one's own body and thereby increased feelings of self-esteem. Competitive games allowed for the venting of youthful angst in an acceptable and controlled environment. Further, the sporting contests fueled the imagination, giving rise to the hope that greatness was within the grasp of those who worked hard and played by the rules.

Learning to read, the basic building block for all higher learning, has always been at the heart of an elementary education. At the time of the first great waves of immigration, reading took on an even greater role. Reading in the newly adopted English language was seen as a means to "Americanize" the young citizenry. At the turn of the century, reading textbooks were sorely in need of modernization. Still in use in many schools were the McGuffey Readers. The readers were named for their originator, William McGuffey, a professor of ancient languages and a Presbyterian minister. In McGuffey's view, religion and education complemented one another to such an extent that they were presented simultaneously. The books, first published in the mid-1830s, saw wide use for seventy years, but eventually, despite all efforts to keep it current, the text proved to be hopelessly out of date. The field was opening to new methods and innovations to assist young people attain reading skills.

What has been the best method for teaching children to read? The answer, even with the benefit of hindsight, remains unclear. During the twentieth century, teaching theories were plentiful, as was the criticism that each generated. One theory suggested that the twenty-six character alphabet be expanded to forty-four characters. The additional characters were to be used to more accurately convey letter and word sounds. Once reading skills were attained, the extra characters were to be dropped in favor of the traditional alphabet. Another theory held that teaching letter combinations was superior to teaching individual letter sounds. Additionally, the letter combinations were to be tied to corresponding colors to better display contrasting sounds.

But for better than half the century, the method that proved to be the most pervasive was based upon the "whole word" theory. The whole word method encouraged what was often referred to as "sight-reading," a kind of big picture approach to learning. The student was taught, often by repetition, to identify whole words through memorization. This method did not rely much on the use of phonics and as a result delayed the teaching of some confusing English language rules until a higher grade level. Students were taught to ascertain word meanings from the context of the sentence and through the accompanying illustrations. It was a theory that would become known for its notable characters.

The development of the new reading program was without question an enormously difficult task. It carried with it a responsibility to the nation's parents and their children that cannot be overstated. Obviously, the pressure to produce results was extreme, especially in light of variables

**❶**

**NUMBERS WE NEED- WORKBOOK INTERIOR**
Authors: William A. Brownell and Fred Weaver
Illustrators: Hazel Hoecker and A and J Jousset
Publisher: Ginn & Co

**❷**

**NUMBERS WE NEED -WORKBOOK INTERIOR**
Authors: William A. Brownell and Fred Weaver
Illustrators: Hazel Hoecker and A and J Jousset
Publisher: Ginn & Co

## Do You Know These Put-Together Stories?

1. ___ cowboy + ___ cowboys = ___ cowboys

2. ___ horses + ___ horses = ___ horses

3. ___ + ___ = ___          4. ___ + ___ = ___

| 5. | 6. |
|---|---|

| 7.  | 8.  | 9. |
|---|---|---|
| _____ | _____ | _____ |
| _____ | _____ | _____ |

$4 + 1 =$   3  ⑤          $2 + 3 =$   5  4          $2 + 1 =$   3  4

$1 + 3 =$   ④  5          $1 + 2 =$   4  3          $3 + 2 =$   5  6

$1 + 1 =$   2  1          $1 + 4 =$   5  3          $2 + 2 =$   3  4

$3 + 1 =$   2  4          $2 + 2 =$   5  4          $2 + 3 =$   4  5

Book One                                                                           29

---

### Pairs of Take-Away Stories about 7 – 1 and 7 – 6

1.

___ Indians in all

Cover 1 Indian.   ___ Indians are left.   $7 - $ ___ $= $ ___

Cover 6 Indians.   ___ Indian is left.   $7 - $ ___ $= $ ___

The pair of take-away stories is  $7 - 1 = $ ___   $7 - 6 = $ ___

2.

___ in all

Cover 6.   $7 - $ ___ $= $ ___

Cover 1.   $7 - $ ___ $= $ ___

3.

___ in all

Cover 1.   $7 - $ ___ $= $ ___

Cover 6.   $7 - $ ___ $= $ ___

4. Pairs of stories help.   $7 - 1 = 6$ helps you know  $7 - $ ___ $= $ ___ .

88                                                                      Book One

**3** 📖📖📖

**THE NEW WE WORK AND PLAY**
Authors: Williams S. Gray et al
Illuatrator: Eleanor Campbell
Publisher: Scott, Foresman & Co
Reprinted by permission of
Addison-Wesley Educational
Publishers, Inc. Copyright © 1951 by
Scott, Foreman & Co

**4** 📖📖📖📖

**SALLY DICK AND JANE**
Authors: Helen M. Robinson and
Marion Monroe and A Sterl Artley
Illustrator: Bob Childress
Publisher: Scott, Foresman & Co
Reprinted by permission of
Addison-Wesley Educational
Publishers, Inc. Copyright © 1962
by Scott, Foreman & Co

**5** 📖📖📖

**THINK-AND-DO BOOK- WORKBOOK**
Authors: Helen M. Robinson et al
Illustrator: George McVicker
Publisher: Scott, Foresman & Co
Reprinted by permission of
Addison-Wesley Educational
Publishers, Inc. Copyright © 1962
by Scott, Foreman & Co

**3**

# THINK-AND-DO BOOK

*for use with* **The Three Pre-Primers**

*The New Basic Readers*

SALLY
DICK AND JANE

*The New Basic Readers*

**4**    **5**

that were beyond the control of the developers. The program had to be equally valid in the North as in the South, function for both the rich and the poor, and at least consider the cultural differences of the great melting pot. Once success was achieved, there was little time to rest on one's laurels, for the material had to be updated in subsequent editions to implement innovative teaching methods. To achieve all of these goals in the short term was remarkable enough. For those goals to be so consistently met that they became the standard required a long-standing commitment to excellence seldom seen in any field or undertaking.

Such was the case for the team who introduced America to Sally, Dick, and Jane. The development stage for the series began in 1927 and was given direction when Zerna Sharp, a reading consultant, took a stroll along the shore of Lake Michigan. At the beach Sharp observed the communication characteristics of the children at play. She noticed that the children made their points in a clear and succinct manner. They often repeated their thoughts in brief sentences. The repetition of speech and the abbreviated sentences, Sharp recognized, were a result of immature vocabularies. Nevertheless, it formed a style of communication, a language all its own. Sharp theorized that the cadence of "child speak" and its familiarity to children would form the groundwork for a successful reading program. Sharp brought her idea up through the chain of command at Scott, Foresman and Company, publishers. After some debate, the tenets of her theory were adopted into the program and underwent further development.

The publishing house gathered a talented team including educators, illustrators, writers, consultants, child psychologists, and editors. Thanks to Sharp, the writers now had a style from which to pen their text, but story content remained a question. The team opted for themes that were most familiar to the students. Stories often concerned play and family life. The stories, though short, had a definite introduction, body, and conclusion. In addition to their obvious use in reading instruction, the writers designed the stories to entertain and foster a love for reading.

Another consideration the writing team faced was vocabulary building. The writers recognized that without a sustained effort to increase vocabulary, the program would be a failure. They determined that they would introduce new words at a rate of one or two (never more) per page depending upon the reading level. The new words would be used repeatedly in the pages directly following their introduction. They were to be repeated further, but to a lesser degree, in other stories throughout the remainder of the book. The team's approach to vocabulary building continued beyond the confines of a single volume. In an effort to retain words already mastered, words were reintroduced in as many as three successive books.

The team turned its attention to the illustrations that were to accompany the text, recognizing that the artwork was a potent learning tool. The illustrations are colorful pieces, full of fun and humor, serving not only to enhance the text but to also assist in word meaning and sentence expression. All of these and many other elements were considered, reconsidered, and debated before the series began publication in 1930.

The team had long planned that the nucleus of the series be a family whose most prominent members were the children. The working names of the children while the series was under development were "the boy" and "the girl". When first-graders opened the first of Scott, Foresman's Elson Basic Reading pre-primers, they met a brother and sister team named Dick and Jane. The fledgling students found in Dick and Jane a pair of children with authentic personalities who were fun loving and who shared the sibling experience in a realistic manner. In short, the students identified with the characters and accepted them as fellow travelers. Learning became more fun and less tedious. Most importantly, it worked. Students found success in the reading program, and that success stimulated success in other areas of study.

Although the series had been fully developed and completed for presentation, it was also a program that was a work in progress. Scott, Foresman called in consultants to comment and advise on the effectiveness of the program. The publisher contacted school administrators and educators for input as well, and employed field personnel who sat in on classroom reading circles to view firsthand the presentation of their curriculum. From those sessions, the field personnel gathered innovative

FUN WITH
OUR FRIENDS

# MORE FUN WITH OUR FRIENDS

### Guess Who

Sally said, "See my cars.
See my cars go up, up, up.
One, two, three.
Up go my three little red cars."

89

## THE NEW
### GUESS WHO

**①** ▢▢▢▢

**FUN WITH OUR FRIENDS**
Authors: Helen M. Robinson, et al
Illustrators: Bob Childress and Jack White
Publisher: Scott, Foresman & Co
Reprinted by permission of Addison-Wesley
Educational Publishers, Inc.
Copyright © 1962 by Scott, Foreman & Co

**②** ▢▢

**MORE FUN WITH OUR FRIENDS BOOK 1**
Authors: Helen M. Robinson, et al
Illustrators: Richard H. Wiley , et al
Publisher: Scott, Foresman & Co
Reprinted by permission of Addison-Wesley
Educational Publishers, Inc.
Copyright © 1962 by Scott, Foreman & Co

**③** ▢▢▢▢

**THE NEW GUESS WHO**
Authors: Helen M. Robinson et al
Illustrator: Richard H. Wiley
Publisher: Scott, Foresman & Co
Reprinted by permission of Addison-Wesley
Educational Publishers, Inc.
Copyright © 1962 by Scott, Foreman & Co

**④** ▢▢▢▢

**THE NEW GUESS WHO TEACHER'S EDITION JR. PRIMER**
Authors: Helen M. Robinson, et al
Illustrator: Richard H. Wiley
Publisher: Scott, Foresman & Co
Reprinted by permission of Addison-Wesley
Educational Publishers, Inc. Copyright ©
1962 by Scott, Foreman & Co

Father said, "Oh, Sally.
It is fun for you to play here.
But we have work to do.
Run and play with the red ball.
You can have fun with that."

Jane said, "Spot! Spot!
You can not play here.
Go away, Spot."

90

**THE NEW GUESS WHO- INTERIOR**

Author: Helen M. Robinson, et al
Illustrator: Richard H. Wiley
Publisher: Scott, Foresman & Co
Reprinted by permission of Addison-Wesley Educational Publishers, Inc.
Copyright © 1962 by Scott, Foreman & Co

**THE NEW GUESS WHO-INTERIOR**
Author: Helen M. Robinson et al
Illustrator: Richard H. Wiley
Publisher: Scott, Foresman & Co
Reprinted by permission of Addison-Wesley Educational Publishers, Inc.
Copyright © 1962 by Scott, Foreman & Co

Dick said, "Come here, Father!
Come and see what Spot did."

Sally said, "Oh, Dick.
I can do that.
I can do what Spot did."

172

Sally said, "Look! Look!
I did something funny."

Jane said, "I want to do that.
Dick and I can do it."

Father said, "Here, Puff.
I will help you do it."

92

Dick said, "Look here, Mother.
See what we did.
Guess who this big one is."

"Guess who this is," said Jane.

"Guess who this is," said Sally.
"And see the two little ones.
Guess who! Guess who!"

93

## On Cherry Street

THE GINN BASIC READERS

**100**
EDITION

**2**

# My Little Green Story Book

## REVISED EDITION

THE GINN BASIC READERS

**1**

THE GINN BASIC READERS

## Friends Far and Near

REVISED EDITION

**3**

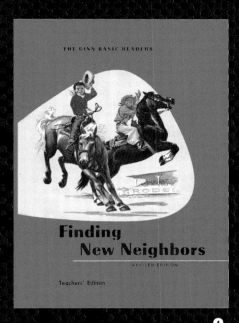

④

⑤

teaching ideas from practicing teachers. Scott, Foresman evaluated these ideas for effectiveness and, if proved successful, incorporated them into the next updated reader.

Another area where successful classroom experiences were shared was the Teacher's Edition, a volume similar in appearance to the students' books, but in addition to the stories and illustrations, it was a fully annotated guide for the instructor. To assist in teaching there were talking points, questions for the reading group, and story objectives. The objectives included vocabulary words and tie-ins to the Think-and-Do Book. The Think-and-Do Books were workbooks designed to challenge the student beyond the confines of rote learning. They were an interactive medium between Dick and Jane and the student. Lessons involved tasks such as choosing a word to complete a piece of dialogue between characters or choosing the appropriate facial expression for a character in a given scene. For students experiencing difficulty in the Basic Reading Program, there were "Dick and Jane" readers with material that accommodated special needs. Scott, Foresman also developed books for pre-schoolers. These wordless volumes prepared future readers for the program. Children experienced holding and "reading" books just like grownups. They could follow uncomplicated stories through a series of illustrations.

The program developers revised the readers in other ways too, not strictly along educational lines. Additional characters were added. A baby girl, Sally, joined the family. As the "little kid," Sally often required some degree of assistance from her big brother and sister, which, of course, was readily given. Sally was the most playful of the three children and had something of a mischievous quality to her character. Spot the dog and Puff the kitten played supporting, often humorous roles. In the revision process, the characters' style of dress was updated as well. For this purpose, researchers used current children's clothing catalogs as references. Undoubtedly, children recognized that they or their classmates were attired in a manner very similar to the books' characters. Even the physical appearance of the characters evolved into a slightly older, more sophisticated look. The revisions to the illustrations were not limited to the characters; an assortment of modern conveniences was added and automobiles were frequently updated.

The team responsible for this work changed as well. As the original developers of the program left Scott, Foresman and Company, new educators, psychologists, writers, and illustrators arrived. America was changing as well. Topics never before considered for inclusion in a school curriculum were opened for study and discussion. This was especially true in the area of race relations and equality. The education system played a role in the struggle for equality when in 1954 the U.S. Supreme Court ruled that segregation violated the Constitution based on unequal access to educational opportunities in its decision in Brown v. Board of Education of Topeka.

In the 1960s, America's true ethnic colors were depicted in the pages of the Basic Reading Program. New to the neighborhood and living next door to Sally, Dick, and Jane was a family of African-Americans. There were the twin

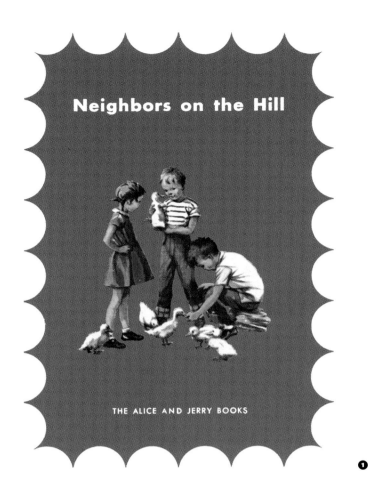

❶ 📖

**NEIGHBORS ON THE HILL**
Authors: Marjorie Flack and Mabel
O'Donnell
Illustrators: Florence and Margaret
Hoopes
Publisher: Row, Peterson & Co

❷ 📖

**ANYTHING CAN HAPPEN**
Authors: Mary Geisler Phillips and
Mabel O'Donnell
Illustrator: Dorothy Todd
Publisher: Harper & Row

❶                    ❷

girls, Penny and Pam, and their brother, Mike. The family routines and situations of these new characters and their parents mirrored life in the Sally, Dick, and Jane family. Additionally, the new family provided positive role models to the series, and their presence obviously strengthened the neighborhood. This began a new era for the series in which more characters of varied ethnic backgrounds graced the illustrations and storylines of the Basic Reading Program.

Despite the revisions and the updated instruction methods, the program had a number of detractors who questioned the series' very foundation, the whole word theory. The concerns over this theory were given a voice with the publication of Rudolf Flesch's *Why Johnny Can't Read*. Flesch's book examined the whole word or sight method and proclaimed it a failure. He strongly suggested that phonics was the basis of any successful reading program. Flesch reasoned that not only was the phonics approach a better method for teaching reading, but it was easier for the student as well. The Basic Reading Program had some phonics instruction but not enough, cited the critics. As a result, they said, many children attained reading skills too slowly, some not at all.

Unquestionably, the phonics approach had its merits, but the methods utilized in the Basic Reading Program had a proven track record. From

its inception in 1930 until 1970 when the "Sally, Dick, and Jane" series was discontinued, eighty-five million school children learned to read with the program. The achievements of the Basic Reading Program extended beyond the classroom. The recipients of this instruction continued to use learned skills into adulthood, furthering advancements in science and technology, medicine, and the arts. Moreover, those skills fed the hunger for information. Educating the electorate and thereby, in no small measure, helping to preserve freedom and democracy — that was the gift of reading, the greatest of all educational gifts. For the characters who delivered those gifts, there were rewards as well; Sally, Dick, and Jane passed into the status of American cultural icons.

Competition among textbook publishers offered local school districts many choices. The "Sally, Dick, and Jane" readers proved to be the most popular. However, not all districts subscribed to the Scott, Foresman Basic Reading Program. Instead, some chose the "Alice and Jerry" series published by Harper & Row. Others opted for the Ginn program, which featured the exploits of Susan and Tom. Still other districts chose the work of publisher D.C. Heath and Company whose characters were Ned and Nancy. Most of the non-Dick and Jane titles bore at least a passing resemblance to the Scott, Foresman and Company volumes. However,

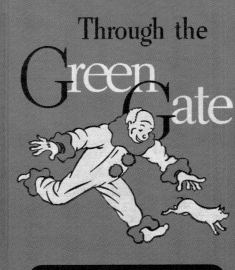

THE ALICE AND JERRY BOOKS

**③** 📖

**THROUGH THE GREEN GATE**
Author: Mabel O'Donnell
Illustrators: Florence and Margaret Hoopes
Publisher: Row, Peterson & Co

**④** 📖

**THROUGH THE GREEN GATE**
Author: Mabel O'Donnell
Illustrators: Florence and Margaret Hoopes
Publisher: Row, Peterson & Co

## Miss Lizzie

Someday you may go to Friendly Village. Of course, when you get there, you will want to see all your old friends, Alice and Jerry, Bobby and Billy, and Paddy and all his pets.

You will want to call on Mr. Carl, and say "Hello" to Mr. Andrews in his fruit store on River Street.

Maybe Cobbler Jim will let you sit on the end of his workbench, and talk to his old black cat while he mends your shoes.

5

**1**

**①**

**TIP AND MITTEN**

Authors: McKee, Harrison, McCowen, Lehr, Durr

Illustrator: Lilian Obligado

Publisher: Houghton Mifflin Co

**②**

**FLICKA, RICKA, DICKA AND THEIR NEW FRIEND**

Author: Maj Lindman

Illustrator: Maj Lindman

Publisher: Albert Whitman & Co

Used by permission of publisher.

**③**

**FLICKA, RICKA, DICKA AND THE BIG RED HEN**

Author: Maj Lindman

Illustrator: Maj Lindman

Publisher: Albert Whitman & Co

Used by permission of publisher.

**④**

**SNIPP, SNAPP, SNURR, AND THE SEVEN DOGS**

Author: Maj Lindman

Illustrator: Maj Lindman

Publisher: Albert Whitman & Co

Used by permission of publisher.

FLICKA, RICKA, DICKA AND
THEIR NEW FRIEND

By

Maj Lindman

ALBERT WHITMAN
& COMPANY

Chicago  Illinois

**2**

Father said, "It is a fine idea."

The three little boys took Dick for a long walk.

there was one program unlike any other.

For a pen name, Theodor Geisel chose a title of status and applied it to his middle name to become Dr. Seuss. The good doctor's practice was a shot of rollicking good fun with a healthy dose of nonsense. It began as a two-part assignment. The first was to write and illustrate a first grade level book from a prepared list of 225 words. The second part was to make it fun. To write an original manuscript with such limited word usage was a daunting enough task, but to expect it to be fun was an outrageous request. Outrageous was exactly what they got. It was called *The Cat in the Hat*, and it began with a theme familiar to all children: the boredom of being stuck indoors on a rainy afternoon.

The story is told from the perspective of a young boy. With their mother out for the day, the boy and his sister sit idly at a window waiting out the storm. Nearby in a bowl, a fish sleeps peacefully. With a mighty bump, the door is thrust wide to produce a tall-hatted cat sporting a bow tie and an umbrella. To the amazement and eventual dismay of the children, the cat performs a series of tricks. The fish, speaking as the children's conscience, leans out of the bowl to declare that tricks and cats are not welcome while mother is away. Soon the fish is incorporated into the show, balanced with an array of household items by the cat riding atop a ball. More disaster ensues. The cat is joined by his confederates, Thing 1 and Thing 2, who add to the mayhem. Finally, the fish spies the mother, and the kids put an end to the wildness and toss out their unwanted guests. With feelings hurt, the cat departs leaving the children with a giant mess and no time to clean up before their mother enters. The children know that they're in trouble; but just when all appears lost, the cat returns riding a kind of multi-armed cleanup contraption and the order of the house is restored in the nick of time.

*The Cat in the Hat* was a pure joy for the young reader — a funny story written in a series of wonderful, ridiculously contrived rhymes and a host of characters depicted in a wholly unusual and whimsical manner. It was part comic, part real book, and all fun. It was also a phenomenal success in terms of sales. Soon a series of supplemental readers were under development for use in and out of the classroom.

The newly established publisher, Beginner Books, brought the works of Dr. Seuss and other talented writers and illustrators, including Berenstain Bears authors Stan and Jan Berenstain, to an eager marketplace. The hallmark of Beginner Books was originality and creativity. No author exemplified those qualities more than the man who started it all, Ted Geisel. As Dr. Seuss, Geisel entertained and instructed through an array of unforgettable characters and story titles including *Green Eggs and Ham*, *The Foot Book*, and *Horton Hears a Who*. Perhaps no author better instilled in children that reading was a pleasurable undertaking than did Dr. Seuss.

Educational pursuits were not limited to the curriculum of each school district. The Girl and Boy Scouts offered programs that taught young people the value of service to their community and readied them for leadership roles in their adult lives. Another area of instruction, largely spiritual but with secu-

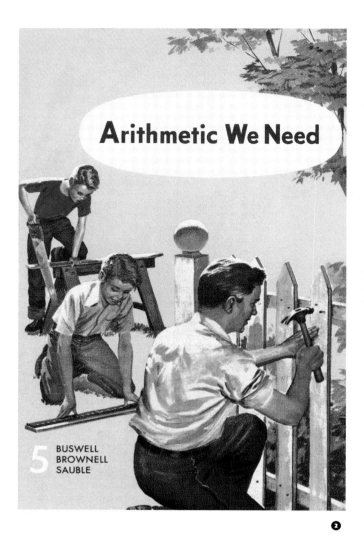

**①** 📖

**LANGUAGE FOR DAILY USE 4TH EDITION #3**
Authors: Mildred A. Dawson, et al
Illustrator: Unknown
Publisher: Harcourt, Brace, & World
Reproduced by permission of Harcourt, Inc.

**②** 📖

**ARITHMETIC WE NEED**
Authors: Busswell, Brownel, Sauble
Illustrator: Unknown
Publisher: Ginn & Co

lar applications, was Sunday school. These classes often began with simple Bible stories and crafts for the youngest students and ran to complex theory and Biblical discussion for high school youth. There was another choice in instruction that did not require joining an organized group or club. One did not even have to attend class or pass an examination upon completion. Its students were often described as being self-taught. It was an institution like no other, where one remained anonymous while reaching beyond the boundaries that society often placed on the individual. It was available to anyone who could read. For in America in the twentieth century, young people were blessed with a multitude of resources no farther away than their public library.

The rise in popularity of sporting events in the last century was nothing less than a cultural phenomenon. In the beginning, baseball was king, both in terms of the national game and in local participation. It seemed that every town, no matter how small, had at least a team or two. Larger cities sported a considerable number of amateur and semi-professional teams. There were teams that were without a home field. These teams barnstormed across the country picking up games as they went. And, of course, there were the big league teams that played the game from early spring into late summer; each raced for the pennant and with it an opportunity to play in the fall classic, the World Series.

In the early days, football was primarily a school sport. It was a fall activity, which was linked to other events and rituals held in its honor. There were pep rallies, bonfires, and homecoming dances. Before professional leagues were formed, football players joined barnstorming teams at the end of their collegiate careers. Like football, basketball seemed especially well suited for school play. Its niche was as a winter/spring game. The popularity of basketball eventually spread from the gymnasium to city and homemade courts.

A number of other sports garnered a faithful following based largely along geographic lines. Such was the case with hockey. These sports offered Americans opportunities to participate on several levels. One might choose to play the game or attend as a spectator. A fan might follow the game through radio broadcasts or through newspaper coverage. This variety of media allowed fans to keep current with the doings of their favorite teams. As a result, the individual was not only entertained; he often felt part of the game. For many, particularly immigrants, the sporting world offered a path of entry to and inclusion in the new land. There seemed to be nothing more American than identifying with a favorite team and sharing fellowship with like-minded individuals. The sports fan fraternity even offered membership to those with opposing loyalties, for if enjoyment could be found with a group of fellow boosters, imagine the enjoyment of arguing the merits of one's own team with the opposition.

For the young people of these early times there was allure beyond the shared experience of fandom or even the contest itself. It was a love for the giants who played the games; names such as Mathewson and Thorpe were awe-inspiring. This was a new kind of hero, to be sure, not based in the world of serious adult endeavors, but instead rooted in the world of play. There were sports heroes for every taste with nicknames to match their endless gallantry. There was the Bambino, the Brown Bomber, the Galloping Ghost, and a host of others. Later still there would be a hero who would transcend sports and define courage and strength for all Americans. Jackie Robinson changed the nation from his spot on a baseball diamond in Brooklyn.

Young athletes had their own reasons to love the games they played. Each contest offered opportunities for individual heroic performance, and for the victors there was the pleasure associated with athletic conquest. Even players with limited skills enjoyed a certain status by being a part of a team and, though their playing time was short, it did not cut into their dreams. After all, it was common knowledge that many of the greatest sports stories came about with the insertion of a substitute who changed the outcome of a contest. There was another positive aspect to athletics, one that reached beyond the camaraderie of the team: the unique relationship that developed between the coach and his players.

This relationship is highly complex: part student and teacher, recruit and drill sergeant, containing elements of both love and hate. It is a shared struggle. Both parties are on an impossible quest for perfection. There are lessons in winning with humility and losing with dignity. At times, it is a one-sided arrangement. But in the endless practice sessions, the coach and the player prepare each other for what lies ahead.

The position of coach or manager in dealing with his players is both professional and personal. Between the coach and his employers, it is a

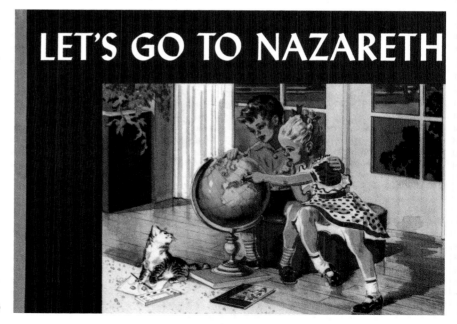

## THE CAT IN THE HAT

Author: Dr. Seuss
Illustrator: Dr. Seuss
Publisher: Beginner Books
Used by permission of Random House
Children's Books, a division of Random
House, Inc. Trademark & Copyright © by Dr.
Seuss Enterprises, L.P. 1957, 1985.

## GREEN EGGS AND HAM

Author: Dr. Seuss
Illustrator: Dr. Seuss
Publisher: Beginner Books
Used by permission of Random House
Children's Books, a division of Random
House, Inc. Trademark & Copyright ©
by Dr. Seuss Enterprises, L.P. 1960,
1988..

## ONE FISH, TWO FISH, RED FISH, BLUE FISH

Author: Dr. Seuss
Illustrator: Dr. Seuss
Publisher: Beginner Books
Used by permission of Random House
Children's Books, a division of Random House,
Inc. Trademark & Copyright © by Dr. Seuss
Enterprises, L.P. 1960, 1988.

❹

## 365 BEDTIME STORIES

Author: Alice Sankey
Illustrator: Ellen Segner
Publisher: Whitman

❶

❷

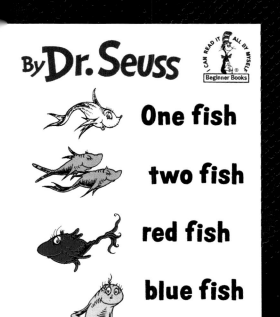

bottom-line position, a relationship based on winning. When managing the press and booster clubs, it is a public relations job. A coach may be considered a success if he functions well with several of the elements of the position. The great ones somehow handle it all, and one of these was a coach for Long Island University, Basketball Hall of Famer Clair Bee.

Lovers of sports information and statistics can have a field day with the accomplishments of Clair Bee and his basketball teams. At his first college coaching assignment, Rider College, his record was an outstanding 53 and 7. As a coach at LIU, Bee's won-lost record was a staggering 357 and 79. His teams completed two seasons in which they were undefeated. In an amazing thirteen-year stretch, his LIU teams racked up a 222 and 3 at-home record. Twice his teams were NIT champions. He was credited for the development of the 1–3–1 defense. He assisted in the development of the 3-second rule and the 24-second rule in the NBA, which gave the professional ranks a new lease on life. He was considered the greatest defensive strategist of his time. When Dr. James Naismith, the game's inventor, penned his book *Basketball: Its Origins and Development*, he chose Clair Bee to write the introduction. In addition to the Basketball Hall of Fame, Bee was enshrined in the Madison Square Garden Hall of Fame and the LIU Sports Hall of Fame.

Bee gloried more in the education his players received than in the victories they shared. He considered himself, foremost, a teacher whose concern for his players was not limited to their athletic output. He cared about these young men and their post-playing lives and provided leadership to help his players move into successful and productive careers. Bee strongly believed in a moral code that included integrity, courage, sportsmanship, and personal responsibility. He reinforced those values in a series of juvenile-based sports books he wrote which starred his All-American hero Chip Hilton.

Mary Hilton was a widow living in the town of Valley Falls. She was known as a hardworking, kind, and supportive mother. When we meet her son William "Chip" Hilton, he is a junior in high school employed part-time at the Sugar Bowl, a sweet shop off the town drugstore, where he mans the fountain as a soda jerk. His father, "Big Chip," had been the chief chemist at Valley Falls Pottery and had been killed in an industrial accident while saving a co-worker. The accident occurred just before Chip entered high school. We learn that Big Chip was an extremely gifted athlete, an All-American football and basketball player. Like his son, Big Chip had played for Valley Falls High under Coach Henry Rockwell. Rockwell was a strong disciplinarian who understood well the games he coached and the boys who played for him. In Chip he had a hardworking, versatile athlete who was immensely coachable.

Standing 6' 2" and weighing in at 170 pounds, Chip was one of those athletes who is so agile and smooth that his playmaking appears effortless. But those who know Chip know better. That effortless touch he brings to the games is the product of countless hours of practice and instruction. Tough, aggressive, fair, and honest, the boy is always prepared to play. He relies on

**❶** 

**BABY'S CHRISTMAS**
Author: Ester Wilkin
Illustrator: Eloise Wilkin
Publisher: Western Publishing Co
Used by permission.  Golden Books Publishing
Company, Inc.  Copyright © 1959, 1987.  All
rights reserved.

**❷** 

**FROSTY THE SNOW MAN**
Author: Annie North Bedford
Illustrator: Corinne Malvern
Publisher: Golden Press

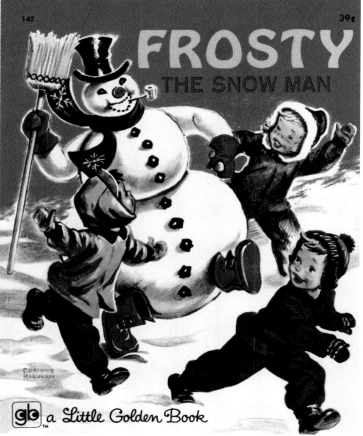

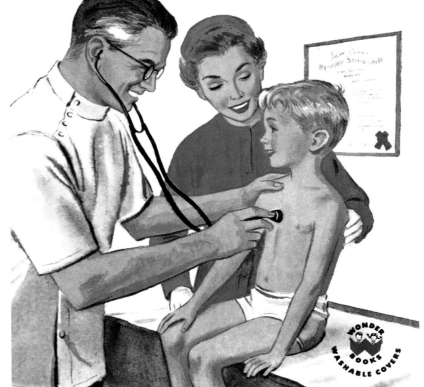

**BEDTIME STORIES**

Authors: Variety of authors
Illustrator: Gustaf Tenggren
Publisher: Golden Press
Used by permission. Golden Books
Publishing Company, Inc. Copyright ©
1968. All rights reserved.

**A VISIT TO THE DOCTOR**

Authors: Berger, Tidwell, and Haseltine
Illustrator: Vic Dowd
Publisher: Wonder Books

**CHITTY CHITTY BANG BANG**

Author: Jean Lewis
Illustrator: Gordon Laite
Publisher: Golden Press

his instincts during competition, but not solely. His quick thinking often carries the day. He is that rare combination of a gifted, thinking athlete with an outstanding work ethic. Add this to his leadership abilities, his even temperament, and his blond-haired good looks, and you have in Chip Hilton the personification of the American Golden Boy.

To his credit, author Clair Bee understood that little dramatic effect was served by perfection in life or sport. To that end, Chip doesn't win them all, and not all his personal relationships are positive ones. Sometimes he experiences personal struggles, just as any teenager would. The cast of characters that are his teammates share in his struggles and bring problems of their own to the stories. Among those characters are Biggie Cohen, Soapy Smith, and Speed Morris.

Chip and the boys begin their adventures at Valley Falls High and continue them at State University. There is sports action in summer vacation leagues and in industrial league play. Chip even works out with and serves as something of a consultant to a professional team. The stories involve all manner of drama in the athletic contest, and Bee explores strategy in some depth.

But there were other issues to be considered in the "Chip Hilton" books. Bee examines the sometimes arbitrary methods employed by selection committees choosing teams for tournament play. He looks at adult jealousy and power grabbing when several members of the community attempt to force Coach Rockwell into retirement. And he writes of the most unwelcome element in amateur sports: the professional gamblers' influence. In more than one of the books, race relations serve as potent subject matter. This is a series of books that does not suffer from what might be seen as the narrow scope of sports. The storytelling is, for all the heroics involved, surprisingly realistic. This is especially true in terms of the dialogue between the characters and is evidence of the author's knowledge of young men and how they communicate.

❶

❷

**All About
the ARCTIC
and ANTARCTIC**

allabout
books
20

Written and illustrated by
**ARMSTRONG SPERRY**

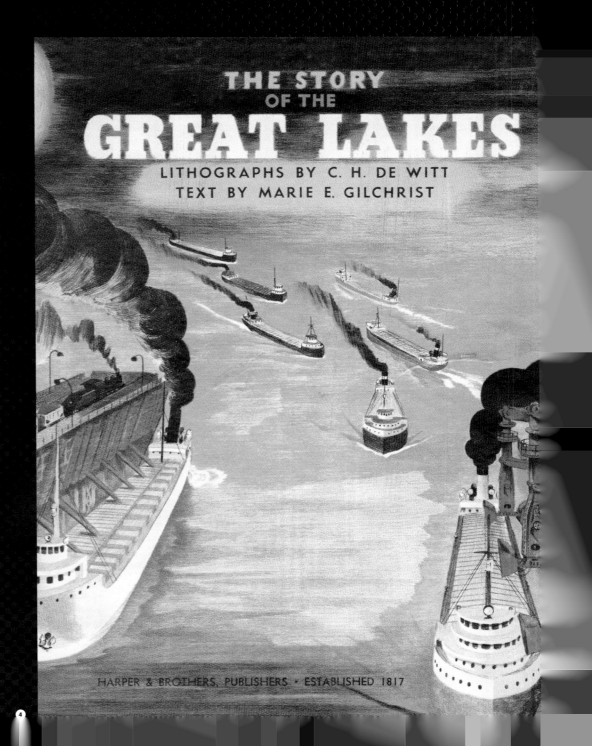

THE STORY
OF THE
GREAT LAKES
LITHOGRAPHS BY C. H. DE WITT
TEXT BY MARIE E. GILCHRIST

HARPER & BROTHERS, PUBLISHERS · ESTABLISHED 1817

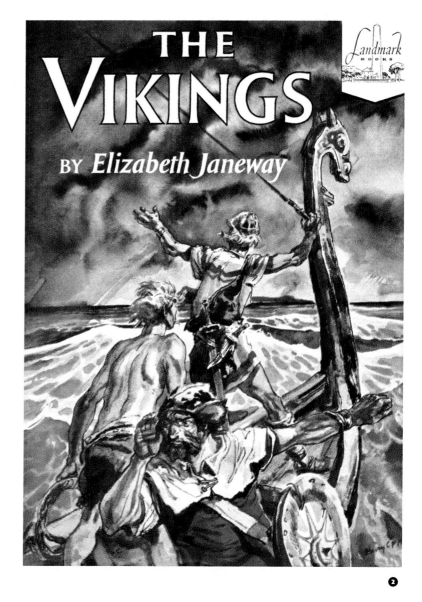

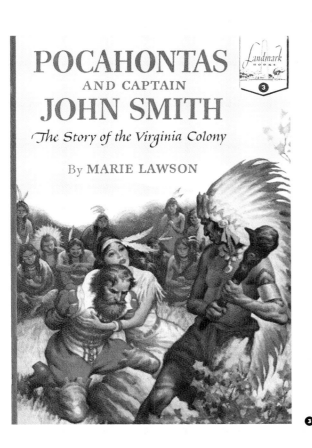

**④** 📖

**MARJORIE DEAN HIGH -SCHOOL SOPHOMORE**
Author: Pauline Lester
Illustrator: Unknown
Publisher: A L Burt Co

**⑤** 📖

**MARJORIE DEAN HIGH-SCHOOL JUNIOR**
Author: Pauline Lester
Illustrator: Unknown
Publisher: A L Burt Co

Bee's experience and personal qualities show through in other ways as well. In Chip Hilton, the author created a hero often visited by adversity. In Chip's case, that adversity only strengthens his character and enhances his resolve. "The Chip Hilton Sports" series teaches lessons in self-discipline and responsibility, a course of study which teacher Bee imparts as well as anyone.

In general, book illustrations are provided for the purpose of enhancing the text and often, in the case of jacket art, as a device to stimulate sales. The illustrations for elementary-school reading books carry a greater burden. The students rely heavily upon these illustrations in their efforts to decode the text. The quality of the illustrations in a reading book may well have a direct bearing on the success of the entire program, and they are highly instructional in nature. The work largely depicts cause-and-effect situations. Usually no more than one illustration occupies a single page. By advancing a single thought, each depiction becomes complete and lends itself to be understood as standing alone with that page's text. As a result, students quickly learn to depend on the illustrations to help them accomplish their reading goals.

The illustrations are so highly representational of the text that the work offers seemingly little in the way of artistic expression for the illustrator in comparison to other forms of illustration we have examined. Given these "rules" of reader illustration, the pictures could be unimaginative, even dreary or wooden. That is simply not the case. For in spite of the restrictions imposed upon the artists, the illustrations in most readers are interesting, lively, and often humorous.

Beginning with the outstanding work of Eleanor Campbell, the "Dick and Jane" series was graced with strong illustrators. Their work features laughing children with sparkling eyes, which seem to say, "Come along with us. This is going be fun." Just as the text promotes the characters as role models, so does their depiction in the illustrations. The children display white smiles and combed hair and wear clean clothes, which provide a lesson in hygiene, unnoticed and unrelated to the story. The outdoor environment for the series is as sunny as the characters' dispositions. In most stories, we find nary a cloud.

In this cheery outdoor atmosphere is all manner of wholesome distraction. From swing sets and wagons to kites and bikes, there is always plenty to keep the children happily occupied. The interior of the characters' home is tidy and comfortable. The characters' personal possessions are on display here too. We note stuffed animals, frolicking kittens, and school projects or crafts in various stages of development.

Over the long life of the series, the illustrators made many revisions to the general look of their work. The characters' appearances received several updates and, in a move toward more realism, began to be depicted with a look that reflected that of their readers. The color palette changed too. The bright, somewhat sharp colors of the earlier editions slowly receded into the softer pastels of the later books. An example of this change and of the general intent of a reader illustration can be found in the book: *The New Guess*

**1**

**BERT WILSON'S FADEAWAY BALL**
Author: J.W. Duffield
Illustrator: H.G. Richards
Publisher: Western Printing

**2**

**GARRY GRAYSON'S HILL STREET ELEVEN**
Author: Elmer A. Dawson
Illustrator: Walter S. Rogers
Publisher: Grosset & Dunlap
Reprinted with the permission of Pocket Books,
a division of Simon & Schuster, Inc.
Copyright © 1926.

**3**

**THE HIGH SCHOOL PITCHER**
Author: H. Irving Hancock
Illustrator: Walter Hayn
Publisher: Altemus

**4**

**THE HIGH SCHOOL BOYS' CANOE CLUB**
Author: H. Irving Hancock
Illustrator: Walter Hayn
Publisher: Altemus

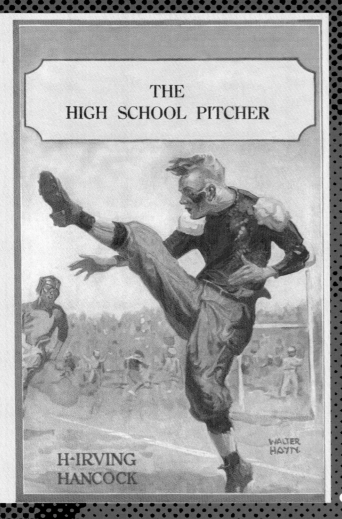

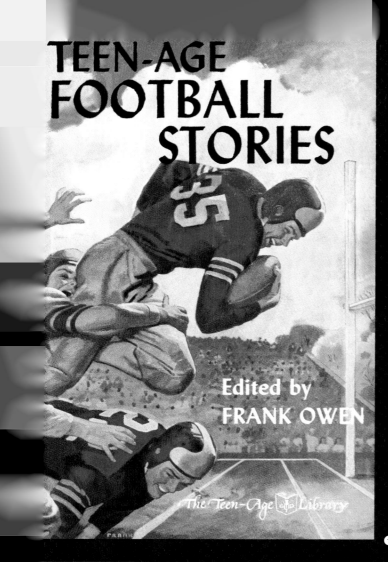

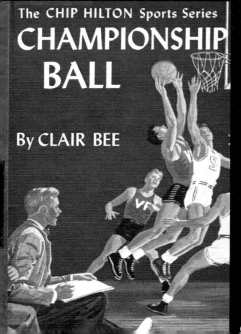

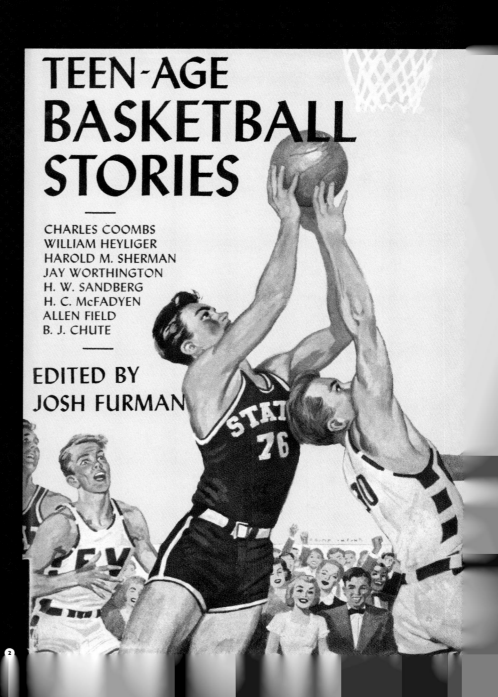

**①** 📖

**TEEN- AGE FOOTBALL STORIES**
Editor Frank Owen
Illustrator: Frank Vaughn
Publisher: Grosset & Dunlap

**②** 📖

**TEEN-AGE BASKETBALL STORIES**
Editor Josh Furman
Illustrator: Frank Vaughn
Publisher: Grosset & Dunlap

**③** 📖📖

**CHAMPIONSHIP BALL**
Author: Clair Bee
Illustrator: Frank Vaughn
Publisher: Grosset & Dunlap
Used by permission of Cindy &
Randy Farley

*Who*. The chapter entitled "Guess Who" featured the work of illustrator Richard H. Wiley. In this last story of the reader, some rules of illustration were relaxed to allow for the increased sophistication of the student on the verge of completing this portion of the program.

The story opens on a warm, sunny day. In the foreground, Sally is playing with her toy cars on sacks, which are neatly stacked on the lawn. In the text, Sally explains her play activities to her sister Jane. In the illustration, Jane smiles politely upon her younger sibling, but clearly she is distracted from her original interests. Body language gives her away. For Jane is only partially turned to listen to her sister, and her feet remain pointed toward her original focus: a do-it-yourself project undertaken by Dick and Father. It appears that the two are constructing a concrete sidewalk. At this point, we can assume that the sacks on which Sally is playing have been placed on the lawn only temporarily, for the sacks probably contain material for the project. Rounding out the illustration are the family pets. Puff the kitten watches Sally play while Spot the dog bounds toward the work site.

In the text on the following page, two of the characters communicate similar ideas. First, Father kindly asks Sally to play elsewhere and not interfere with the building project. Next, Jane attempts to shoo Spot away from the wet concrete. While at first glance we might think the text equates a young child with a family pet, the illustration quickly puts the notion to rest. Here we see that the sacks of material are indeed intended for the project. The sacks are heavy as evidenced in Father's effort in picking one up. He is bent over holding the lopsided sack; a vein on his neck is prominently raised, his partially obscured face pinched in response to the heavy load. A red ball lies at his right foot; Puff is slightly behind him to his left. With the burden of the heavy sack and the virtual gauntlet of toys and pets for him to stumble through, is it any wonder that Father should want Sally to move out of the way as a safety consideration? Meanwhile, Dick and Jane work to finish the surface of the concrete before it hardens. Spot is seen at the edge of the new sidewalk, paw outstretched. The illustration indicates that Jane's remarks are meant to discourage Spot from marring the still wet surface.

The next page's text in the first paragraph is a message from Dick requesting Father's attention. The accompanying illustration relates the situation. Spot, before departing the site, places a perfect paw print in the drying concrete. Sally, following her Father's request, leaves the area and is at Dick's side inspecting the paw print with some interest. The second paragraph follows the conversation between Sally and her brother as

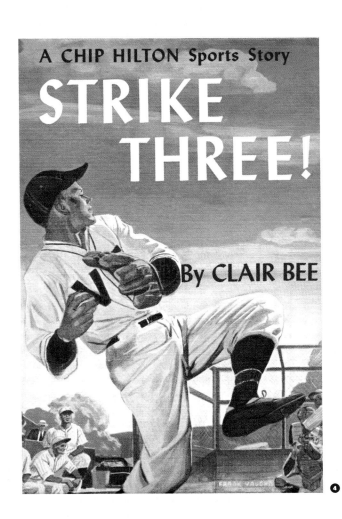

❹ 📖📖

**STRIKE THREE!**
Author: Clair Bee
Illustrator: Frank Vaughn
Publisher: Grosset & Dunlap
Used by permission of Cindy &
Randy Farley

❺ 📖📖📖

**FENCE BUSTERS**
Author: Clair Bee
Illustrator: Unknown
Publisher: Grosset & Dunlap
Used by permission of Cindy &
Randy Farley

she reports that she can mimic the actions of Spot. A separate illustration accompanies this exchange, showing Sally with her foot poised above the new concrete. It is easy to imagine what happens next.

The following page shows the sidewalk with a paw print and a footprint. Sally is clapping, obviously pleased with what she has done. The other kids, hands on their hips, look upon the markings in the concrete. Father too is kneeling close by, holding Puff, a slight smile on his face. The text imparts Sally's glee, Jane's interest in permitting her and Dick to add their footprints to the walk, and Father's joining in by helping the kitten place its paws in the wet surface.

The next page concludes the story, as it must, with the whole family participating in the fun. Mother joins the crew and looks on as the smiling children point at their sidewalk decorations. In the last illustration of the story, the new sidewalk sports a total of five prints. The accompanying text relates the children's delight in asking Mother to "Guess who, guess who."

This is a story in which the illustrations not only promote an understanding of the text but support other cognitive skills as well. There is a sense of well being and caring within the family that is not readily evident in the written material. Further, the sense of fun and youthful mischievousness is lost in the text but apparent in the illustrations. These are illustrations worthy of study, capable of keeping up with and challenging the student's fertile imagination, thereby keeping the program's material valid and alive.

For Theodor Geisel the usual rules of reader illustration apparently did not apply. His illustrations are not rooted in realism nor do they advance single thoughts confined to a page at a time. Instead, each illustration is a visual horn of plenty spilling forth an array of characters unlike any seen before. The illustrations make no pretensions of espousing the coziness of home and hearth; they are much too sophisticated and complex in their originality for that. Indeed, the depictions broke new ground in children's readers and offered images that were wildly entertaining and amusing while being somewhat startling and unsettling. For perhaps the first time, youngsters saw that artistic expression came in many forms.

In *The Cat in the Hat*, Geisel depicts the cat with half feline-half human features, a creature that walks erect and has the ability to speak. Beyond the physical aspects, the character has unlimited ability to convey thought and emotion. Somehow the cat can display the ability to reason, show merriment and surprise, even disappointment and shame. At the story's conclusion, the cat exhibits pride and triumph. By the cat's own actions and demeanor and through the reactions of the children in the story, the cat appears simultaneously threatening and nonthreatening. This is a complex idea to be sure; a suggestion that all that is encountered is not easily quantified and categorized. By serving as both writer and artist, Geisel achieves a unique balance between text and illustration resulting in some of the most original, thoughtful, and entertaining work the genre has ever seen.

A number of fine illustrators plied their craft to educational texts outside of the school curriculum. A fine series and forum for quality juvenile

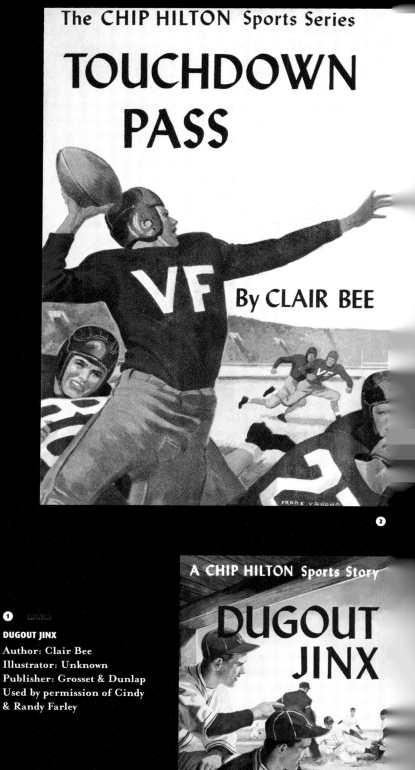

**1**

**DUGOUT JINX**
Author: Clair Bee
Illustrator: Unknown
Publisher: Grosset & Dunlap
Used by permission of Cindy & Randy Farley

A CHIP HILTON Sports Story

FRESHMAN QUARTERBACK

By CLAIR BEE

**2** 

**TOUCHDOWN PASS**
Author: Clair Bee
Illustrator: Frank Vaughn
Publisher: Grosset & Dunlap
Used by permission of Cindy
& Randy Farley

**3** 

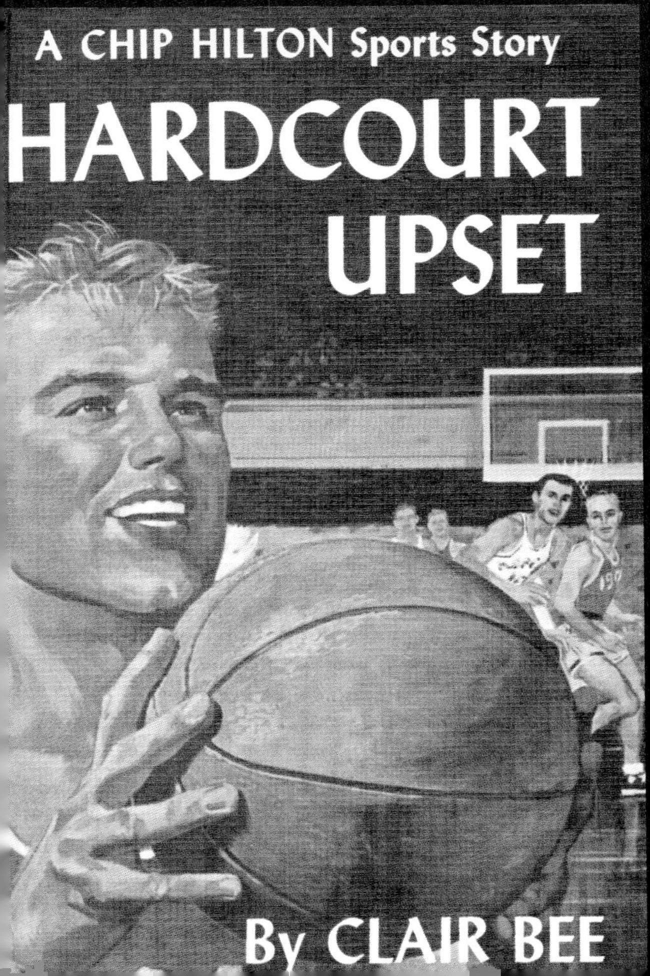

**FRESHMAN QUARTERBACK**
Author: Clair Bee
Illustrator: Unknown
Publisher: Grosset & Dunlap
Used by permission of Cindy
& Randy Farley

**4** 

**HARDCOURT UPSET**
Author: Clair Bee
Illustrator: Unknown
Publisher: Grosset & Dunlap
Used by permission of Cindy &
Randy Farley

**5** 

**COMEBACK CAGERS**
Author: Clair Bee
Illustrator: Unknown
Publisher: Grosset & Dunlap
Used by permission of Cindy &
Randy Farley

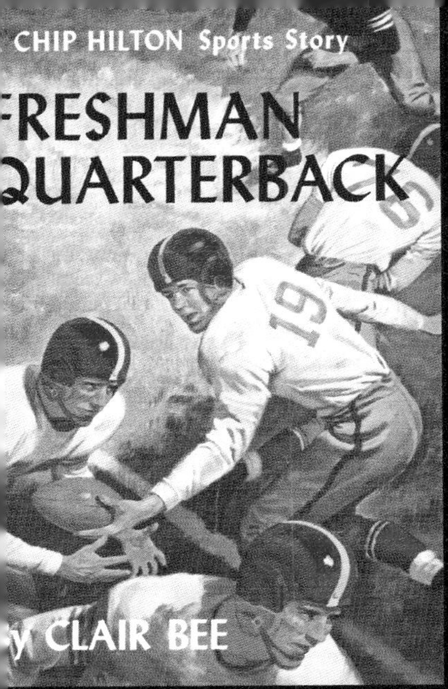

A CHIP HILTON Sports Story

HARDCOURT UPSET

By CLAIR BEE

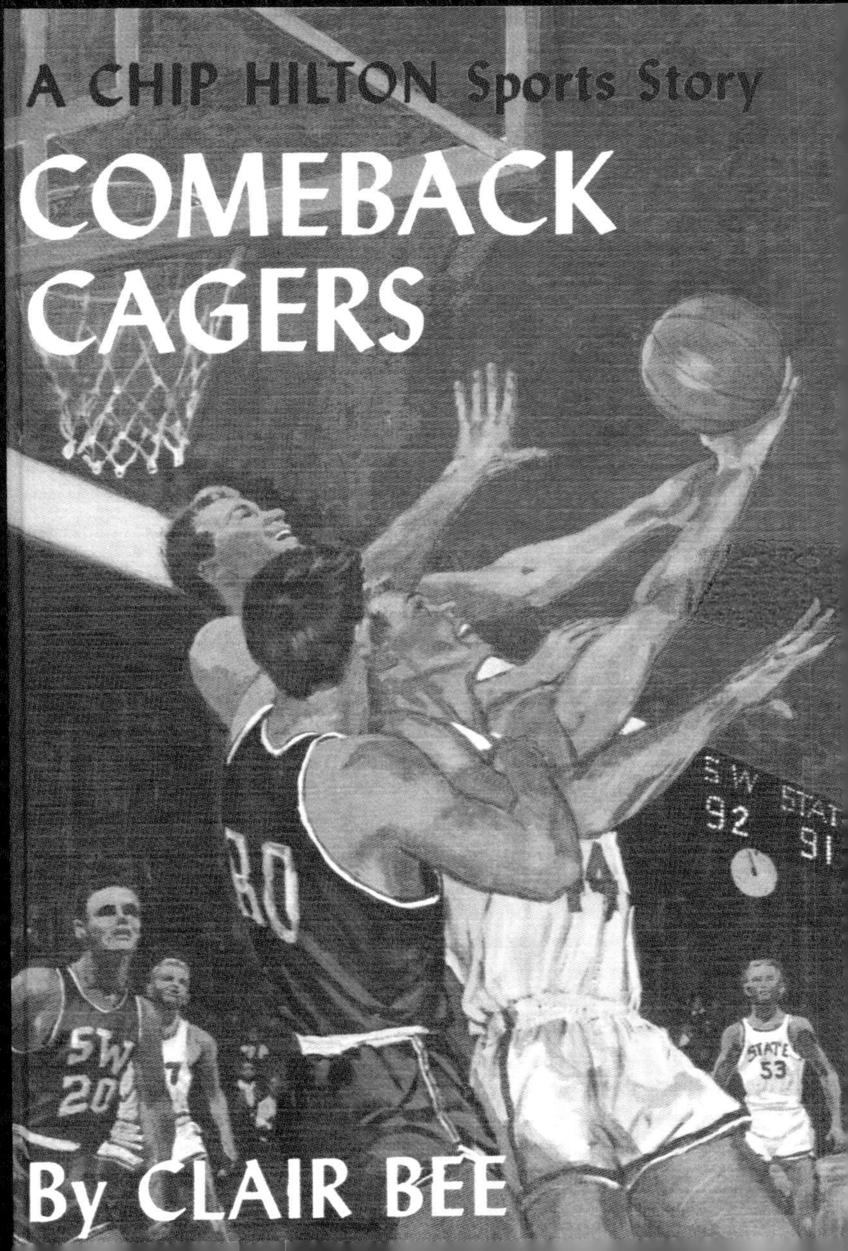

A CHIP HILTON Sports Story

COMEBACK CAGERS

By CLAIR BEE

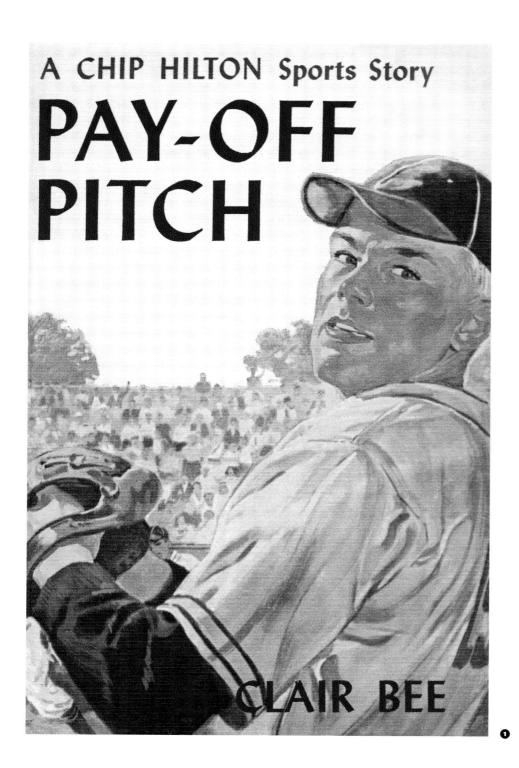

❶ ▢▢

**PAY-OFF PITCH**
Author: Clair Bee
Illustrator: Unknown
Publisher: Grosset & Dunlap
Used by permission of Cindy & Randy
Farley

❷ ▢▢

**PITCHERS' DUEL**
Author: Clair Bee
Illustrator: Unknown
Publisher: Grosset & Dunlap
Used by permission of Cindy &
Randy Farley

❸ ▢▢▢

**CLUTCH HITTER!**
Author: Clair Bee
Illustrator: Frank Vaughn
Publisher: Grosset & Dunlap
Used by permission of Cindy &
Randy Farley

❹ ❺

Picture 1.

Father is sitting at table, admiring pumpkin that he has just finished carving into a jack-o-lantern for the children. Children are all standing around the table admiring it, too. Spot, in foreground, has his forepaws up on the table, looking curiously at the pumpkin. Jane, looking at Spot and pointing to the pumpkin, is saying:

"Look, Spot.

Oh, look.

Look and see.

Oh, see."

*Use up + down -*
*Jump ↑*

*Use Puff - getting hind foot in something on table -*
*Spot*

Picture 2.

Spot has jumped up on table and is exploring pumpkin, tipping it a little as he puts his nose into the hole in the top. All the others watch him with interest. Dick might be saying:

"Oh, look.

See Spot.

Spot sees something."

**① ZERNA SHARP, CREATOR OF DICK AND JANE**
Often referred to as "the mother of Sally, Dick, and Jane," Zerna Sharp was a reading consultant, teacher, and elementary school principal. Photo used by permission. Photo courtesy of the Clinton County Historical Society, Inc.

**② COACH CLAIR BEE**
Clair Bee, author of the "Chip Hilton" books, pictured here in his Merchant Marine uniform during World War II, where he attained the rank of Lieutenant Commander. He also served with the U.S. Army during World War I as an infantryman in Europe. Used by permission. Photo courtesy of Cindy & Randy Farley

**③ ④ COLOR OUTLINE (OF DICK AND JANE ILLUSTRATION DIRECTIVES)**
An actual "Dick and Jane" reader in development. This rarely seen look into the process reveals the importance of an elementary schoolbook's illustrations. The completed text, in quotations, tells a small portion of the story. The accompanying directives to the artist clearly demonstrate the larger storytelling possibilities of the illustrations. Used by permission. Courtesy of the Clinton County Historical Society, Inc.

Picture 3.

Spot has tipped pumpkin entirely over on his head. His head is raised so that he looks very funny. All the children and father are laughing, and Dick says:

"Oh, oh, look.

See Spot.

See funny, funny Spot."

Picture of Spot
(looking startled, if possible)

*Picture story*

S P O T

*PP possibly*
*OK 1 Pg 9 5.00 pd*

Mildred Sprague

writers and illustrators was the "All-about Books" published by Random House and featuring scientific illustrations by award-winning illustrators. The depictions are of such quality that many could be applied to adult text. Among the highly skilled All-about illustrators was Thomas W. Voter, longtime staff artist and director of scientific illustration in the art department of New York's American Museum of Natural History.

Another area of illustration requiring work that strongly supported the text was Sunday school literature. Not only do the illustrations promote the storyline and the values brought forth in the written material, but also they carry strong messages of their own. This extension of the text had extremely positive applications including the furthering of racial equality evident in a number of the books published years prior to the civil rights movement. Even the most time-honored spiritual messages profit greatly from the works of gifted illustrators.

Nearly all effective sports illustrations depict action game situations. In the case of the jacket illustration, the rendition must show athletic struggle, player against player. In this struggle, the ultimate triumph and glory that is sports is realized. The contorted faces freeze-framed amid athletic warfare fuel the imagination and draw us to the story.

The premise of the sports illustration is based upon this struggle as well as conquest and heroism, but a successful depiction requires still more. The illustrator must have more than a passing understanding of the athletic contest he or she is to depict and possess considerable knowledge of anatomy and movement.

A great practitioner of the form is illustrator Frank Vaughn. Vaughn, who received training at the New York Phoenix School of Design, found success in all manner of illustration, from magazine and advertising work to a vast array of juvenile subject matter. His work on the "Chip Hilton" books defines the sports dust-jacket illustration.

In the first book of the series, *Touchdown Pass*, Vaughn portrays all elements of the genre in their truest form. Above the crush and onslaught of the opponents' defensive linemen rises quarterback Chip Hilton. Embossed upon his broad chest against his crimson jersey are the white initials VF for his beloved Valley Falls High School. Hilton stands among those who would tackle him. He pays them no mind, for his attention is not upon his personal safety. Instead he intends to push down field and vanquish the opposition. His weapon of choice is the forward pass; his arm is cocked in readiness as he sets his sights on a receiver in the distance. The receiver is closely guarded but in position to catch a pass if it can be expertly thrown. Hilton, running out of time and options, is ready to do just that. The scene explodes with action, but the payoff, we know, is contained within the pages of the text. It is Vaughn who introduces us to this story ensuring a successful handoff from illustrator to author.

The same is true of the illustration for *Championship Ball*, the first of the "Hilton" basketball stories. The action is set against a dramatic blue background, which contrasts well with the court's rich hardwood flooring. The scene is of a fight for a Valley Falls offensive rebound. Two cagers leap for the ball, their momentum causing their bodies to slam together in a mid-air collision. The illustrator clearly understands that basketball's long-held reputation as a noncontact sport is a myth. Also, two players are poised in wait pending the outcome of the rebounding struggle. Their positioning is pivotal to the ongoing play. But there is something more here, something that draws our eyes away from the unfolding action. It is Chip Hilton attired in street clothes, his foot wrapped in bandages. He is cheering on his team while keeping some sort of record on a tablet. We are well aware of his athletic prowess and what he means to this Valley Falls team, so we must wonder what role he is accomplishing on the sidelines and what is the cause of his injury. We also wonder if his damage is permanent and if his sports career is in jeopardy. These are the kinds of questions a fine cover illustration poses. This is a sports illustration that realistically depicts an athletic contest and lends legitimacy to the text. A writer, a publisher, or a reader can ask no more of an illustrator.

❺

❺ ▭▭

**ALICE IN WONDERLAND "THE END"**
Author: Lewis Carroll
Illustrator: Maraja
Publisher: Grosset & Dunlap

# Acknowledgments

Joe and Cheryl wish to thank the many friends, family, and professionals who supported them with this project in a variety of ways, by lending their prized book collections, through advice, or by the granting of permission.

To our sons, Derek Homme and James Homme, for innumerable hours of patience, endurance, and understanding during the writing of this book.

To Ed and Sheila Homme, for their immeasurable help. A supportive family is the key to a project such as this.

A personal thank you to our valued friend, Carol Jane Seidlitz, for her generous assistance during this and many previous projects, for her energy, encouragement, and especially for her enduring friendship.

A special thank you to Julie Ede, Hugh Ashlock, and Tony and Mary Carpentieri, who contributed to such a degree that the book would not be what it is without their invaluable assistance.

Grateful acknowledgments to Dr. R. Christopher Goodwin, the Estate of Harold L. Goodwin, and the John Blaine/Rick Brant Trust for permission to reprint the Rick Brant illustrations. Spindrift Island, the series titles "Rick Brant Science-Adventure Stories," "Rick Brant Electronic Adventure Series," and the lightning bolt logo are all registered trademarks.

A thank you to Nancy Hart of the Clinton County Historical Society for authorization to reprint the illustration outline and photograph, and for her aid in the Dick and Jane research.

To Cindy and Randy Farley who graciously provided biographical information about Clair Bee, his photograph, and who also approved our request to reprint the original Chip Hilton illustrations.

Bill Gillies, Jr., son of the late illustrator Bill Gillies, and his daughter Kim Gillies VanHeynigen were also of significant assistance with information, photographs, and permission.

Illustrator Rudy Nappi was generous with his knowledge and permission.

It is with tremendous admiration for the legacy of N.C. Wyeth that we thank Andrew and Betsy Wyeth for their consent to reprint the illustrations from Deerslayer.

Brooks Garis, grandson of Howard R. Garis, provided illustrations and permission, for which we are grateful.

Grateful acknowledgment to Penguin Putnam Inc. for its assistance and letter of nonobjection for the use of selected Grosset & Dunlap book covers.

We also wish to thank those who offered inspiration and/or assistance:

Charlotte Allen, Jim Bowers, Cathy Cervantes of C & M Used Books, Ci's Unique Antiques, Pat Davenport, Kate Emburg, Susan Hermansen-Jent, John Humphrey, Ray Johnson, Gary Kobayashi, Dan Burke, V. Louise Kellogg, Bob King, Lorie Kirker of Alaskana Books, ladies of Bishop's Attic and the Palmer Public Library, the Utilities Section, Mary Adam Landa, Jay & Roberta Landgren of The Book Bank, Louise of the Bookstall, Anne Nolting, Jim Ogden, Della Palmer, Karen Plunkett-Powell, Carol Reed, LaDonna and Mary of Remember When Antiques, Linda Joy Singleton, Jim Towey, and for their continuing inspiration, the Fabs and the boys from Hawthorne, plus the numerous individuals with whom Joe and Cheryl brainstormed ideas.

# Value Guide

The authors have assigned values to vintage juvenile books based on several factors. At the heart of the matter is desirability and condition. Although rarity of a book plays a part in determining its value, rarity is not the last word in placing a price or value on a work.

For instance, the "Nancy Drew" titles were produced in great numbers and were widely distributed. Despite their relatively plentiful number, the "Nancy Drew" books have only increased in value for collectors. The tremendous popularity of the series has sustained a high level of interest and desirability for collectors and fans of the series. Conversely, a book or series that has attained a small readership and has little more than a regional following usually generates little in the way of collector interest, even though the books may be rare.

The desirability of a book is predicated on its jacket art as well. The "sizzle" that originally sold the steak continues to interest buyers in vintage juvenile books. Cover art may be found in several styles, including paste-on illustrations, dust jackets, and picture covers. Books without dust jackets or cover illustrations are generally considered less desirable and valuable.

The old real-estate axiom relating to the three most important words for that business as "location, location, location" may be easily adapted to collectors of juvenile books. For collectors the words might be, "condition, condition, condition." While condition is an important consideration in the purchase of any collectible item, it can be especially challenging in assembling a fine collection of juvenile literature. The books, by the very nature of their intended consumer group, are often well worn. Page corners are bent to serve as bookmarks, notes or scribbling may appear throughout the text, and snack food may be present - even identifiable - decades after the fact. A perusal of any vintage book catalog or on-line auction site will find all manner of defect description including scrapes, marks, and stains due to a price sticker, dampness, and tape residue. There may be loose or missing pages and flap or spine damages, and there may be dust jacket chipping, darkening, or fading. Collectors are obviously a particular lot when it comes to matters of condition.

Other factors apply to book collecting. There are often a host of variations or formats for each title. Some are obvious, such as the updating of the cover illustrations, while other variations are apparent to only the most studied collector. Variations may include the update of storylines, quality of the paper, changes in endpapers, and texture of the book cover. There are claims to first editions, which in the case of series books may be highly suspect. Buyer beware! There are books that were published for mail order clubs and books that were once loaned by libraries that have less collectibility than others do. Truly, a book cannot be judged solely by its cover.

The juvenile book-collecting business requires a lot of study and research. This is certainly true if it is your business or if you have interest enough to immerse yourself in the hobby. But price and value alone do not determine the enjoyment that one receives from a personal collection. Literature and art are both in the eye of the beholder; enjoy the hobby as an informed consumer but, most importantly, enjoy it.

The illustrations presented in this book have been restored to their original beauty. While specimens of their quality exist, they are relatively few.

For the purposes of this value guide, the authors have used a grading code of Very Good, as this is the most commonly found grade. A work in Very Good condition is one that has been well cared for and is complete. It contains a fully readable text without loose or missing pages. It has a secure binding and is a generally clean edition. There may be indications of wear and a few minor defects present, such as small tears or creasing on the dust jacket.

The book icons found in the captions correspond with the value key below.

Value Key

| $5.00 — $15.00 | 📖 |
| $20.00 — $30.00 | 📖📖 |
| $35.00 — $55.00 | 📖📖📖 |
| $60.00 — $85.00 | 📖📖📖📖 |
| $100.00 — $230.00 | 📖📖📖📖📖 |
| $250.00 & up | 📖📖📖📖📖📖 |

Naturally, higher values than those listed correspond with volumes in better condition. As stated earlier, variations in juvenile book printings are plentiful; check with your local antiquarian bookseller for additional information. There are also a number of clubs, on-line sites, and newsletters that can be of assistance to everyone from the novice collector to those with more advanced interests. Bear in mind that prices listed in this book are for collectible items and are therefore relative. Actual value depends on what the market will bear. This is a general price guide intended for the enjoyment of collectors of juvenile books.

# Selected Bibliography

Allen, Douglas and Douglas Allen, Jr. *N.C. Wyeth, the Collected Paintings, Illustrations and Murals*. New York: Bonanza Books, 1972.

Axe, John. *The Secret of Collecting Girls' Series Books*. Grantsville: Hobby House Press, Inc., 2000.

Best, James J. *American Popular Illustration, A Reference Guide*. Westport: American Popular Culture, 1984.

Billman, Carol. *The Secret of the Stratemeyer Syndicate: Nancy Drew, Hardy Boys, and the Million Dollar Fiction Factory*. New York: Ungar Publishing Company, 1986.

Bowen, Ezra, Mary Y. Steinbauer, John R. Martinez, George Constable, Anne Horan, Gerald Simons, and Bryce S. Walker. *This Fabulous Century 1900-1910*. Vol 1, Time Life Series (New York: Time Life Books, 1969).

Dell, John Edward and Walt Reed. *Visions of Adventure, N.C. Wyeth and the Brandywine Artists*. New York: Watson-Guptill Publications, 2000.

Farah, David. *Farah's Guide*, 11th ed. SynSine Press, 1999.

Heller, Steven and Seymour Chwast. *Jackets Required, An Illustrated History of American Book Jacket Design, 1920-1950*. San Francisco: Chronicle Books, 1995.

Johnson, Deidre. *Edward Stratemeyer and the Stratemeyer Syndicate*. New York: Twayne Publishers, 1993.

Johnson, Edna, Evelyn R. Sickels and Frances Clarke Sayers. *Anthology of Children's Literature*, 4th ed. Boston: Houghton Mifflin Co, 1970.

Jones, Diane McClure and Rosemary Jones. *Collector's Guide to Children's Books 1950 to 1975 Identification and Values* Vol 1. Paducah: Collector Books, 2000.

Jones, Diane McClure and Rosemary Jones. *Collector's Guide to Children's Books 1850 to 1950 Identification and Values* Vol 2. Paducah: Collector Books, 1999.

Kingman, Lee, Joanna Foster, and Ruth Giles Lontoft. *Illustrators of Children's Books: 1957-1966*. Boston: The Horn Book, Inc., 1972.

Knight, Melanie, Linda Tracy, Rosemarie DiCristo, Patricia DeLucia, Nancy Mejia, and Lorraine Rogers. *A Guide to Judy Bolton Country*. Rheem Valley: SynSine Press, 1997.

Mahony, Bertha E., Louise Payson Latimer, and Beulah Folmsbee. *Illustrators of Children's Books: 1744-1945*. Boston: The Horn Book, Inc., 1970.

Mattson, E. Christian and Thomas B. Davis. *A Collector's Guide to Hardcover Boys' Series Books 1872–1993*. Newark: MAD Book Company Publishers, 1997.

McCallum, Jack. *Chip Hilton*. Sports Illustrated, January 7, 1980, pages 52-60.

Munro, Eleanor. *Originals: American Women Artists*. New York: Simon and Schuster, 1979.

Petteys, Chris. *Dictionary of Women Artists, an International Dictionary of Women Artists Born Before 1900*. Boston: G.K. Hall & Co., 1985.

Scharnhorst, Gary and Jack Bales. *The Lost Life of Horatio Alger, Jr*. Bloomington: Indiana University Press, 1985.

*Something About the Author*, Vols 1, 2, 3, 4, 5, 7, 11, 13, 17, 20, 21, 23, 24, 26, 27, 28, 31, 34, 39, 41, 43, 51, 52, 67, 75, 88, 100.

Sutherland, Zena, Dianne L. Monson, and May Hill Arbuthnot. *Children & Books*, 6th ed. (Glenview: Scott, Foresman and Company, 1981).

Tuckerman, Henry T. *Book of the Artists*. New York: James F. Carr Publisher, 1967.

Viguers, Ruth Hill, Marcia Dalphin, and Bertha Mahony Miller, *Illustrators of Children's Books: 1946-1956*. Boston: The Horn Book, Inc., 1958.

Wyeth, Betsy James, ed. *The Wyeths by N.C. Wyeth, The Intimate Correspondence of N.C. Wyeth 1901-1945*. Boston: Gambit, 1971.


BIBLIOGRAPHY of NON PRINT SOURCES:

www.britannica.com

www.happyhollisters.com

Microsoft Encarta Encyclopedia 2000 Software